CHEZ PANISSE DESSERTS

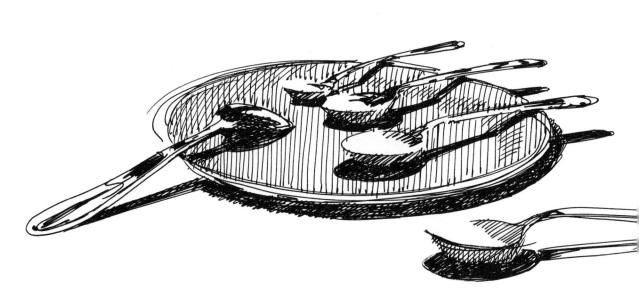

ILLUSTRATIONS BY WAYNE THIEBAUD

CHEZ PANISSE DESSERTS

BY LINDSEY REMOLIF SHERE

PREFACE BY ALICE WATERS

RANDOM HOUSE  NEW YORK

To my family, especially to Charles

Library of Congress Cataloging in Publication Data
Shere, Lindsey Remolif, 1935–
Chez Panisse desserts.
   Bibliography: p.
   Includes index.
   1. Desserts.   2. Chez Panisse.   I. Title.
TX773.S4277 1985   641.8'6   84-42997
ISBN 0-394-53860-9

Manufactured in the United States of America
Design by Patricia Curtan
2 3 4 5 6 7 8 9
First Edition

ACKNOWLEDGMENTS

My thanks to Alice Waters for believing in this book and to all my partners at the restaurant for their support over the years. Many thanks also to all the people who have worked with enthusiasm and dedication in the pastry department at Chez Panisse—Diane Dexter, Lisa Goines, Gayle Ortiz, Mark Peel, Joe Schwab, Steve Sullivan, John Sutherland, Craig Sutter, Sarah Tenaglia, Mary Jo Thoresen, Diane Wegner, Deborah Welch, Julia Wishy, and Clay Wollard.

My gratitude to Pat Curtan and Elaine Ginger for their many hours of devoted work on the copy of this book, to Michael Edwards and Thérèse Shere for their considerable editing and rewriting help, and to my husband, Charles, for the innumerable hours he spent typing. To the friends, colleagues, and relatives, especially Charles and Giovanna who were always on the spot, my thanks for their willingness to taste yet another dessert.

Special thanks to Gayle Wilson for her tireless and cheerful dedication to the research for this book, and to Bill Fujimoto at Monterey Market for sharing his expertise and allowing me to taste and learn constantly.

Pat Curtan and Wayne Thiebaud are responsible for making this a beautiful book; I can't thank them enough. And my appreciation to Jason Epstein for his patience and confidence, and to Becky Saletan, for her guidance and her hard work.

Many thanks are due to all the people who gave so generously of their time and their expertise: Jim Dodge, Stanford Court Hotel; Bob Gelhar, Oregon Filbert Commission; Charlotte Glenn, Le Marche Seeds International; Sibella Kraus, Greenleaf Produce; Esther Nelson, North Willamette Experiment Station; George Ossey, formerly of C and H Sugar; Annabelle Post, *Sunset* Magazine; Bill Sutherland, Pacific Organics; Milt Torn, Torn Ranch; Dr. George York, University of California at Davis; and Bob Youngman, Oregon Department of Agriculture.

And above all my gratitude to the cooks and writers whose work has guided and inspired me in my work at the restaurant: James Beard, Ada Boni, Robert Courtine, Curnonsky, Elizabeth David, M.F.K. Fisher, Richard Olney, and Waverly Root, to name just a few.

CONTENTS

PREFACE

I think this is a very special cookbook. It is a collection of recipes created over the last thirteen years by Lindsey Shere, the pastry chef at Chez Panisse. The recipes reflect a unique aesthetic, shaped by the fusion of Lindsey's personal inspiration with that of the restaurant. Guided and stimulated by the philosophy and resources of Chez Panisse, Lindsey expresses her almost ethereal sense for balancing flavors and combining tastes. Her desserts are restrained—yet exotic, and wild. They leave you charmed, surprised, and satisfied.

The ever-changing single-menu format of the restaurant has greatly influenced our choices of what dishes to cook and how to prepare them, and of how to combine different flavors and textures into a harmonious menu. The attempt to marry the elements of a menu that includes dessert has been illuminating. In a more conventional restaurant the pastry chef has no way of knowing what other courses will be ordered, so the desserts are planned to be generally appealing. Often there is an entirely separate dessert menu that offers extravagant portions of sweet desserts. At Chez Panisse it is important for the dessert to complement and harmonize with the spirit of the menu, to capture a balance between the aromatic and the pungent. This quality is certainly as elusive for desserts as for any other part of the meal. I think dessert should be the finishing touch. It should be just the right flavor and texture to complete the meal, something to amuse and surprise the palate one more time—never overwhelming or dulling.

A firm commitment to cooking with the highest quality local, seasonal, fresh ingredients underlies everything we do at Chez Panisse. The restaurant has developed a network of sources over the years, beginning with backdoor deliveries of lavender, violets, herbs, Meyer lemons, rose geraniums—all from friends' backyards. Our suppliers now include a large group of growers who cultivate varieties of fruits and berries that were not previously available in the markets. I believe that these hand-selected foodstuffs should be approached with a fresh attitude and a curiosity that will encourage us to take full advantage of them.

When a stranger (covered with little scratches) turned up on our back doorstep laden with ripe blackberries and a bunch of not-so-ripe, still red ones, Lindsey, knowing they wouldn't work for tarts, used them instead to make a fantastic glaze. A friend growing fraises des bois for us discovered that Quinalt strawberries grow beautifully in our climate, and now supplies them regularly. Excellent ingredients are the heart of this very special dessert cuisine. Wherever you are, you can no doubt uncover wonderful local berries, fruits, and nuts that will work for these recipes.

There is something very handmade about these desserts. It has to do with working with fragile foods in their brief moment of ripeness—capturing the perfume quickly before it dissipates—making ice cream in small batches to be eaten right away—or gathering rose petals and bringing them into the kitchen to candy. It also has to do with just the look of them, the varying shapes and colors of the ingredients, and with the aesthetic of the cook. Lindsey's love for one-of-a-kind antique serving dishes inspired me to go on long and costly shopping expeditions for old, mismatched Limoges china to complement the subtle beauty of these desserts.

Lindsey has pursued surprising and unlikely presentations that rely on classical methods and combinations. And she always applies the good cook's critical attitude to her work, a never-ending process of tasting, and tasting again—and never taking for granted the qualities of the ingredients, or the way the flavors and textures will blend. New insight seems to come from renewed evaluation.

We have learned to enjoy waiting for the fruits of the season to appear—anticipating those juicy white peaches in the summer, the second crop of figs in the fall, the persimmons at Thanksgiving, the blood oranges in the spring. This book is organized according to ingredients and seasons so that when you come home from the market with the perfect peach, you can easily find out more about it, and find a recipe using it. I believe these recipes will give you great pleasure if you use the best of what is available, and always trust your instincts.

Alice L. Waters
JUNE 1985

1

THE BASIC
REPERTORY

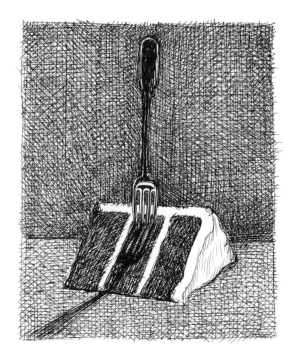

T HE RECIPES in this chapter are the building blocks of dessert making and are, for the most part, simple in themselves. Each embodies a fundamental technique that, when used singly or in combination, is at the heart of the recipes that follow.

Custards are the simplest of desserts, made of cream and milk thickened with egg yolks. They lend themselves to innumerable flavorings and are the base of ice creams, Bavarian creams, baked custards, and many sauces. Pastry cream, as well as its variation, frangipane cream, is another basic custard. It can be thickened with flour as well as eggs and is the base of countless fillings, soufflés, and fruit tarts. In combination with the simple short crust pastry and fresh or poached fruit, it offers many possibilities for beautiful, rewarding desserts. A Bavarian cream is an egg custard thickened with gelatin—a delicate-textured, very versatile cream that can be flavored with almost any fruit or liqueur.

The short crust pastry, pâte sablée, which is used for fruit tarts and almond tarts, has a texture very like butter cookies; the method of cutting butter into flour applies to both and results in a very tender crust. Sponge cakes and Ladyfingers teach you how to make eggs work for you as leavening in simple cakes that can be the beginning of a dramatic Bûche de Noël.

Savarins and brioches are light and buttery yeast doughs that can be served as breakfast pastries, rum babas, or Christmas cakes with candied citrus and currants. Slices of toasted brioche make delicious croutons for savory hors d'oeuvres, or, sugared and browned, a cookielike accompaniment to dessert.

Crêpes are thin, lacy pancakes. The batter can be varied with different choices of flour or the addition of chopped nuts. Crêpes are good served simply with butter, sugar, and perhaps Grand Marnier or another liqueur, or with warm fruit butters. Or they can be crisped in the oven to a cookielike texture to hold ice cream and sherbet.

Langues de Chat are crisp, flat cookies with rounded corners that make them look like cats' tongues. They can accompany almost any ice cream or pudding, and can be molded to form cups for ice cream and mousse. Served in this way, these cookies provide the important accents of texture and flavor to any soft, light–flavored dessert.

Caramel, in its many forms, is an essential ingredient in many of these recipes. A simple caramel syrup can be used to flavor mousses, soufflés, ice creams, and custards. It can be a crisp, golden coating for whole fruit, or turn a plain apple tart into Tarte Tatin. Combined with fruit purées, caramel makes a delicious sauce for ice cream or baked fruit. Angel hair is a beautiful garnish of caramel threads to spin around a dessert.

Many people find puff pastry intimidating and mysterious. It is the most delicate of all pastries and seems complicated because there are so many steps involved, but each step is in itself simple. After you make puff pastry a few times it will be easy. It makes a delicious alternative to short crust pastry for plain fruit tarts, especially if baked in a wood-burning oven. Caramelized puff pastry cookies are crisp and perfect with soft-textured desserts like mousses and fruit compotes.

Once you master the techniques and methods found in these basic recipes and understand the principles at work, you will be able to make almost any dessert imaginable. But what will make you a really good dessert cook is your alertness to flavor, scent, and appearance, and especially your sensitivity to the dessert as a complementary part of a whole meal.

FLAVORED SUGARS

For scented sugars, use fresh rose geranium or other scented geranium leaves, violets, or rose petals. They must be perfectly dry. Put a leaf for each cup of sugar in a tightly closed container and keep for a week or two before using. Layer the violets or rose petals with the sugar and let stand until the sugar is scented. This will take about a week, depending on how fragrant the flowers are. Use these scented sugars for butter cookies or in cakes. For vanilla sugar or vanilla powdered sugar, sink a piece of whole vanilla bean into your sugar container and let stand for a week or two. If you are in a hurry, split the vanilla bean in half lengthwise, scrape the tiny black seeds from it into the sugar, and mix together to distribute the vanilla. This will flavor the sugar in minutes.

Vanilla beans are the seed pods of the vanilla orchid, *Vanilla planifolia*. The pods or the extract made from the pods are invaluable for flavoring many desserts. The pods should be split in half lengthwise and the soft pastelike seeds scraped out with a small knife. Both they and the pod are used for flavoring. The pods can be rinsed, dried, and reused if they are still scented. Use them to scent sugar, as above, or steep in a jar of brandy or Cognac to make your own vanilla extract.

CRÈME CHANTILLY

The cream used in all these recipes is the whipping cream available in the local supermarket. I never use ultra-pasteurized cream because it seems to lose all its flavor in processing.

4

Whip the amount of cold fresh cream needed for your recipe until it mounds softly and will just barely hold its shape. The volume will approximately double after it is whipped. There should be no hint of graininess, which is the first sign that the cream is overbeaten and turning to butter. Stir in vanilla and sugar to taste. Or you may flavor the cream with spirits or liqueurs, wine, fruit purées or jams, or the reduced liquid from poached fruit.

CRÈME FRAÎCHE

Makes 1 cup: *1 cup whipping cream · 1 teaspoon buttermilk*

Warm the cream in a non-corroding saucepan to 95°F. Stir in the buttermilk. Pour into a glass or plastic container, cover loosely, and put in a warm place (about 75°F is good) for 12 to 24 hours, or until the cream has thickened slightly. Stir well, cover, and store in the refrigerator until you need it. The tangy taste will gradually get stronger, but the cream will keep for a week to 10 days in the refrigerator. To make more, follow the above directions but substitute 1 tablespoon of your crème fraîche for the buttermilk. You can continue to make it this way indefinitely.

CRÈME ANGLAISE

Makes a generous pint: *2 cups milk · 3 tablespoons sugar · 1-inch piece of vanilla bean · 4 egg yolks*

Warm the milk with the sugar and the split, scraped vanilla bean in a non-corroding saucepan to dissolve the sugar, stirring occasionally. Whisk the egg yolks to break them up, but don't make them foam or you will not be able to see when the custard is properly cooked. Whisk a little of the hot milk into the egg yolks to warm them. Return to the pan and cook the custard, stirring constantly, until it coats the spoon. Test it by drawing a finger across the spoon. If this leaves a trail in the custard, the custard has cooked to the right point. Be sure to take the pan off the heat

5

while you test—or you will have scrambled eggs on the bottom of the pan. The custard can also be tested with a thermometer—it will be cooked properly at 170°F to 175°F.

Using a strainer to remove any little lumps of cooked egg, pour the cooked custard into a refrigerator container. Be sure your containers are sweet smelling, especially if they are made of plastic. Put the vanilla bean back in the custard to flavor it further until you are ready to use it. Cover tightly and chill. Remove the vanilla bean and whisk the custard smooth just before you are ready to use it.

VANILLA ICE CREAM

Makes 1 quart: *4-inch piece of vanilla bean · 1 cup half-and-half · 2 cups whipping cream · ⅔ cup sugar · 6 egg yolks*

Split the vanilla bean in half lengthwise and scrape the fine black seeds into a non-corroding saucepan. Add the vanilla bean pod, half-and-half, cream, and sugar, and warm the mixture, stirring occasionally, until the sugar has dissolved.

Whisk the egg yolks just enough to mix them and whisk in some of the hot half-and-half mixture. Return to the pan and cook over low heat, stirring constantly, until the custard coats the spoon (when you draw a finger across the custard coating the back of the spoon, your finger should leave a clear trail).

Strain through a medium-fine strainer to remove any lumps that may have formed, scraping as much of the vanilla bean through the strainer as you can. Strain the custard into a storage container, recovering the vanilla bean pods from the strainer and putting them in the container to flavor the ice cream mixture while it chills. Cover the container tightly and chill the custard thoroughly. When you are ready to freeze the mixture, remove the vanilla bean pods. Freeze according to the directions for your ice cream maker.

Frozen desserts should be stored in non-reactive containers—plastic or glass—tightly covered. Aluminum foil must not contact their surfaces. They should be stored at 0°F for best quality, but warmed to 5°F to 7°F before serving.

6

PASTRY CREAM

Makes 2½ cups: *2 cups milk* · *⅓ cup flour* · *6 tablespoons sugar* · *6 egg yolks* · *1 to 2 tablespoons unsalted butter* · *Vanilla extract or other flavoring to taste*

Scald the milk—that is, heat it to just under boiling. Mix the flour and sugar in a heavy non-corroding saucepan. Beat the egg yolks until thick and light colored. Thoroughly whisk the hot milk into the mixed flour and sugar and cook over medium heat, stirring constantly, until the mixture has boiled for a minute or two.

Whisk a little of the mixture into the egg yolks to warm them and stir back into the flour mixture. Mix well, being sure to incorporate all the flour mixture from the sides of the pan, and cook over medium heat, stirring constantly, until the pastry cream begins to hold a slight shape. It should cook to 170°F. It is important to cook the pastry cream thoroughly after adding the egg yolks; this cooks an enzyme that otherwise makes the cream break down. The first time you make pastry cream, use a thermometer. Note how it looks at 170°F; from then on you can just cook it until it looks right. Don't ever let it boil.

Remove from the heat and stir in the butter, then put through a medium-fine strainer. Cool and whisk occasionally to keep a crust from forming; or cover with plastic and refrigerate until cool, then whisk to smooth it out. Stir in vanilla to taste, or vanilla and a spirit or liqueur that is appropriate to whatever the pastry cream will be used for. Don't overbeat after cooking or the cream will thin out—a useful thing to remember, because you can thin it, if it is too thick, by beating it. Beat it when cold, just before using, to smooth and thin it slightly—it should look shiny, and mound lightly when layered in a tart.

Use this pastry cream to fill tarts, cakes, puff pastry desserts, cream puffs, or éclairs. It keeps in the refrigerator up to five days if chilled right after it is cooked.

To make Frangipane Cream: Make one recipe pastry cream, above, and after straining it, add 3 finely crushed Italian macaroons with a few drops of kirsch to taste. This is delicious for Peach, Nectarine, Pear, or Apricot tarts.

7

VANILLA BAVARIAN CREAM

Makes about 1 quart: *1¾ cups milk · ½ cup sugar · 3-inch piece of vanilla bean · 6 egg yolks · 1 tablespoon plus 1 teaspoon gelatin · ¼ cup cold water · 1¼ cups whipping cream*

Heat the milk, sugar, and the split and scraped piece of vanilla bean in a non-corroding saucepan to just under boiling. Whisk the egg yolks just enough to mix them and stir in some of the hot milk mixture. Return to the pan and cook over low heat, stirring constantly, until the mixture coats the spoon. Strain the custard into a bowl.

Sprinkle the gelatin over the cold water in a small pan and let soften a few minutes. Dissolve over low heat—it should not get hotter than 105°F to 115°F. If the temperature should go over 150°F the gelatin will denature and lose its jelling power. Stir the dissolved gelatin into the custard. Whip the cream until it holds very soft mounds when some of the cream is dropped from the beaters.

Set the bowl of custard over ice water and stir constantly, scraping the sides of the bowl with a rubber spatula. When the custard is slightly thickened and cooled, quickly whisk it into the whipped cream. Finish by folding it with a rubber spatula to be sure that the two mixtures are thoroughly mixed. Rub a 1-quart mold very lightly with a paper towel moistened with sweet almond oil. (Sweet almond oil can usually be bought at pharmacies: it is a light flavorless oil perfect for oiling molds for jelled desserts. If you can't find it, substitute another light flavorless oil.) Pour the Bavarian mixture into the mold and chill at least 6 hours.

To unmold, carefully run a table knife around the sides of the mold to loosen the Bavarian. Set a serving plate on top and invert. Tap or shake gently. If the Bavarian does not come out, lift one edge of the mold and slip the knife between it and the Bavarian to release the vacuum.

Serve in a pool of lightly sweetened berry purée and garnish with berries. Or serve with sliced peaches, or with Warm Chocolate Sauce. Accompany with Bow Ties or other crisp cookies.

FROZEN MOUSSE

Makes 3½ cups mousse, enough to fill the center of a 1½-quart bombe:
½ cup sugar · ⅜ cup water · 4 egg yolks · 1 cup whipping cream · Pernod, Cognac, Chartreuse, Armagnac, kirsch, vanilla extract, or other flavoring of your choice

Heat the sugar and water in a small saucepan and boil until the temperature reaches 220°F on a candy thermometer. Meanwhile, beat the egg yolks in a small bowl until they are very pale and light and they form a ribbon for 1 second when the beater is lifted. Pour the hot syrup slowly in a thin stream into the egg yolks, beating them constantly and being especially careful to beat the yolks well when you start adding the syrup so the eggs don't curdle. Then set the bowl over ice water and beat until thick and cold. The mixture should hold a ribbon for 3 seconds when the beater is lifted.

Whip the cream stiff with the chosen flavoring and quickly fold it into the cold egg yolk mixture. You will need about 1 tablespoon of Cognac or Armagnac for this much mousse, but only ⅜ teaspoon of Pernod or ½ teaspoon of Chartreuse. The flavoring should be added to your taste, and in an amount that will complement the other flavor of the finished bombe. Taste and adjust the flavoring, if necessary, and pour into a bombe mold lined with sherbet. Freeze the bombe until firm. Put a final layer of your choice of sherbet on the top and freeze again until firm.

This is the basic recipe I use to make the filling for sherbet bombes. I don't think it works well with ice creams, but its light creamy texture is a perfect foil for fruit sherbets and it can carry all sorts of spirits and citrus peels as flavoring. There seems an almost endless possibility for flavor combinations, and the desserts can be made to look either subtle or striking. You can make different designs in the slices by enclosing the mousse on all four sides with sherbet. If you are using only ice creams or sherbets, you can make even-sized layers for a striped appearance, or angled layers that are deep on one side and shallow on the other—use your imagination.

As well as offering their variety of taste and visual appeal, these wonderful desserts leave you free to entertain at the table—they *must* be made ahead of time. At the restaurant we use stainless steel loaf pans so that we will be able to cut similar-looking slices for everyone, but if you have a true bombe mold, use it and bring the whole dessert to the table to serve it.

To unmold the bombe, dip it in cold water, run a knife around the edge, and invert on a serving plate or tray. Return to the freezer, uncovered, to harden the surface again, then cover and leave in the freezer until serving time.

FROZEN CARAMEL MOUSSE

Makes a generous quart: *8 egg yolks · 3 tablespoons water · ⅞ cup sugar · ½ cup boiling water · 1⅝ cups whipping cream · 1½ teaspoons vanilla extract, to taste*

Beat the egg yolks until pale yellow and stiff enough to hold a ribbon for 1 or 2 seconds when the beater is lifted from the mixture.

Make the caramel: Put the 3 tablespoons water in a small, heavy, light-colored saucepan. Sprinkle in the sugar and let it stand to absorb the water. Do not mix it. When the water is absorbed, boil the mixture until it turns pale gold. Be careful that it doesn't get too dark or the mousse will taste burned. To check the true color, tip the pan so you are looking only at a thin layer. You can put the pan back on the heat if the caramel isn't dark enough, but note that the heat of the pan will continue cooking it even when it is removed from the heat. Have the boiling water ready. Remove the pale gold sugar mixture from the heat and set the pan in the sink. Pour the boiling water into it carefully: this stops the cooking and prevents further browning of the caramel. Stand well back when doing this so as not to be burned by the spattering caramel.

Set the pan back on the heat and simmer just until all the caramel has dissolved, stirring constantly. Pour the caramel in a very thin stream into the beaten egg yolks, beating constantly so the eggs don't curdle. Set the mixture over a bowl of ice and beat until it is cool and holds a soft shape. Then whip the cream with the vanilla until it mounds softly, and fold it thoroughly into the egg yolk–caramel mixture. Both mixtures must be beaten stiff enough that they won't separate while freezing. Pour into a container or parfait glasses and freeze.

10

Frozen caramel mousse is delicious with many kinds of fruit and can be used in a number of composed desserts. Garnish individual servings with a caramelized walnut, or with a raspberry on a rosette of crème Chantilly.

SHORT CRUST PASTRY

Makes one 9-inch pastry shell: *1 cup flour · 1 tablespoon sugar · ¼ teaspoon salt · ¼ teaspoon grated lemon peel · ½ cup unsalted butter, not too cold · 1 tablespoon water · ½ teaspoon vanilla extract*

Mix the flour, sugar, salt, and lemon peel. If you use salted butter, omit the salt. Cut the butter into ½-inch slices and work it into the flour mixture with your hands or a pastry blender until the butter is in mostly cornmeal-size pieces and the mixture is beginning to hold together—the softer your butter is, the faster this will happen. You can make this pastry with butter that is quite soft, as it might be in the summer, as long as you don't work it too much. Combine the water and vanilla and work it into the flour-butter mixture just until the pastry is blended and will hold together if you press it. Gather it into a ball and wrap it in plastic. Let it rest for 30 minutes so the flour will absorb the moisture more completely. At this point you can wrap the pastry in foil and freeze it for up to a month.

Press the pastry into a 9-inch tart pan, making sure that you have a layer of even thickness over the bottom and the sides. If the thickness is uneven, some parts will bake too much before other parts are cooked. Do not use a black tart pan; the shell may burn if you do. Before baking, set the shell in the freezer for 30 minutes or overnight, wrapped in foil. You don't need to fill the shell with beans before baking: this pastry doesn't shrink much. Bake in a preheated 375°F oven for about 25 minutes, or until the shell is light golden brown and baked all the way through.

I have found that about an ounce of this pastry is needed for each inch of pan size, so if you have an 11-inch tart pan you would need to make about two ounces more of pastry—or about a fourth again as much as this recipe.

To make almond-flavored pastry: Omit the grated lemon peel and add a few drops of almond extract with the vanilla extract.

BUTTER COOKIES

For 4½ dozen small cookies, or half as many 2½-inch cookies: *1 cup unsalted butter · ¾ cup sugar · 1 egg yolk · 1 teaspoon vanilla extract, or ½ teaspoon grated orange peel plus ¼ teaspoon orange flower water, or ½ teaspoon grated lemon peel, or 1 ounce sweetened chocolate · 2 cups flour · ⅛ teaspoon salt*

I find these cookies taste richer when I use half unsalted and half salted butter. If you use salted butter, be sure to omit the salt called for above.

If the butter is not soft, cut it in ½-inch-thick slices, put it into a metal mixing bowl, and heat it briefly in order to melt about an eighth of it. Let it stand a few minutes for the temperature to equalize and soften the rest of the butter. Cream the butter until it is light and fluffy, add the sugar, and beat until fluffy again. Add the egg yolk and beat until light again. If you are using chocolate, melt it over hot water and then let it cool briefly. Beat the chocolate, or whatever other flavor you are using, into the butter-egg yolk mixture. Work in the flour, and the salt if you need it, until just evenly mixed. The dough will be soft, but manageable if you handle it lightly.

Shape the cookie dough into rolls any size you like. I usually make rolls about 1¼ inches in diameter, shaping the dough by rolling it in plastic wrap. After chilling it I slice it, unwrapped, to make little one- or two-bite cookies. You can also make the rolls and then flatten them to make bar-shaped cookies.

Or you can divide the dough and make half of it chocolate and the other half orange or vanilla. Pat each piece of dough flat into a ¼-inch-thick long rectangle on plastic wrap. Chill them slightly until you can move them easily but the dough can still be rolled. Lay one rectangle on top of the other, leaving about ¼ inch of the bottom one showing on one long edge. Begin a tight roll on that edge, turning the exposed ¼ inch over the top layer to start the roll. This will give you a spiral design when you slice the dough.

When the cookie dough is rolled, chill it. Slice it straight or on the diagonal a scant ¼-inch thick and lay the cookies on a baking sheet at least 1½ inches apart. Bake in a preheated 350°F oven 10 to 12 minutes, depending on their size, or until they are golden brown on the bottom and very lightly browned on top. These are best baked shortly before serving time and kept in a tightly closed container to maintain crispness.

LANGUES DE CHAT

For 30 cookies, 2½ by ½ inches: *¼ cup soft unsalted butter · ⅓ cup sugar · A few drops of vanilla extract · A pinch of salt · 2 egg whites, at room temperature · ⅓ cup flour*

Cream the butter, sugar, vanilla, and salt until fluffy. Beat in the egg whites just enough to blend them and then the flour only until mixed— do not overbeat. Butter and flour a baking sheet. Using a pastry bag with a plain round ⅜-inch opening, pipe out tongues about ½ inch apart. Hold the tip almost vertical to the baking sheet and very close to it so that you get a very thin layer of batter.

Bake in a preheated 425°F oven for 4 to 5 minutes, or until the cookies have browned lightly around the edges but are paler in the center. Remove them immediately from the baking sheet to a cooling rack. If they harden before you can take them off the sheet, return the pan to the oven briefly to soften them again.

Store Langues de Chat in an airtight container until serving time.

COOKIE CUPS

For 12 to 14 cups: Make one recipe of Langues de Chat batter (see preceding recipe). Butter and flour a heavy baking sheet that will not flex in the oven and mark 5-inch circles on the pan—use a demitasse saucer or something of similar size for a guide. Spread a slightly rounded tablespoon of the batter as smoothly as you can on each circle. Have some custard cups or individual brioche tins ready to use for forming the cups.

Bake in a preheated 425°F oven for 4 to 5 minutes, or until they are golden brown almost all over. Set out the custard cups upside down. Quickly remove the cookies from the baking sheet and lay them over the cups with the bottom side of the cookies up. Pinch the cookies in gently around the cups to make a fluted shape. Hold them until they have cooled slightly and have set, then remove to a rack to cool. If the remaining cookies cool too much to form, set them back in the oven for a few moments to soften again. Store the cooled and finished cups in an airtight container until ready to serve. They can be served filled with any kind of ice cream and sauce.

To make Nut Cookie Cups: Follow the above recipe, but just before you bake the cookies sprinkle the top of each one with about ½ teaspoon very finely chopped walnuts, black walnuts, almonds, hazelnuts, or pecans. You will need 2 or 3 tablespoons for this recipe. Bake and form as directed.

CRÊPE BATTER

Makes about 1 quart batter, enough for 32 crêpes 6 inches in diameter:
2 cups milk · ¼ teaspoon salt · ½ teaspoon sugar · 4 tablespoons unsalted butter · 1¼ cups flour · 1 tablespoon vegetable oil · 3 eggs · ½ cup beer

Heat the milk, salt, sugar, and butter until the butter has melted. Measure the flour into a mixing bowl, make a well in it, put in the oil, and break in the whole eggs. Mix slightly with a whisk or an electric hand mixer to incorporate some of the flour. When it starts to thicken, add the warm milk mixture, little by little, beating it well until smooth. When you have added a little over 1 cup of milk, or enough to make a medium-thick batter, continue to beat until it is quite smooth, adding the rest of the milk mixture gradually. Mix in the beer and strain into a refrigerator container.

Chill the batter for at least 2 hours before frying. I always make it the day before I am going to use it; by that time the flour has surely absorbed as much liquid as it can and has also relaxed after the beating process.

14

The batter will keep for five days to a week with no problem. The crêpes can also be fried several hours before you want to use them, then kept stacked and tightly wrapped in plastic.

To fry the crêpes: Let the batter warm slightly; there probably will be a layer of congealed butter on the top. If you are in a hurry, skim off that layer, put it in a pan and warm it, stirring all the while, until melted; then stir it back into the rest of the batter.

Heat your crêpe pan until a drop of water sizzles when you throw it in the pan. You may rub the pan with butter and wipe it out with a paper towel to keep the first crêpe from sticking; you won't need to do it again. Lift the pan off the heat and ladle about 2 tablespoons of the batter into the center of the pan. (Measure 2 tablespoons of water into your ladle to see how full you will want it when you dip up the batter.) There shouldn't be any more batter than will stick to the bottom of the pan in a thin layer when you pour it in.

Tilt and rotate the pan immediately to make the batter run around the edge and cover the rest of the bottom evenly, then set the pan back on the heat. If you didn't get enough batter to cover the bottom of the pan, drizzle a bit more into the empty spaces. Try not to get too much batter in the pan, or the crêpe will be thick and soggy. The batter should bubble when it hits the pan and make little holes that go all the way through the crêpe. That way you will have very delicate, lacy crêpes that can be crisped easily. Brown the first side—it takes about 1 minute on my stove over a medium-hot flame. If the edge browns too fast, run a silver knife around the edge of the pan to loosen just the thin edge of the crêpe so it will be pulled away from the pan and won't burn while the rest is browning. To turn the crêpe, lift one edge with a silver knife. Check to see if it is browned enough; if so, lift the crêpe and turn it over with your hands. Cook the second side for about 1 minute also and turn out on a piece of plastic wrap. The side that browns first is the right side of the crêpe and it should be brown and lacy.

Stack the crêpes right side down as you fry them so they are ready to fill as you take them from the stack. Wrap them in plastic; they will keep for several hours at room temperature, or overnight in the refrigerator if you don't want to use them immediately.

You can also serve the hot crêpes straight from the pan. Drizzle them with melted sweet butter, sprinkle with sugar and Grand Marnier or some other liqueur, fold to a quarter circle, and eat immediately.

To crisp the crêpes for an ice cream filling: Heat the oven to 375°F and put as many crêpes as will fit in a single layer on a rack—a cooling rack will do. They must be spaced apart for air to circulate around them. Set the rack over a cookie sheet, making sure air can circulate under the crêpes, and put it in the oven. Start checking them after about 2 minutes. When they are crisp all around their edges but you can still fold them in the center, take them out and let them cool, folded in half, on another rack. Repeat until you have one for each serving, then put them on plates. Fill with the ice cream and shake a little powdered sugar over the tops. Drizzle with sauce, if you like, and serve.

I usually use peanut oil in this recipe, but you can substitute walnut or hazelnut oil, depending on how the crêpes are to be used and what they will be served with.

To make Buckwheat Crêpes: Substitute ¼ cup plus 1 tablespoon buckwheat flour for an equal amount of the regular flour.

To make Black Walnut Crêpes or Pecan Crêpes: Add 3 tablespoons milk to the basic crêpe batter. Chop ½ cup (2 ounces) black walnuts or pecans and add them to the batter just before you are ready to fry the crêpes.

Serve the crêpes brushed with melted butter and sprinkled with sugar and Cognac, or serve crisped, filled with Pear Ice Cream (page 50) and drizzled with Cognac Caramel Sauce (page 261).

SPONGE CAKE

For a 9-inch cake: *6 eggs • ¾ cup sugar • 1 teaspoon vanilla extract • ⅔ cup all-purpose flour • ⅓ cup cake flour • ⅛ teaspoon salt • ½ teaspoon grated lemon peel*

Butter and flour a 9-inch springform pan. Whisk the eggs and sugar over hot water or above a flame to warm them slightly. Remove from the heat, add the vanilla, and beat until the mixture holds a 3-second ribbon. Sift the flours, measure, and add the salt. Sprinkle the grated lemon peel over the beaten eggs and sift some of the flour over. Using a whisk, fold

16

it in quickly but gently and only partially. Give the whisk a shake each time you bring it up through the batter. It will help break up any lumps of cake flour. Continue sifting more of the flour over, folding in about three-fourths of each addition, until all the flour is added. Finish folding quickly. Pour the batter into the springform pan and bake in a preheated oven at 325°F for 35 minutes or so, until the top springs back when lightly pressed.

To serve, slice the cake in half crosswise, fill it with fruit curd, and ice it with whipped cream. Or slice it in half or thirds, sprinkle with rum, and fill with zabaglione. Ice with whipped cream and garnish with finely chopped candied orange or tangerine peel.

LADYFINGERS

For about three dozen 3-inch ladyfingers, 1-inch wide: *3 eggs · 6 tablespoons sugar · ½ cup sifted cake flour · ⅛ teaspoon salt · 1½ teaspoons orange flower water or other flavoring · ¼ teaspoon cream of tartar · Vanilla powdered sugar to shake over (page 4)*

Butter and flour two baking sheets. Separate the eggs and beat the yolks with half the sugar until they are very light and hold a 3-second ribbon. Whisk in the flour and salt until it is just mixed and stir in the orange flower water. Warm the egg whites slightly over hot water or swirl above a gas flame until barely warm. Beat them with the cream of tartar until they hold stiff peaks. Beat in the remaining 3 tablespoons sugar until they again hold stiff peaks. Fold in the egg yolk mixture quickly. Be careful not to deflate the whites or you will have flat ladyfingers.

Using a pastry bag with a plain ½-inch round tip, pipe the batter quickly onto the baking sheets, leaving about an inch of space between the cookies. Shake or sieve a thin layer of the vanilla powdered sugar over the tops of the cookies. Bake in a preheated 325°F oven for 10 to 15 minutes depending on the size of the cookies, or until they have just begun to brown slightly around their edges. Let them stand on the baking sheet about a minute after coming from the oven to firm up a bit, then remove to cool on a rack. You can shake more of the sugar over them at this

17

point if you want a heavier coating. You can also bake the cookies about 5 minutes longer to make dry, crisp cookies.

Use ladyfingers for lining molds for Bavarians, or serve them with various fruit desserts. The crisp ladyfingers are delicious with ice creams and sherbets.

CREAM PUFFS

For about 40 small puffs, or a Saint-Honoré ring and 26 to 28 small puffs: *1 cup water · 6 tablespoons unsalted butter · ⅛ teaspoon salt · ½ teaspoon sugar · 1 cup flour · 4 to 5 eggs · Optional: 1 egg yolk · Optional: 2 teaspoons whipping cream*

Preheat the oven to 400°F.

To make the puffs: Heat the water, butter, salt, and sugar in a heavy saucepan. When it boils, remove from the heat, add the flour all at once, and quickly stir it in until the mixture is smooth. Return to medium heat and cook, stirring, until the dough makes a ball in the pan and follows the spoon. It will be quite stiff. Heat a minute or two longer to cook the flour thoroughly. Remove from the heat and pour into a mixing bowl. Break one of the eggs into the center and beat until it is smoothly mixed in. Add 3 more eggs this way. If you think the dough is as soft as it can be and still hold a shape, there is enough egg in it. Otherwise, break the fifth egg into a bowl, beat it with a fork, and add half of it to the dough, beating it in well. Add the remaining half egg if you think it is needed. This is an important step: since the eggs provide the leavening for the dough, you want to work in as many as possible without making the dough too liquid. It should be glossy and smooth and just hold its shape.

Butter a baking sheet or line it with parchment paper and put the dough into a pastry bag with a tip with a ½-inch plain opening. Pipe mounds 1¼-inches wide by 1-inch high about 1½ inches apart onto the sheet. Or you can spoon heaping teaspoonfuls of dough onto the sheet. If you want to glaze the puffs, beat the egg yolk and cream with a fork and brush on the tops of the puffs only. If the glaze drips onto the baking sheet, it will glue the puff down and keep it from rising. If you are going to dip the

18

puffs in caramel, as for the Saint-Honoré Cake, they needn't be glazed.

Put the puffs in the oven and immediately turn the heat down to 375°F. Bake the puffs for about 15 minutes, or until they are golden brown and well puffed. Take them from the oven, prick each one with the tip of a sharp knife in an inconspicuous place, and put them back into the oven for 5 minutes to dry out. Cool on a rack. If you are not using the puffs within an hour, crisp them in a 375°F oven for a few minutes shortly before filling.

The puffs can be filled with all sorts of flavored creams and served with fruits, fruit sauces, or chocolate sauce. They can also be filled with savory mixtures and served as appetizers. They are the basis of the Saint-Honoré Cake, and can also be made into éclairs filled with different pastry creams.

SAVARIN

Makes 5½ cups dough, enough for a 10-inch bundt pan or a 9-inch spring-form pan, for 16 to 20 servings: *1½ tablespoons dry yeast · ¼ cup warm water · 8 eggs · ½ cup less 1 tablespoon milk · 2 tablespoons sugar · ¾ teaspoon salt · 1-inch piece of vanilla bean · 3¾ cups flour · 1½ cups unsalted butter*

Sprinkle the yeast over the warm water in a small bowl. Put the whole unshelled eggs in another bowl, cover with hot water to warm them, and set aside. Put the milk, sugar, and salt in a small saucepan. Split the vanilla bean lengthwise, scrape out the tiny black seeds, and add the seeds and pod to the milk mixture. Warm the mixture until the sugar and salt have dissolved. Measure the flour into a large mixing bowl. When the yeast bubbles, stir in enough of the flour from the mixing bowl to make a soft dough. Let it rise until double and bubbly.

Make a well in the remaining flour and break the warmed eggs into it. Pour in the warm milk mixture, leaving the vanilla pod behind, and add the yeast mixture. Whisk this all together until smooth. Cut the butter in ½-inch thick slices and lay them over the top of the dough. Cover and set aside in a warm place to rise. The dough will rise faster without the butter, but if you put the butter on top it will be the same temperature as the dough when you are ready to beat it in. When the dough has risen double, beat in the butter until it is well mixed and smooth.

Savarin is traditionally baked in a ring mold, but I like to use a bundt pan or even a 9-inch springform pan. Fill whichever pan half full. Let rise in a warm place again until the dough just reaches the top of the pan, and set it, without jarring, into a preheated 350°F oven. Bake for 55 minutes to 1 hour, or until it is firm, golden brown, and pulling away from the sides. You can slide it out of the pan onto a rack near the end of the baking to check the browning of the sides. They should be golden brown, too.

For the syrup: *2 cups water · 1 cup sugar · ¾ to 1 cup kirsch*

While the cake is baking, make the syrup: Boil the water and sugar together for a few minutes, remove from the heat, and let cool slightly. Add the kirsch. When the cake comes from the oven, prick the top with a fork and turn out onto a baking sheet—one with sides, not a flat one. Ladle the syrup over the savarin gradually while it is still warm and let it stand to soak up the syrup from the bottom of the pan, spooning some over the top occasionally.

For the glaze: *½ to ¾ cup apricot jam · 1 teaspoon kirsch*

When the syrup has been absorbed, heat the apricot jam to boiling and add the kirsch. Brush the cake with the jam, reheating as necessary. Move the cake carefully to a serving plate. When you are ready to serve it, heat the jam again and brush on another coat. The first coat usually soaks in, so the cake will be much prettier if you brush on a second.

Serve with strawberries, cherries, or poached pineapple sections, garnished with crème Chantilly.

RUM BABAS

To the recipe for the savarin add 6 tablespoons currants and 4 tablespoons golden raisins that have been slightly warmed with a little rum to plump them. Stir them in after you have beaten in the butter. Fill baba molds a third full with the dough, let it rise to within ¼ inch of the top, and bake as for the savarin. This will take 15 to 20 minutes. Or bake in a large pan as for the savarin. Substitute rum for the kirsch in the syrup. Serve with crème Chantilly.

I like to bake these in individual brioche molds at the restaurant, where I glaze them, split them two-thirds across to make hinged sandwiches, and pipe in crème Chantilly so it oozes from the center of the cakes. In any case, do serve babas with crème Chantilly.

This recipe is essentially that given in Prosper Montagné's *Larousse Gastronomique*.

BRIOCHE

Makes a generous 2½ pounds dough, to fill two 9-inch cake pans: *1 tablespoon dry yeast · ¼ cup warm water · 4 cups flour · 2 tablespoons sugar · 1 teaspoon salt · 6 eggs · 1½ cups unsalted butter*

Brioche is versatile. Use it to enclose main courses like salmon coulibiacs, as savory appetizers before dinner, and in many ways as dessert. Cut in ½-inch slices, sprinkle with sugar, and glazed briefly under the broiler, it makes a delicious substitute for cookies with fruit desserts. You can also use it for an elegant bread pudding. The chilled dough can be rolled out, filled with cinnamon-sugar mixtures, and baked for breakfast pastries. Brioches can also be baked, then hollowed out to contain fruit or pastry cream mixtures.

Sprinkle the yeast over the water in a small bowl and set aside 10 minutes or so until it bubbles. Mix the flour, sugar, and salt in a large bowl. If the eggs are cold, put them unshelled in a bowl and cover with hot water to warm them. When the yeast mixture is bubbly, stir in about 7 table-spoons of the flour mixture from the large bowl until it forms a smooth, light batter. Set aside in a warm place, preferably between 75°F and 95°F, and let it rise until double. Make a well in the flour mixture and break in the eggs. Scrape in the yeast and beat with a wooden spoon, or in a food processor or mixer, until the dough is smooth.

Slice each stick of butter into 4 lengthwise strips and distribute them over the top of the dough. Adding the butter in this way, without working it into the dough, permits the yeast to accomplish the first rising without

21

having to work against the butter. The butter will also warm to the same temperature as the dough. Cover and let rise in a warm place until tripled in bulk. This will take about 1½ hours.

Punch the dough down and beat in the butter until the dough is satiny and smooth. You may knead it in by hand but it is much easier to use a machine for this job. This dough is too soft and sticky to knead in the usual way—work it by picking it up and slapping it down on the board. The dough will be stringy and hard to work with at first, but as the butter is assimilated it will become very smooth, satiny, and light. When the dough is smooth put it back in the bowl to rise until double, about 1 hour. You may also refrigerate it to let it rise slowly overnight, covered with a plate weighted with a heavy object.

The long, slow rise will give the brioche a fine texture. Take it directly from the refrigerator and shape it without letting it warm. There is so much butter and egg in the dough that as soon as it warms it becomes sticky and hard to manage. If the dough has had the second rise at room temperature, you will have to chill it to make a freeform shape like a ring, or to roll the dough for a cinnamon roll. If the dough is to be baked in pans or molds, divide it into pieces large enough to fill the pans half full, work each piece very briefly to a tight ball, and put it in a buttered pan. Let the dough rise, covered, to the top of the pans, until it does not spring back when pressed gently with the fingertips. You may want to brush the top very lightly with a mixture of eggs and cream or milk—this will make the brioche a rich golden brown. Bake in a preheated 375°F oven until golden brown and firm: for individual brioches this will take about 20 minutes, for an average size loaf, 35 to 45 minutes. Remove the brioche from the baking pan and cool on a rack.

PIE CRUST

Makes a little more than one pound, enough for two 9-inch pie shells:
*2 cups unbleached all-purpose flour · ⅜ teaspoon salt · ⅛ teaspoon sugar ·
5 tablespoons cold salted butter · 6½ tablespoons cold unsalted butter · 3 tablespoons vegetable shortening · 3 tablespoons plus 1 teaspoon ice water*

Mix the flour, salt, and sugar in a bowl. Cut the salted butter in pieces
⅓-inch thick and quickly cut them into the flour mixture until it is the
texture of cornmeal. You can do this with a pastry blender, with your
hands by rubbing quickly and lightly between your fingers, or in an
electric mixer or food processor. Cut in the unsalted butter and the vegetable shortening until they are in larger pieces, about ⅛ to ¼ inch in
diameter. This helps to make the dough flaky. Sprinkle in the 3 tablespoons
ice water, tossing the dough lightly with a fork to moisten it evenly. Use
another teaspoon of water if necessary to make the dough hold together.
Stir the dough with the fork until it has come together in small lumps
and there is no dry flour left.

   Divide the dough in half and press it into two balls. Be careful not to
knead it—just squeeze it together. Kneading activates the gluten, which
makes the dough tough. However, if the dough is crumbly, knead it
together very briefly. Wrap tightly in plastic and chill for at least 4 hours.
During this time the enzymes in the flour will mellow the gluten to permit
the water to be absorbed completely; this conditioning will help to prevent
shrinkage and toughness later.

   To roll the pastry, flour your board or marble lightly and roll the dough
quickly into a 12- to 13-inch circle ⅛-inch thick. Fold it in half to move
it, or roll it loosely around the rolling pin, then unroll it over your pie
plate. Ease the pastry gently, without stretching it, into the contours of
the pie plate. If you stretch the dough now it will shrink back to its
original size when you bake it.

   For a single-crust pie: Cut off the pastry about ½ inch beyond the edge
of the pan. Turn the crust under the rim of the pan, even with the edge,
and crimp it with a fork; or make a scalloped edge by pressing and
crimping it with your fingers. Prick the bottom all over with a fork.

   At this point I always freeze the dough for 15 to 30 minutes or longer.

23

This helps to relax the dough and keep it from shrinking. I always prebake the shells for single-crust pies, and I have found that it isn't necessary to weight the shell with beans or the like if I line the frozen shell tightly with a piece of aluminum foil. If you prefer, fill the foil with beans.

Bake the lined shell in a preheated oven at 375°F for about 20 minutes, or until the pastry is set and dry on the bottom. Remove the foil, turn the heat down to 350°F, and continue baking another 10 to 15 minutes, or until the crust is golden brown. Cool. Now the pastry is ready for any filling, whether it is to be baked again or not. If the edge of the filled pie begins to brown too much while baking, cover with a strip of foil for the rest of the baking period.

For a two-crust pie: Trim the pastry of the bottom crust even with the edge of the pan. Fill the pastry and brush the rim with water. Quickly roll out the top crust ⅛-inch thick and 1 or 2 inches larger than the pan. Fold or roll up on the rolling pin as before and lay over the filling. Cut excess pastry off ½ inch beyond the edge of the pan and press the crusts together all around the edge to seal them. Fold the edge under the bottom crust and crimp the edge as before. Glaze the crust as directed in your recipe, and incise a design ¹⁄₁₆-inch deep into the top of the pie, cutting all the way through in a few places to make vents for steam to escape while baking. Bake as directed in the individual recipe.

At the restaurant we have fun with those incised designs, drawing leaves, leaves and fruit, abstract designs, things that look like spiderwebs, people's initials, designs that suggest the sizes of serving pieces—anything we can think of. Sometimes we make cutouts from extra scraps of dough, sticking them to top crusts by brushing them with water—you can use small cookie cutters or truffle cutters for that, or cut them freehand.

PUFF PASTRY

Makes about 2¾ pounds of dough, enough for 3 or 4 tart shells: *2¾ cups all-purpose flour (12 ounces)* · *1 cup cake flour (4¼ ounces)* · *1¼ teaspoons salt* · *2½ cups cold unsalted butter (1¼ pounds)* · *2 tablespoons lemon juice* · *1 cup ice water*

Mix the flours and the salt together in a bowl, and take out ½ cup and set aside. Cut ¾ cup (6 ounces) of the butter into the flour until the mixture has the texture of cornmeal. Put the lemon juice in a measuring cup and add enough ice water to make 1 cup in all. The lemon juice helps relax the gluten in the flour; this will make the rolling of the dough easier. Add the water to the flour mixture, tossing with a fork to mix it evenly. Press it together; don't knead it or strands of gluten will develop in the dough and toughen the pastry. Add a bit more water if it is needed to make a soft dough. Gather the dough into a ball, squeezing to make it hold together, and flatten it to a ¾-inch-thick circle.

At this stage the dough is called the *détrempe.* Wrap the détrempe well in plastic and refrigerate for 30 minutes. It is important that the first four turns be made while the butter is cold, but malleable—if it hardens, the butter layer will break inside the dough, perhaps even break through it. It is important to follow the timings given here for this reason. After about 15 minutes, cut the remaining butter into ½-inch pieces and beat with a wooden spoon or rolling pin, or in a mixer, until it is smooth. There should be no lumps. Work in the reserved ½ cup flour until it is smoothly mixed. The butter should still be cold—about 60°F is good if you want to check the temperature. Form the butter into a square about ¾-inch thick, wrap in plastic, and lay it on top of the détrempe in the refrigerator so their temperatures will be identical.

When the détrempe has rested 30 minutes, quickly roll it on a lightly floured board or marble to a square ½-inch thick. It should be a little more than twice the size of the square of butter. Set the butter diagonally across the center of the square of dough and fold the corners of the dough tightly over the butter like the flaps of an envelope, enclosing it completely. Brush off any excess flour and pinch the dough closed tightly. Be sure to keep your rolling surface lightly floured at all times, but always brush any loose flour off the dough before you fold it or it will not stick together. The loose flour will also turn gray in the baking. Quickly roll this to a rectangle ½-inch thick and about 8 inches by 24 inches, trying always to keep the corners as square as possible.

In this first rolling, roll from the center out to but not over the edge. You want the butter to spread in an even layer to the edges of the dough; if you roll over the edges before the butter spreads to the edge, there will be a double thickness of dough with no butter layer. This is important: The dough rises in baking when the moisture in the butter vaporizes from the heat and forces the dough to expand. It is the many layers of butter trapped between the layers of dough that makes the pastry rise properly. It is best to use a large ball-bearing rolling pin. Lean and put your weight on the rolling pin rather than pushing with your arms. Roll from the center out, alternating directions. Roll the dough to the desired size quickly, in as few motions as possible. Rolling too much at this point will make the dough elastic and tough. If at any time the dough begins to be stretchy, chill it for 20 minutes before continuing.

Fold the left-hand third of the dough over the center, brush off excess flour, and then fold the right-hand third over that. The rolling and folding you have just done is called a *turn*. Rotate the dough 90 degrees. Roll again to a rectangle ½-inch thick and about 8 inches by 24 inches. Fold in thirds again and wrap and chill for 30 minutes. You have completed the first two turns.

After the 30 minutes of chilling, make two more turns, always rotating the dough 90 degrees before making the next turn. It helps if you form the habit of always placing the top flap of dough to your left. Chill the dough for 45 minutes more. Then make two more turns and chill the dough about 2 hours before its final rolling and shaping. If at any time the dough softens or becomes elastic so you can't roll it properly, wrap it and chill it for 20 minutes or so. If the butter in the dough is too cold to roll smoothly, let the dough rest a few minutes on the board until you can roll it evenly.

The pastry will rise its highest if you shape it and bake it within 2 hours of the final turn. You may also keep it two or three days in the refrigerator, well wrapped, or several months in the freezer. To freeze, cut the pastry in quarters; each will be enough for one tart shell. Wrap them tight in foil. Before using, defrost overnight in the refrigerator. You can also freeze rolled tart shells or individual pastries, using the following instructions, if they are wrapped airtight. Glaze and bake them straight from the freezer.

To roll tart shells: Cut a piece of puff pastry weighing 10 to 12 ounces. Always use a sharp knife to cut the pastry or you will pinch its layers together, spoiling their ability to rise in the oven. For the same reason, never cut by sliding the knife through the pastry. Push the knife straight down, then lift it out and move it to the next position, pushing straight down again for the next cut.

Keep your rolling surface lightly floured so the pastry won't stick, but always brush off any excess flour before folding or layering the pastry. Roll it into a large circle about ⅛-inch thick. Using something like an 11-inch tart ring as a guide, make straight cuts about 1 inch outside its edge to make a rough octagon about 13 inches in diameter. Move the dough to a pizza pan or a baking sheet, then gently lift it and re-form it into a round. Brush the outer inch of the pastry with water. Roll the edge inward to make a rim, pinching it down at intervals to secure the edge to the bottom. Work quickly so the dough doesn't warm and soften. This will make an informal tart shell about 9 inches in its inside diameter.

Prick the bottom all over with a fork, and chill it or freeze it. If they are tightly wrapped, puff pastry shells will keep refrigerated for two or three days or frozen for several months. They will rise highest and have the most delicate texture, though, if you bake the dough within a couple of hours of making the final turns and doing the final shaping.

Bake the shells in a preheated 400°F oven for 10 minutes. After 5 minutes, prick the shells and press the bottom down gently to keep it from puffing, repeating this every few minutes until the bottom is set. Turn the heat down to 350°F after the first 10 minutes and bake for about 15 minutes more, or until the sides are baked through and the tart shell is golden brown.

To roll individual puff pastries: Again, always keep the dough cold, the rolling surface lightly floured, and use a very sharp knife or cutter. Cut a piece of the dough large enough to allow about 1½ ounces of pastry for each individual piece. Roll out quickly until ⅛-inch to 3/16-inch thick. Before you cut the dough, lift it gently from the board or marble and let it retract. This prevents the pieces from shrinking after you cut them.

Small pastries can be cut with any shape cutter you like—as long as it is sharp. You can also cut squares, rectangles, and the like with a knife. For a single serving, I cut them about 2½-inches to 3-inches square, or in shapes with an equivalent area. As soon as they are cut, turn them over and set them on a lightly moistened baking sheet. This will make the pastry adhere evenly to the pan and help it rise evenly in the oven. Chill them on the pan in the refrigerator or freezer for 10 to 15 minutes. You can cut small decorations for the top of pies, tarts, or individual pastries with sharp truffle cutters or other tiny cutters. You can also make tiny freehand diamonds, leaves, or other shapes with a sharp knife—these should be chilled also. When you are ready to bake, brush the tops of the pastries with an egg-and-cream glaze, set these decorations in place, and glaze them also. If you like, use a sharp knife to incise a design ¹⁄₁₆-inch deep in the top of the pastry.

Set in a preheated 400°F oven, bake 10 minutes, reduce the heat to 350°F, and bake 15 to 20 minutes more, or until golden brown. Cool slightly, loosen with a spatula, and finish cooling on a rack.

To use scraps: Whenever possible, leftover puff pastry should be brushed free of excess flour, stacked in layers, pressed together, and chilled. Use such scraps when making tarts whose fruit fillings will be baked in the shell, or for various kinds of cookies where the amount of rise is not important.

PALM LEAVES

Roll out scraps on a board with sugar instead of flour. Roll into a rectangle and give the pastry a turn, sprinkling liberally with sugar. Let rest 15 minutes, then roll out into a long rectangle. Moisten the top very lightly with water, sprinkle with sugar, and fold the edges up the length of the rectangle to meet in the center. Press with the rolling pin to seal. Moisten the top of the pastry again very lightly, sprinkle with sugar, and fold in half lengthwise. Press with the rolling pin to seal and chill the strip of pastry. Slice cookies ¼-inch to ⅜-inch thick straight down through the strip of pastry. Place the cookies flat on a wet baking sheet. Leave the

28

space of one cookie between them. Bake in a preheated 350°F oven, and watch carefully after 15 to 20 minutes. When the bottoms are a golden brown caramel, flip them over with a spatula and return to the oven for 5 to 8 minutes, or until both sides are caramelized. Watch carefully—the cookies will burn very easily at this stage. Remove and cool on a rack. Serve immediately or store in an airtight container.

BOW TIES

Roll scraps of pastry ⅛-inch thick on a board sprinkled with sugar instead of flour. Cut the dough into rectangles 2½ inches by 1 inch. Twist each one twice in the center to make a bow-tie shape and lay on a chilled baking sheet. You may freeze them at this point or you may bake them after chilling them for 30 minutes. Bake in a preheated 400°F oven until golden brown and glossy on the bottom, 8 or 9 minutes. Turn them quickly with tongs and return to the oven for 2 to 4 minutes more, or until they are glossy brown on both sides. Some may finish baking before others; remove them to a cooling rack as they finish baking.

TWISTS

Roll scraps of pastry ⅛-inch thick on a board sprinkled with sugar instead of flour. Cut strips of pastry 5 inches to 7 inches long and ½-inch wide or so. Twist them 3 to 5 times and lay on a baking sheet. Chill for 30 minutes or freeze. Bake as for Bow Ties, above.

The caramel on all these cookies attracts moisture from the air, so serve them fairly soon after baking, or store immediately on cooling in an airtight container.

COUNTRY STYLE PUFF PASTRY

Makes about 2¼ pounds dough, enough for three 9-inch tart shells: *2½ cups unbleached flour · ¾ cup rye flour · 1 teaspoon salt · 2 cups cold unsalted butter (1 pound) · 1 cup ice water*

Combine the two flours and salt and mix them well. Set aside ½ cup of the mixture. Cut ¼ pound of the butter into small pieces and cut them into the flours with a pastry blender until the mixture resembles coarse meal. Add the ice water, tossing the flours with a fork until mostly mixed. Turn out onto a board and finish mixing by pushing it together with your hands and a pastry scraper, just until the mixture holds together in a ball. Wrap in plastic and refrigerate for an hour. This dough will be a little sticky, so be sure to keep the surfaces it comes in contact with floured.

Put the remaining ¾ pound of butter on a lightly floured board or between sheets of waxed paper and pound it with the rolling pin until it is malleable but not warm. Work in the reserved ½ cup of flours, pushing everything together with your pastry scraper until the flour is mixed in, being careful not to warm the butter too much. Wrap this in plastic and mold it into a square about ¾-inch thick.

Flour your rolling surface lightly and roll the dough into a rough 12-inch square. This dough is stickier than puff pastry usually is—use plenty of flour for rolling, but brush off any excess before folding. Put the butter in the center and pull the four sides up to cover it completely, being sure they overlap slightly in the center. Brush off any loose flour and press the pastry together to seal the edges over the butter. Roll the package lightly to make a rectangular shape, rolling from the center out and alternating directions. Now roll the package into a rectangle about ½-inch thick, being careful not to roll over the ends. Fold the left-hand third of the dough over the center third, brush off excess flour, and fold the right-hand third over that. This is the first turn. Rotate the dough 90 degrees and make one more complete turn, wrap well in plastic, and chill for another hour. Then make two more turns in the same manner, being careful to flour the board and rolling pin and then to brush off the excess. Chill for another hour and then make the fifth and sixth turns. Chill again, preferably overnight, before rolling for tart shells.

This makes delicious pastry for apple tarts, and also for savory tarts of all kinds—try it for a meat pie.

CLAY'S QUICK PUFF PASTRY

Makes about 3½ pounds of dough, enough for four or five 9-inch tart shells: *3½ cups all-purpose flour (14 ounces) · 1½ cups cake flour (6 ounces) · 1½ teaspoons salt · 3¼ cups unsalted butter (1 pound 10 ounces) · 2 tablespoons lemon juice · 1 cup ice water*

Mix the flours and salt together and set aside. Cut the butter into pieces ½-inch square and lay them on a baking sheet. Chill in the freezer until very hard. When the butter is hard, cut it into the flour mixture in a mixer, using the paddle, or in a food processor. Stop when the butter is cut into pieces about ¼ inch in diameter. Put the lemon juice in a measuring cup and add ice water to make 1 cup in all. Add this to the butter–flour mixture and mix only until moistened. The dough should not hold together yet.

Turn it out onto a lightly floured board or marble and press together into a rectangle. It will look very rough, with large chunks of butter showing. Press it hard enough to make it hold together, but do not knead it or the dough will toughen. Roll the rectangle out ½-inch thick. Fold one narrow end over the center third of the dough and fold the other end over that, making three layers of dough. Try to keep all the corners as square as possible so the layers build up evenly in the dough. Work as quickly as you can so the dough doesn't get warm. Working on a cold marble slab makes this much easier.

Refrigerate the dough for a few minutes any time it starts to soften. Give the dough package a quarter-turn, and roll it into a ½-inch-thick rectangle again. Fold it in thirds again. Repeat the rolling and folding twice more. Each of these operations is called one turn. After you have made these first four turns the dough will begin to look quite smooth.

Wrap the dough well in plastic and chill for an hour. Make two more turns; then chill for another hour to let it rest. The dough is now ready to be rolled for tarts or other desserts. You will get the highest rise from

31

your puff pastry if you shape and bake it within 2 hours of the final turn, but it can be stored in the refrigerator, tightly wrapped in plastic, for up to three days. It can also be kept frozen for several months.

CARAMEL

I use caramel reasonably often in these desserts for the richness of flavor and variety of texture it gives. You may have to try making caramel a few times to get the feel of how quickly the color changes and how it tastes when it gets too dark, but it is very easy to work with once you understand it. Always try to boil sugar for caramel in a light-colored saucepan so you can easily check the color as it deepens. It is important to keep a bowl of ice water at hand when you work with caramel, both to set the pan in to stop the cooking and to use for first aid if you should ever spatter yourself. Caramel burns terribly because it is very hot, from 310°F to 350°F, and it sticks to you. When I am adding liquids to hot caramel I try to set the pot in the bottom of my sink so that any spattering hits the sides of the sink instead of me. Even then I stand back, and even then I get burned occasionally.

Sugar crystals slow down the caramel-making process. When sugar is boiled long enough the sucrose breaks down into dextrose and levulose to form invert sugar, which does not crystallize easily. The caramel-making process can be speeded up by slow boiling, or by the presence of an acid like lemon juice or tartaric or citric acid. The acid should be added after boiling has started, at 220°F.

CARAMEL SYRUP

Makes ¾ cup: *1 cup sugar · 1⅓ cups hot water*

Put the sugar in a small, light-colored saucepan and add ⅓ cup of the water. Let it stand until the sugar is moistened. If you stir it to make it dissolve faster, you run the risk of putting sugar crystals on the side of

32

the pan; this encourages the sugar to crystallize while cooking and slows down the process immeasurably. Cook over medium to high heat, swirling the pan occasionally so the syrup won't begin browning on the outside edges. Continue cooking until the sugar is a light gold color, then take off the heat; the caramel will continue to darken. When the color is deep gold, carefully pour in the other cup of water. Return to the heat and cook, stirring constantly, until all the caramel has dissolved. Pour into a jar. This syrup will keep indefinitely in the refrigerator. Add it to fruit purées to sweeten them for sauces, or use it to flavor custards, or to line molds for custards.

CARAMEL FOR UPSIDE-DOWN TARTS

Makes enough for 1 tart: *½ cup sugar · 2 tablespoons unsalted butter*

Put the sugar and butter in a 9-inch black iron frying pan or a tinned copper tarte Tatin pan. The butter makes an opaque caramel the color of which can be checked in a black iron pan. Heat over medium to high heat, stirring constantly. The mixture will thicken and then begin to color. When it is light brown, take it from the heat and continue stirring it until it doesn't color any more. It should be a rich golden brown when finished. If it isn't dark enough, return it to the heat and cook until it is, always remembering that it will continue to darken just from the heat of the pan. Always stir until it has cooled and thickened slightly so a burned layer won't form on the bottom. When the caramel has reached the right color and is cooled and thickened, arrange the fruit over it according to your recipe.

PRALINE

Makes about 2 cups: *1 cup nuts (almonds, hazelnuts, or walnuts)* · *1 cup sugar* · *⅓ cup water*

Butter a baking sheet and chop the nuts coarse. Put the sugar in a pan and pour the water over it. Let it stand until the sugar is moistened and then cook it over medium to high heat until the syrup is golden. Take it off the heat and stir in the nuts with a wooden spoon. Return the mixture to the heat and cook just until the caramel liquefies again, then immediately pour it onto the buttered baking sheet. Spread it quickly with your spoon to a thin layer and let it cool. Be careful when you handle the baking sheet—it will be very hot at first. When it has cooled, pulverize the praline in a mortar, blender, or food processor, or chop it by hand. Store in a tightly covered jar in the refrigerator, where it will keep for weeks.

CARAMEL FOR DECORATIONS

Makes about a dozen individual cages: *½ cup sugar* · *2 tablespoons water* · *2 tablespoons corn syrup*

Put the sugar and water in a small, light-colored saucepan and let stand until the sugar is moistened. Add the corn syrup and cook over high heat, swirling the pan occasionally, until the syrup is light gold. Remove from the heat and set the pan in ice water to stop the cooking. When the caramel has cooled to about 250°F, it will be syrupy and you should be able to spin a thread with it. You can use it to make various kinds of decorations and cages. To make flat lace decorations, dip an ordinary fork into the caramel, then drizzle it in freeform threads on a buttered baking sheet, making decorations of almost any size and shape you care to. Be sure to keep the caramel at the right temperature, reheating it slightly as you need to. If you have an electric burner you may be able to regulate the temperature precisely—you will have to experiment.

These caramel threads can be formed into cages to cover fancy desserts, either for individual servings or even to cover a whole cake. To make individual cages, butter the outside of the bowl of a ladle. Again using a fork, pull threads of caramel back and forth across the ladle, crisscrossing them to build up a nestlike convex cage. As soon as the caramel is firm, but still warm, use scissors to clip off any threads around the bottom edge so the cage will sit flat, then gently slip it off the ladle to a buttered or parchment-lined baking sheet. As soon as you have finished, store in an airtight container with waxed paper or parchment between the layers. Serve these as soon as possible; caramel tends to condense moisture from the air and turn soggy.

Be careful when you eat these cages—the caramel is very brittle, even glassy, and the sharp ends of the threads can easily cut your mouth.

2

APPLES,
PEARS,
AND QUINCES

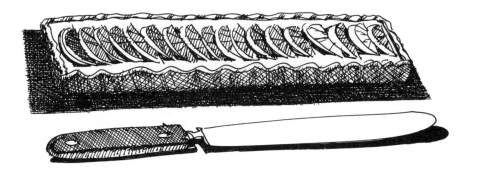

FOR ME apples mark the beginning of fall with its thinning light and its somber colors. It is time for apple tarts, charlottes, pies—comforting, satisfying desserts. Plain charlottes made with good McIntosh apples have a rustic appeal, with their golden toasted bread-and-butter shell surrounding a delicious apple purée; a sharp raspberry or red currant sauce adds sophistication. Similarly, crème fraîche or vanilla ice cream is the simplest complement for a mellow, buttery Tarte Tatin—but the dry herbal flavor of Chartreuse Ice Cream would be more adventurous, ending perfectly a dinner featuring game that might have grazed on such herbs.

To harmonize with an American menu, I would choose to accompany an apple tart with cinnamon ice cream, taking advantage of the traditional pairing of these flavors. For a menu inspired by foods of the Touraine, I might intersperse poached prunes with the apples, recalling the delicious prunes characteristic of that region. And for a Basque dinner, I might serve the tart with ice cream flavored with that flowery liqueur Izarra. The taste of the apples should always be foremost; accompanying flavors are secondary accents, there to add nuance and to tie the dessert in with the rest of the meal. Do use your own local apple varieties because the most flavorful ones, like California Gravensteins, often do not travel.

Pears are the workhorses of winter desserts. Their subtle perfume is enhanced by many flavors and, in turn, enhances them—anise, caramel, raspberry, Sauternes, Muscat, Cognac, Armagnac, and Late Harvest Riesling combine especially well with pears. Bosc pears are best poached whole or used halved in tarts to show off their graceful shape. The winy flavor and firm texture of Bosc and Winter Nelis pears are particularly suited to upside-down tarts, with their strong caramel flavor. Buttery Comices, the most delicately perfumed and smoothest textured of all, can be stuffed and baked and served with various flavors of ice cream or sabayon. Any pears can be made into fruit compotes with other fruits of the season.

Quinces have a heavenly perfume and turn a glorious red when cooked long enough. Keep a basket of them on your table and they will scent the whole house. An apple tart with a few slices of poached quinces is a study in fall colors, the russet and glossy brown echoing the changing leaves outside. One of the loveliest of fall fruit compotes is made of white poached pears, dark figs, and fresh red raspberries, with quinces and their pink syrup.

39

APPLE AND CALVADOS STRIPED BAVARIAN

For 8 to 10 servings: Apple layer: *1 pound McIntosh apples · 2 tablespoons water · 3 tablespoons sugar, to taste · 1½ teaspoons gelatin · ¼ cup cold water · ½ cup whipping cream · 1 teaspoon calvados, to taste*

Quarter, core, and peel the apples and slice them thin into a non-corroding saucepan. Add the water and cook, covered, stirring often, until they have broken down and you can whisk them into a coarse purée, about 15 minutes. Press the apples through a very fine strainer and measure 1 cup of smooth purée. Stir in the sugar. Sprinkle the gelatin over the cold water in a small pan and let stand a few minutes to soften. Dissolve the gelatin over medium heat, stirring or swirling it until it is hot, 115°F to 120°F. Stir the gelatin into the apple mixture and set aside to cool. Stir it occasionally while you make the calvados custard layer. Whip the cream with the calvados until the cream mounds very slightly when some is dropped from the beaters. Reserve the whipped cream to be added later.

Calvados layer: *1¼ cups milk · ½ cup sugar · 6 egg yolks · 1 tablespoon gelatin · ¼ cup cold water · 1 cup whipping cream · 1 tablespoon calvados, to taste*

Heat the milk with the sugar until the sugar has dissolved, stirring occasionally. Whisk the egg yolks to break them up and stir some of the hot milk mixture into them. Return to the pan and cook over low heat, stirring constantly, until the custard coats the spoon. Strain into a bowl. Sprinkle the gelatin over the cold water in a small pan and let it soften for a few minutes. Whip the cream with the calvados as you did for the apple layer and set aside. Dissolve the gelatin as you did before and stir it into the warm custard. Set the bowl of custard over a bowl of ice water and stir it constantly with a rubber spatula, always scraping the bottom and sides of the bowl where it touches the ice water to keep lumps of gelatin from forming there. Cool it until it looks thick and is beginning to set. Remove from the ice water bath and quickly whisk it into its whipped cream. Fold it from the bottom with your rubber spatula to be sure that it is thoroughly mixed.

Oil a 1½-quart bombe mold or stainless steel loaf pan very lightly by rubbing it with sweet almond or other tasteless oil on a paper towel.

Measure 1¾ cups of the custard, pour it into the mold, and refrigerate it until it has just barely set, about 15 minutes. Meanwhile, cool the apple purée over the ice water as you did for the calvados custard or, if it has already thickened, whisk it to smooth it out. When it is cool, fold in its whipped cream quickly. When the bottom layer has set in the mold, pour the apple mixture gently over it and spread it lightly to even it out. Chill again until just barely set; it will probably take longer to set than the first layer. When it has barely jelled, whisk the remaining calvados custard to smooth it and pour it over the apple layer. Cover well and chill at least 6 hours or overnight.

To unmold, run a table knife around the edge to loosen the bombe, put the serving plate on top and invert both. Serve the bombe with Langues de Chat. It is a very light, delicate dessert, pleasing after a rich meal. I think its pale beige and cream colors need no garnish.

HOT APPLE CHARLOTTES

For 6 to 8 individual servings: *5 pounds McIntosh apples · 6 tablespoons water · 4-inch piece of vanilla bean · 4 tablespoons unsalted butter · Sugar to taste · About a pound of firm white homemade-type bread or pain de mie, unsliced · 6 to 8 tablespoons unsalted butter, melted*

McIntosh apples work well for this recipe because they are juicy, very flavorful, and break down easily when cooked. Any tart juicy cooking apple should work.

Quarter, core, and peel the apples. Slice them thin into a non-corroding saucepan and add the water. Split and scrape the vanilla bean, add it and the 4 tablespoons butter to the apples. Cook over low to medium heat, stirring often, until the apples have broken down. You want to have a coarse applesauce, not a fine purée. Continue to cook over low heat until the purée has cooked down to 3½ or 4 cups and is stiff enough to hold a shape. It should not be juicy or it will soak into the bread. Flavor it to taste with a little sugar, but leave it somewhat tart. Chill. This much can be done a number of days ahead.

Remove the crusts from the bread and cut it into ¼-inch slices. You will need 4 or 5 slices for each charlotte, depending on the size of the loaf. Melt the butter and brush both sides of each slice with it. Using a cookie cutter, cut some of the slices into rounds to fit snugly into the bottoms of your individual soufflé dishes. Then cut small shinglelike pieces of bread to the height of the soufflé dishes and an inch or a little more wide. Put the rounds into the bottoms of the soufflé dishes and line the sides with the little shingles, overlapping them slightly to form an enclosure for the apple mixture. Set the lined cups aside until you are ready to bake the charlottes. This much can be done early on the day you are serving the dessert.

About 45 minutes before serving, fill the soufflé dishes with the apple mixture to about ¼ inch below the top of the bread. Cut a round of bread for the top of each that will fit inside the circle of bread and completely enclose the apple mixture. Butter both sides and press it on top of the dish. Bake the charlottes in a preheated 400°F oven about 15 minutes, or until the bread is golden brown. You can find out how the charlottes are browning by turning each one over onto a wide spatula and then lifting the soufflé dish off it. If it is not golden brown, put the dish back and return it to the oven for a few minutes. When done, the charlottes should hold a perfect shape unless the apple purée was not reduced enough. When the charlottes are finished, take them from their dishes immediately and set them on a rack so they won't steam.

Cool about 10 minutes and serve with Red Currant Sauce, Apricot Sauce, or Raspberry Caramel Sauce on one side, and heavy cream on the other.

APPLE CRISP

For 6 servings: *½ cup walnuts · ⅞ cup flour · ⅓ cup brown sugar · 4 teaspoons granulated sugar · ⅛ teaspoon cinnamon · ⅓ cup salted butter · 4 large apples (about 2 pounds) · A little brandy to taste*

Gravenstein, McIntosh, Winesap, or other flavorful cooking apples are best for this recipe; you should experiment according to season and availability.

Toast the walnuts in a 350°F oven for 4 to 6 minutes. Cool and chop coarsely in a food processor or by hand into about ¼-inch chunks. If the pieces are larger they will burn while the crisp bakes. Make the topping: Put flour, sugars, and cinnamon in a bowl. Work the slightly softened butter in with your hands by rubbing pieces of it lightly and quickly between your fingers, or cut in with a pastry blender. When the mixture is beginning to hold together and look crumbly, work in the cooled walnuts.

Quarter, core, and peel the apples and slice into a bowl. There should be 5 to 6 cups. Sprinkle with a little brandy or a couple of teaspoons of sugar to taste, adding cinnamon if you like. The topping is sweet, so don't oversweeten the apples; they need only enough sugar to bring out their flavor. Put the sliced apples in a shallow unbuttered baking dish— a 9-inch or 10-inch pie pan, a 9-inch square cake pan, or a nice terra-cotta gratin dish. Level them and cover evenly with a layer of the topping.

Bake in a preheated 375°F oven until the topping is golden brown all over and the apples are tender—30 to 45 minutes. If the topping has browned enough but the apples aren't cooked yet, turn the heat down to 350°F and lay a piece of foil loosely over the top.

Serve warm with Vanilla Ice Cream or a pitcher of heavy cream.

CINNAMON APPLE ICE CREAM

Makes a generous quart: *1½ pounds ripe flavorful apples (Gravenstein, McIntosh, or other good cooking apples) · 3 tablespoons water · ¼ teaspoon cinnamon · ¾ cup plus 1 tablespoon sugar · 1⅔ cups whipping cream · 3 egg yolks · Vanilla extract and calvados to taste*

Quarter, core, and peel the apples. Slice thin into a non-corroding saucepan and add the water and cinnamon. Cover and cook over low heat, stirring occasionally, until the apples are soft enough to whisk into a slightly chunky apple purée. Measure out 1⅔ cups and stir the sugar into it. Heat the cream, whisk the egg yolks just enough to mix them, and stir in some of the hot cream. Return to the pan and cook, stirring constantly, until the custard coats the spoon. Strain into a container and stir in the apple purée. Taste and flavor with a few drops each of vanilla and calvados, and chill. Taste again, add more vanilla and calvados if the flavor isn't strong enough, and freeze according to the instructions with your ice cream maker.

Serve with crisp cookies.

APPLE PIE

For 8 servings: *Pie pastry for a 9-inch 2-crust pie (page 23)* · *2 pounds flavorful apples (Gravenstein or McIntosh)* · *3 tablespoons sugar, to taste* · *½ teaspoon cinnamon* · *1 egg yolk* · *2 teaspoons whipping cream*

Roll out the pastry for the bottom crust about ⅛-inch thick, fit it into the pan, and trim the edges even with the edge of the pie plate. Chill. Quarter, core, and peel the apples. Cut them in ⅓-inch to ½-inch slices— you should have 6 cups. Mix the sugar and cinnamon and toss with the apple slices. Taste for sugar: you may need even less if you have sweet apples, more for very tart apples. This amount worked well for medium-tart McIntoshes and Gravensteins; your apples may well be different. Moisten the edge of the bottom shell with water. Heap the apples in the pie shell and roll out the top shell the same thickness as the bottom shell. Lay it gently over the apples, and, without stretching it, press it against the moist edge of the bottom crust to seal it. Cut off the top crust about ½ inch beyond the edge of the pan and fold it under the edge of the crust. Crimp to make a decorative edge. Beat the egg yolk and cream together with a fork and brush the shell with it. Cut designs about ¹⁄₁₆ inch into the top shell if you want to decorate the pie. Make a few cuts through the crust for the steam to vent. Bake in a preheated 400°F oven for 25 minutes; then turn the heat down to 375°F and bake about 10 minutes longer, or until the apples are tender and the crust is golden. If the edges of the crust brown too much before the pie is done, cover them with strips of foil.

Serve warm with Vanilla, Cinnamon, or Pear Ice Cream.

COUNTRY STYLE APPLE TART

Makes 1 tart, serving 8: *One 9-inch country style puff pastry tart shell (page 30), chilled or frozen · About 3 apples · About 1 tablespoon brown sugar · Pinch of cinnamon · 1 egg yolk · 1 tablespoon cream · 1 to 2 tablespoons unsalted butter, melted*

Gravenstein, McIntosh, or any other apple that cooks without drying out is best for this recipe.

Quarter, core, and peel the apples. Slice ¼-inch thick and toss the slices with the brown sugar and cinnamon. Beat the egg and cream together with a fork. Put the tart shell on a baking sheet and brush the edge of the shell with the egg-cream glaze. Arrange the apple slices in even layers in the shell. You may also arrange them in concentric rings or a spiral; if you do, be sure to overlap the slices as much as you can so the finished tart won't be skimpy. (The apple slices should be only two or three layers thick, otherwise they will juice too much when they bake and soak the shell.) Brush the apples with the melted butter.

Bake the tart in a preheated 400°F oven for 10 to 15 minutes, or until the edges are puffed and browned. Turn the heat down to 350°F and bake another 25 to 30 minutes, or until the apples are tender and the bottom of the tart is completely brown. If the top begins to get too brown, lay a sheet of aluminum foil over it until the tart is done.

Serve with crème fraîche or Vanilla Ice Cream.

WARM HONEY-GLAZED APPLE TART WITH CRÈME FRAÎCHE

For a 9-inch tart serving 8: *One 9-inch puff pastry tart shell (page 25), chilled thoroughly or frozen · 3 large McIntosh apples, about 2 pounds · 1 tablespoon sugar, to taste · Optional: 1 teaspoon Cognac · 1 tablespoon unsalted butter, melted · 2 tablespoons honey*

Quarter, core, and peel the apples. Slice about ¼-inch thick and toss with the sugar and Cognac. Put the tart shell on a baking sheet and fill it with the apples. Make an even layer of apples and try not to let any ends stick up because they will burn easily. Brush the layer of apples with the melted butter and put the tart into a preheated 400°F oven. Bake for 30 to 35 minutes, turning the tart occasionally, if necessary, to brown the pastry evenly. Tuck down any edges of the apples that seem to be browning too fast, or push them under other apples. Bake until the apples are tender when you test them with the point of a sharp knife. If the pastry begins to get too brown before the apples are completely cooked, turn the oven down to 350°F and lay a piece of foil loosely over the tart. When done, slide the tart onto a rack to cool slightly. After about 10 minutes warm the honey and brush the apples with it.

Serve while warm with crème fraîche.

GRAVENSTEIN APPLE TART
WITH CINNAMON ICE CREAM

For 8 servings: *One 9-inch puff pastry tart shell (page 25), chilled or frozen · 4 Gravenstein apples · 1 teaspoon to 1 tablespoon sugar · A few drops brandy or Cognac · 1 to 2 tablespoons unsalted butter, melted*

Toss the apple slices, sugar to taste, add a few drops of brandy or Cognac, and arrange them in the tart shell. Brush the apple slices with melted butter and bake in a preheated 400°F oven about 35 minutes, or until the apples are tender and the bottom of the shell is golden brown.

Serve warm with Cinnamon Ice Cream, or serve with Vanilla or Pear Ice Cream.

TARTE TATIN

For one 9-inch tart, to serve 8: *One 10-inch circle of frozen or chilled puff pastry (page 25) or pie crust (page 23), rolled ⅛-inch thick · 2 tablespoons unsalted butter · 6 tablespoons sugar · 1⅔ to 2 pounds McIntosh apples · Optional: a pinch of cinnamon*

Melt the butter in a 9-inch black iron frying pan over medium to high heat and immediately add the sugar, stirring constantly. Cook until it is a golden caramel color, being careful to remove the pan from the heat before the caramel is too dark because the sugar will continue to cook from the heat of the pan. (See the caramel recipe on page 33 for detailed instructions.)

Quarter, core, and peel the apples, slice each quarter in half lengthwise, and toss with the cinnamon if you are using it. Make a ring of apples over the caramel in the frying pan, rounded sides down and narrower tips toward the center. Make another circle of apples in the center. You may have to cut off the tips to make them fit if you are using large apples. If you have cut the tips off some of the apples, distribute the tips in the center so the tart will be a little higher in the center when it is turned out. Set the pastry on top of the fruit, let it stand until softened, and push it down between the fruit and the side of the pan.

Bake in a preheated 400°F oven for 30 to 35 minutes, or until the apples and pastry are cooked. Test with the point of a knife, lifting the pastry slightly to be sure it is cooked through. Remove from the oven and let stand a minute or two to firm slightly, then set a serving plate upside down on top of the pan. Lift the two together, holding the plate as tight as you can against the top of the pan, and flip them over quickly so the juice does not spatter you. If some of the fruit has stuck to the pan, simply rearrange it on the tart.

Serve while still warm with a glass of Sauternes, or garnished with crème fraîche or Vanilla Ice Cream, or with Pear Ice Cream. If you can't serve it immediately it can wait in the pan for 15 minutes or so and be set back into the oven for 5 to 10 minutes to soften the caramel before it is turned out. In this case, shake the pan back and forth a few times before inverting the tart to be sure it is loosened from the pan. It should move freely in the pan before you turn it out.

47

STUFFED BAKED PEARS

For 8 servings: *6 tablespoons unblanched whole almonds · 8 amaretti (small Italian macaroons), wrapped 2 to the package · 6 tablespoons unsalted butter, softened · 1½ tablespoons sugar · 1 egg yolk · ½ to 1 teaspoon kirsch, to taste · 4 very ripe pears, preferably Comice*

Toast the almonds in a preheated 350°F oven for 6 to 7 minutes or until they smell good. They shouldn't be at all brown inside; they are toasted only to bring out their flavor. Crush the macaroons between sheets of waxed paper, using a rolling pin; they should be in tiny chunks, but not a fine powder. Chop the almonds by hand into ⅛-inch to ¼-inch chunks. Beat the butter until very light and fluffy. Add the sugar, then the egg yolk, and continue beating until the mixture is again light and fluffy. Beat in the macaroons and almonds and flavor with kirsch to taste.

Halve, core, and peel the pears. Stuff each with a full rounded tablespoon or more of the stuffing. Bake them in a buttered gratin dish in a preheated 375°F oven for 15 to 20 minutes, or until tender when pierced with the tip of a sharp knife.

Serve these pears with a pitcher of cream to pour over them, or with Late Harvest Riesling Ice Cream, or Beaumes-de-Venise Ice Cream, or maraschino ice cream.

PEAR SHERBET BOMBE
WITH CHARTREUSE MOUSSE

For 8 to 10 servings: *1 quart Pear Sherbet (page 53) · 1 recipe frozen mousse (page 9), flavored with Chartreuse*

Chill a 1½-quart mold or loaf pan in the freezer, then line it with slightly softened pear sherbet as directed on page 9. Line the bottom and sides of the mold evenly with a ¾-inch layer of sherbet. Put this back into the freezer to harden while you make the mousse mixture. Flavor it with Chartreuse and taste it with a little of the sherbet to be sure the balance is good, with neither flavor dominating the other. Fill the bombe to within an inch or so of the top and freeze. When the mousse has frozen, spread a layer of slightly softened sherbet over it to fill the mold to the top. Freeze again.

Remove the bombe from the pan and serve in slices. Garnish with a sprig of mint, and accompany with Bow Ties or other crisp cookies.

PEAR AND WHITE CHOCOLATE BOMBE
WITH WARM CHOCOLATE SAUCE

For 10 to 12 servings: *1 quart Pear Sherbet (page 53)* · *2 cups White Chocolate Mousse (page 243)* · *Pear William or Armagnac to taste* · *1 cup Warm Chocolate Sauce (page 259)*

Chill a 1½-quart bombe mold and line the bottom and sides with an even ¾-inch layer of the slightly softened pear sherbet. Return to the freezer to harden while you make the mousse. Flavor the mousse with a little Pear William or Armagnac and pour it into the center of the mold. Freeze until hard enough to cover with the remaining pear sherbet and freeze again until hard. Unmold onto a chilled serving plate, wrap with plastic, and return to the freezer until serving time.

Serve with a pitcher of the Warm Chocolate Sauce to drizzle over the slices, and accompany with Bow Ties or Lace Cookies.

BAKED CARAMEL PEARS
WITH PECANS OR ALMONDS

For 6 servings: *3 large very ripe Comice pears* · *3 tablespoons unsalted butter* · *3 tablespoons sugar* · *½ cup whipping cream* · *1 to 2 tablespoons pecans or almonds, lightly toasted*

Heat your oven to 375°F. Halve, core, and peel the pears. Choose a flameproof dish such as an enameled iron one, and put the pears in it, rounded side down. Cut the butter into bits and distribute them over the pear halves. Sprinkle with the sugar and put the dish in the oven. Bake

49

for 20 to 30 minutes, basting occasionally with the juices. The pears are ready if tender when pierced in their thickest part with a sharp knife.

Remove the pears from the dish, allowing all the juice to drain back into it and adding any of the undissolved sugar still remaining in the pear cavities. Set the dish over high heat and cook, stirring constantly, until the mixture turns a light caramel color. It will look very thick and bubbly because of the butter and pear juice in it. Pour in the cream and bring to a boil. Cook until the sauce is smooth. It will darken and turn a rich brown when you pour in the cream.

Serve a pear half to each person with some of the sauce spooned over it. Sprinkle with the nuts, chopped medium fine. This is very simple, but the flavors of the ripe pears combine wonderfully with the smooth, rich caramel.

PEAR ICE CREAM

Makes about 1¼ quarts: *1½ pounds ripe pears · 3 tablespoons water · 1½ cups whipping cream · ⅝ cup sugar · 4 egg yolks · A few drops of vanilla extract*

Comice, Bosc, Bartlett, or any other good flavorful cooking pear should be used for this recipe, according to the season.

Quarter, core, and peel the pears. They should be so ripe that the juice oozes from them and they look shiny wherever you cut them. Cut them in rough slices into a non-corroding saucepan and add the water. There should be enough water just to cover the bottom of the pan to keep the pears from scorching until they release their own juice. Cook the pears until they are completely heated through or they will turn brown when you purée them. Purée in a blender or food processor or press through a strainer, and measure 1½ cups.

Heat half of the cream with the sugar in a small saucepan until the sugar dissolves. Whisk the egg yolks in a small bowl just enough to mix them and pour in the warm cream mixture, stirring constantly. Return the egg yolk mixture to the pan and cook over low heat, stirring constantly, until the custard coats the spoon. Strain into the pear purée, add the rest of the cream, and add a few drops of vanilla to taste. Chill. Freeze according to the instructions with your ice cream maker.

Alice and I like this served with Tarte Tatin, or you can fill a crêpe or a cookie cup with it—or serve it alone.

PEAR CARAMEL ICE CREAM

Makes about 1¼ quarts: *1 recipe Pear Ice Cream · 2 additional pears · 4 tablespoons unsalted butter · 4 tablespoons sugar · ½ cup whipping cream*

Make pear ice cream, above, cooking the two extra pears. After you cook the pears, but before you purée them and make the ice cream, take out ½ cup pear juice. Put the juice, butter, and sugar in a small non-corroding saucepan and cook over medium to high heat, stirring constantly, until the caramel turns pale golden brown. Remove from the heat and carefully add the cream, stirring all the while. Return to the heat and cook, stirring, until all the caramel has dissolved. Chill until it is thick enough to swirl into the ice cream, and add it when the ice cream comes from the ice cream maker.

This ice cream needs no embellishment beyond a few Lace Cookies or Bow Ties.

PEARS POACHED IN RASPBERRY SYRUP

For 6 servings: *4 cups water · 1⅓ cups sugar · 2 strips of lemon zest · 1 half-pint basket raspberries · 2 pounds firm ripe Bosc pears (6 medium sized)*

Bring the water and sugar to a boil in a non-corroding saucepan. Cut two lengthwise strips of zest from a lemon with a vegetable peeler, taking care not to cut into the white part under the skin, and add to the syrup. Simmer gently while you purée the raspberries. Pass the purée through a strainer that is fine enough to remove the seeds, and add it to the syrup. Peel the pears with a vegetable peeler, keeping them as smooth and round as possible. Leave the stems on but take off all the peel to the edges of

51

the stems. Pull out the blossom ends with the tip of the peeler. Poach the pears in the barely simmering raspberry syrup for 30 to 35 minutes, or until tender and translucent but not soft. Transfer them gently to a storage container, and chill separately from the syrup. Strain the cooled syrup over the pears through a fine strainer. Chill.

Serve one per person, garnished with a piece of candied violet near the stem end, some of the syrup, and crème fraîche or crème Chantilly. This needs to be served with both fork and spoon.

PEARS POACHED IN RIESLING JUICE

For 6 servings: *1 fifth-sized bottle Riesling grape juice · 2 tablespoons sugar · 2 pounds firm ripe Bosc pears*

Heat the grape juice and the sugar to simmering in a non-corroding saucepan large enough to hold the pears. Peel the pears as smoothly as you can with a vegetable peeler and neatly pull out the blossom end with the tip of the peeler. Leave the stem attached. Add the pears to the simmering grape juice and cook them at a slow simmer for about 30 minutes, or until they are tender and slightly translucent but not mushy. Remove from the syrup to a container and cook down the syrup by one-third. Pour over the pears and chill. Serve with crème fraîche and Lace Cookies.

PEARS POACHED IN SAUTERNES AND HONEY
WITH CRÈME FRAÎCHE

For 6 to 8 servings: *A half bottle of Sauternes · 1½ cups water · ½ cup honey · About 2 pounds firm ripe pears, preferably Bartlett or Bosc*

Combine the Sauternes, water, and honey in a non-corroding saucepan and bring to a simmer, stirring once or twice. Meanwhile, peel the pears neatly with a vegetable peeler and pull out the blossom end with the tip of the peeler. Peel away any bits of skin near the stem but leave the stem attached and the core intact. Drop each pear into the simmering Sauternes

52

syrup as you finish peeling it. Cut a piece of baking parchment to fit over the pears, lay it on top, and continue simmering until the pears are cooked through but are not soft and mushy. You may cook the pears covered with a lid, but the parchment lying right on top of them bastes them better and keeps any pears that might be above the level of the syrup from turning brown. It will take 30 to 40 minutes to cook the pears, depending completely on their variety and ripeness. They will cook a little more from their retained heat after you take them from the syrup. The pears will look slightly translucent when they are done.

When the pears have finished cooking, remove carefully with a slotted spoon and cook the syrup down to about three-quarters of its original volume. Cool the pears and the syrup separately, or the pears will continue to cook in the syrup until it has cooled. When cooled to room temperature, put the pears and the syrup into a container together to chill, preferably overnight. The pears will take on a beautiful golden color from the Sauternes.

Serve the pears standing in a pretty bowl in the syrup, with a little crème fraîche on the side, accompanied by Lace Cookies.

PEAR SHERBET

Makes 1⅛ quarts: *3 to 3½ pounds ripe juicy pears · ¼ cup water · ¾ cup sugar · Optional: kirsch, Pear William, Cognac, Armagnac, or brandy*

Bartlett, Comice, Bosc, Winter Nelis or other full-flavored pears should be used for this recipe, according to the season.

Quarter, core, and peel the pears and cut in rough slices into a non-corroding saucepan. Add water, cover, and cook over low to medium heat about 10 minutes, or until the pears are heated through—this will keep them from turning brown when you purée them.

Purée the pears in a food processor or blender or put them through a strainer. Mix in the sugar while the purée is hot and stir until the sugar has dissolved and you can no longer feel the grains between your fingers. Add a few drops of the flavoring of your choice to taste. Chill and freeze according to the instructions with your ice cream maker.

Serve garnished with a sprig of mint, accompanied with crisp cookies, or serve with Stuffed Baked Pears. This may also be served in combination with Raspberry or Black Currant Sherbet, or can be combined with Chartreuse, Cognac, or Armagnac Mousse in bombes.

PEAR AND ARMAGNAC SHERBET

Makes 1 quart: *4 pounds ripe flavorful pears · 3 or 4 tablespoons water · ¾ cup sugar · 3 tablespoons Armagnac, to taste*

Use good ripe perfumed Bartlett, Comice, Butter, or Primavera pears that ooze juice when you cut into them.

Quarter, core, and peel the pears and cut in thin slices into a non-corroding saucepan. Add enough water to cover the bottom of the pan, cover, and cook over medium heat, stirring occasionally, until the pears are heated through. Purée them in a blender or food processor and stir in the sugar while they are still hot, stirring until it dissolves. Cool. Add the Armagnac, taste, and then add more, if you like. Chill. Freeze according to the instructions with your ice cream maker.

Serve with Lace Cookies or other crisp cookies.

To make a Pear and Cognac Sherbet: Substitute Cognac for the Armagnac.

BUTTER PEAR TART WITH FRANGIPANE CREAM

For 8 servings: *One 9-inch baked short crust tart shell (page 11) · 1 cup frangipane cream (page 7) · ¾ cup sugar · 2¼ cups water · 2-inch piece of vanilla bean · 1½ pounds firm ripe Butter pears · 2 tablespoons apricot jam, preferably homemade · A few drops of kirsch · 1 to 2 tablespoons peeled pistachios, finely chopped*

Make the frangipane cream long enough ahead of serving time for it to chill completely. It will keep for several days. Poach the pears in time for them to chill also.

Bring the sugar, water, and vanilla bean to a boil in a non-corroding

54

saucepan. Quarter, core, and peel the pears and add them to the hot syrup, rounded side down. Cover and just barely simmer about 15 minutes, or until the pears are just cooked through. Remove from the syrup to a plate and chill them. Chill the syrup separately if you want to save it for another use.

When you are ready to assemble the tart, spread the frangipane cream in the bottom of the tart shell. Drain the pear quarters on paper towels and carefully cut them lengthwise into slices about ¼-inch thick. Beginning at the outside of the tart, arrange the slices in circles, each slice overlapping the next halfway. Fill in the center however the slices fit best. Heat the jam until it bubbles and stir in the kirsch. Quickly brush the pears lightly with the glaze, reheating it if it cools and thickens. Sprinkle the pistachios around the edge of the tart or wherever they look nicest.

Serve as soon as possible. No other garnish is needed.

PEAR AND FIG TART

For 8 servings: *One 9-inch puff pastry tart shell (page 25), chilled or frozen; or one 9-inch short crust pastry tart shell (page 11), baked · ¾ to 1 pound small ripe figs · ½ pound ripe Bosc pears · 1 teaspoon sugar · Apricot jam, honey, or reduced fruit poaching liquid for the glaze · Kirsch to taste*

If you are using a puff pastry tart shell, put it on a baking pan. Cut the tough ends from the stems of the figs and slice figs in half. Quarter, core, and peel the pears, being careful not to break them. Arrange the figs in a circle around the edge of either tart shell. Cut the pear quarters in slices ⅓-inch thick and arrange them, slightly overlapping, inside the circle of figs. Sprinkle with the sugar. Bake the puff pastry tart in a preheated 400°F oven about 30 minutes, or until the pastry is golden brown and cooked on the bottom and the pears and figs are cooked. The short crust shell should be baked at 375°F until the fruit is cooked, about 35 minutes. Heat your choice of glaze, add a little kirsch, and brush the fruit with it.

Serve the puff pastry tart immediately with crème fraîche or with Anise, Chartreuse, or Beaumes-de-Venise Ice Cream. Serve the other tart with crème Chantilly—it can wait an hour or two to be served.

PEAR TARTE TATIN

For 8 servings: *One 10-inch circle of chilled or frozen puff pastry (page 25), rolled ⅛-inch thick; or the same amount of pie dough (page 23), rolled about ⅛-inch thick · ½ cup sugar · 2 tablespoons unsalted butter · About 5 medium-size Bosc or Winter Nelis pears · Optional: 1 tablespoon rum, Cognac, brandy, or Armagnac*

Make a caramel in a 9-inch pan with the sugar and butter, following the directions in the recipe for Quince and Apple Tarte Tatin on page 58. Cut the pears in half, core, and peel them. The pears should be ripe and juicy but still firm. Gently toss the pears with the liquor of your choice and arrange them in the caramel, rounded side down and pointed ends to the center. You may need to cut the pears into smaller slices in order to arrange them to fill the center. You may quarter the pears if you prefer— I like the way halves look. You may also intersperse the pears with slices of poached quinces, as prepared for the Quince and Apple Tarte Tatin.

Cut four or five 1-inch slits around the center of the pastry to let steam escape and lay it over the top of the pears. Let it defrost if it is frozen. When the pastry is slightly soft, push the edges down between the pears and the sides of the pan. This will make a pretty, wavy edge because the pastry molds to the shape of the pears.

Set the tart in the middle of a preheated 400°F oven and bake about 30 minutes, or until the pears are tender and the crust is thoroughly browned and baked through. To check the pastry for doneness, you can either lift the crust gently at one edge or you can look at the slits; note that the pastry will always have a moist layer where it meets the fruit. Remove the tart from the oven and let it stand about a minute, then invert a serving plate over the top of the baking pan. Lift the two together, holding the plate as tight as you can against the top of the pan, and flip it over quickly so the juice doesn't spatter you. If some of the fruit has stuck to the pan or slipped out of place, just set it back on the tart and push into place. If a lot of the caramel has run off, spoon it over the pears before it hardens.

Serve warm with crème fraîche, with very lightly sweetened whipped cream, or with Vanilla or Chartreuse Ice Cream.

UPSIDE-DOWN PEAR AND MUSCAT RAISIN TART

For 8 servings: *One 10-inch round piece of puff pastry (page 25), rolled ⅛-inch thick, chilled or frozen · ¾ cup muscat raisins · ½ cup Beaumes-de-Venise wine · 2 tablespoons unsalted butter · 2 tablespoons sugar · 2 pounds ripe Bosc or Winter Nelis pears, or enough to cover the bottom of the pan with halved pears*

Put the raisins in a small non-corroding saucepan and pour over all but 2 tablespoons of the wine. Cover and heat just to bubbling, stir, cover again, and set aside until the raisins have absorbed the wine. Meanwhile put the butter, sugar, and the remaining wine in a black iron frying pan or a tarte Tatin pan. Cook, stirring constantly, until the mixture is golden brown caramel. (See page 33 for detailed instructions on caramel.) Cool.

Halve the pears, peel, and core them. Make a ring of them in the prepared pan, rounded sides down, tips pointing to the center. Fill their cavities with some raisins and distribute the rest among the pear halves. Lay the chilled pastry over the pears and let it soften enough to tuck the edge between the pears and the side of the pan. Cut several slits in the top. Bake in a preheated 400°F oven for about 30 minutes, or until the pears are tender and the pastry is golden brown and cooked. Check it by lifting it gently from the pears or by looking at the slits. Remove from the oven when done and set a serving plate upside down on top of the pan. Lift the two together, hold the plate as tight as you can against the top of the pan, and flip it over quickly so the juice doesn't spatter you.

Serve immediately with crème fraîche.

To make an Upside-Down Pear and Fig Tart, in addition to the pears and pastry, as above:

4 ounces dried figs · 1 cup water · ¼ cup Beaumes-de-Venise wine · 2 tablespoons honey

Heat the figs to simmering with the other ingredients. Cover and cook until very tender, 30 minutes to 1 hour. Cool and store in the syrup.

To make the tart, cut off the tough stem ends of the figs and slice the figs about ¼-inch thick. Continue as in the preceding recipe, arranging the fig slices instead of raisins among the pear halves and in the pear cavities.

QUINCE AND APPLE TARTE TATIN

For one 9-inch tart, to serve 8: One 10-inch circle of frozen or chilled puff pastry (page 25), or pie crust (page 23), rolled ⅛-inch thick · 2 tablespoons unsalted butter · 6 tablespoons sugar · 1⅔ to 2 pounds McIntosh apples · Optional: a pinch of cinnamon · 2 or 3 quinces, sliced and poached in vanilla syrup (page 187)

Melt the butter in a 9-inch black iron frying pan over medium to high heat and immediately add the sugar, stirring constantly. Cook until it is a golden caramel color. Be careful to remove the pan from the heat before the caramel is too dark because the sugar will continue to cook from the heat of the pan. (See the caramel recipe on page 33 for detailed instructions.)

Quarter, core, and peel the apples, slice each quarter in half lengthwise, and toss with the cinnamon if you are using it. Make a ring of apples over the caramel in the frying pan, rounded sides down and narrower tips toward the center. Make another circle of apples in the center. You may have to cut off the tips to make them fit if you are using large apples. Press slices of quince, rounded sides down, between the apple slices. If you have cut the tips off some of the apples, distribute the tips in the center so the tart will be a little higher in the center when it is turned out. Set the pastry on top of the fruit, let it stand until softened, and push it down between the fruit and the sides of the pan.

Bake in a preheated 400°F oven for 30 to 35 minutes, or until the apples and pastry are cooked. Test with the point of a knife, lifting the pastry slightly to be sure it is cooked through. Remove from the oven and let stand a minute or two to firm slightly, then set a serving plate upside down on top of the pan. Lift the two together, holding the plate as tight as you can against the top of the pan, and flip them over quickly so the juice does not spatter you. If some of the fruit has stuck to the pan, simply

58

rearrange it on the tart. The apples will be a beautiful russet color with dark, rosy-russet slices of quince showing between them.

Serve while still warm with a glass of Sauternes, or garnished with crème fraîche or Vanilla Ice Cream. If you can't serve it immediately it can wait in the pan for 15 minutes or so and be set back into the oven for 5 to 10 minutes to soften the caramel before it is turned out. In this case, shake the pan back and forth a few times before inverting the tart to be sure it is loosened from the pan. It should move freely in the pan before you turn it out.

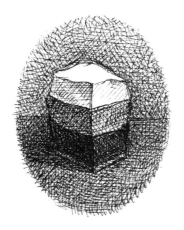

3

CITRUS FRUITS

CITRUS FRUITS make a great contribution to the winter menus at Chez Panisse. They are available in great variety then—navel and Valencia oranges, several kinds of tangerines and tangelos, blood oranges, grapefruits and pomelos, and Meyer and Eureka lemons. Their sharp, tangy flavors and variety of colors—subtle in the juice, strong in the flesh—are particularly welcome after the winter season's heavy, rich meals. Citrus desserts are refreshing; they have the ability to slice through the richness of a roast duck or a cassoulet, balancing and integrating a heavy dinner.

Valencia oranges, and most tangerines and tangelos, make the best sherbets. They also make the prettiest ones, especially if used to fill cups made from their own skins. Navel oranges make the best tarts because they section easily and have few seeds. Perhaps I like them so much because

I remember eating them from the tree throughout my first winter in California—a great luxury for a Midwesterner. I use blood oranges a great deal when they are in season; they have more of a bitter flavor than other oranges, and a more exciting color.

Meyer lemons are not usually available in the market because the tree carries a disease that attacks other citruses. However, they grow in gardens all over Berkeley, a beautiful sight with the soft yellow lemons, and often the flowers, hanging among the glossy dark green leaves. They are one of the hardiest citrus varieties; where winters are too cold, they can be grown in containers and moved indoors. Meyers have a more delicate, complex perfume and a sweeter flavor than the Eureka, the usual market variety, so I cook with them as often as possible. Where only the Eureka is available, you can compensate for its one-dimensional tartness by substituting orange juice for some of the lemon.

Kumquats, with their tart flesh and sweet rind, make a perfect light dessert, when eaten skin and all. Or they can be poached in a light syrup and served with a citrus compote or a cake. Lavender Gems were first available to the restaurant in 1983, although they have been harvested by at least one grower near Indio, California, for a long time. They are a cross between a tangerine and a grapefruit and have sweet pale lavender flesh and the appearance of a tiny grapefruit. They make a lovely sherbet to splash with Champagne and garnish with some shreds of grated peel and a few fruit sections. Clementines, too, are newly available. They are small relatives of the tangerine and can be candied whole or dipped in caramel. If you ever find yourself in Nice, buy some candied Clementines, which are a local specialty. They keep indefinitely and make a delicious butter to fill buckwheat crêpes.

In this part of the country, pomelos, a possible parent of the grapefruit, are available only at Chinese New Year. Look for them in Chinese markets. They make a very fragrant and unusual ice cream. Grapefruit, known mainly as a breakfast fruit, combines with other citruses in compotes or makes a spectacular, cooling sherbet, especially in combination with Champagne.

CITRUS COMPOTE

For 4 to 6 servings: *2 blood oranges · 2 navel oranges · 2 tangerines · 2 cups water · 1 cup sugar · 2 tablespoons brandy or Cognac, to taste*

Wash the fruits and cut the peel from one of each kind of fruit in very thin layers with a vegetable peeler, taking none of the white pith. Cut the strips of peel into thin slivers about ¹⁄₁₆-inch wide. Put them in a non-corroding saucepan, cover with cold water, and bring to a boil. Remove from the heat and let steep for 15 minutes, then drain. Add the water and sugar to the drained peel, bring to a boil, and simmer 20 to 30 minutes, or until a thin syrup forms when you put a few drops on a cold plate. Cool and add brandy or Cognac to taste.

Meanwhile, cut off all the skin from the oranges and tangerines, slicing carefully to remove all the white pith but keeping their round shape. Cut crosswise into ¼-inch to ⅜-inch slices. Alternate layers of the sliced fruit with sprinklings of peel and syrup, preferably in a glass serving bowl. End with peel scattered over the top. The peel will have made pretty little curls. Pour any remaining syrup over the fruit.

Serve thoroughly chilled, accompanied by Langues de Chat and Chocolate Truffles, if you like. This can also be made using a single variety of citrus. When we made this with only blood oranges, Mary Jo Thoresen, one of our pastry assistants, said it was her all-time favorite dessert. Another night we made it with blood oranges, Kinnow tangerines—those took us hours to seed—and Lavender Gems, all put in their separate syrups and served with their own candied peels. It made a beautiful dessert.

CANDIED CITRUS PEEL

4 oranges, or 6 lemons or tangerines, or 2 grapefruits · 1 cup sugar · ½ cup water · 2 tablespoons corn syrup, or ¼ teaspoon cream of tartar · About a cup of sugar for sprinkling the peel

Remove the peel from the fruit in quarter sections. Place in a non-corroding pan and cover with cold water. Bring to a boil and simmer until the white pith begins to look translucent. Let stand in the hot water 15 minutes or so and drain.

Make a syrup of the sugar, water, and corn syrup or cream of tartar. Using a spoon, scrape the white part off the peel as completely as possible. Cut the peel into thin strips and add to the syrup. Cook slowly until the peel is translucent and tender, when the sugar will have penetrated it. Then turn up the heat and cook until the syrup reaches 230°F on a candy thermometer. Have ready a plate or cookie sheet with a layer of sugar sprinkled on it. Put the peel in a strainer to drain off the syrup, and quickly put the drained peel on the sugared plate. Sprinkle the peel with more sugar to cover, then toss with the sugar to separate the pieces, being careful not to burn your hands. Store the candied peel, layered with its sugar, in a covered container in the refrigerator, where it will keep indefinitely.

Serve this candied peel separately as an after dinner candy, or as a garnish for various cakes and tarts.

PINK GRAPEFRUIT AND CHAMPAGNE SHERBET

Makes a generous quart: *4½ to 5 pounds grapefruit, preferably Marsh Ruby · 1 cup sugar · ¼ cup dry Champagne (it can be flat)*

Grate fine the peel of 1 grapefruit into a bowl. Juice the grapefruits and measure 4 cups of the juice. Strain into the bowl with the peel, pushing as much of the pulp through the strainer as you can. Put the sugar in a non-corroding saucepan with about 1 cup of the juice and heat, stirring occasionally, until the sugar has dissolved. Add this to the rest of the juice, then add the Champagne and chill. Freeze according to the instructions with your ice cream maker.

Serve with a little Champagne (not flat!) poured over each serving and garnish with a sprig of mint or a violet.

You can also make this with yellow- or golden-fleshed grapefruit but the sherbet won't have its lovely pale pink tinge.

LAVENDER GEM SHERBET

Makes 1 quart: *About 4 pounds Lavender Gems · ¾ cup sugar · 1 table-spoon Champagne · A few drops lemon juice*

Lavender Gems are a citrus hybrid, a cross between a grapefruit and a mandarin orange, yellow in color, spherical, 2 to 2½ inches in diameter, with flesh tinged a pale pink lavender. The flavor is delicate and sweet, and the peel is sweet and less tangy than that of some other citruses. Lavender Gems make a lovely sherbet.

Wash the fruit and grate the peel from 3 Lavender Gems into a non-corroding bowl. Juice the fruit and measure 4 cups. Strain the juice into the bowl with the peel, pushing as much pulp as possible through the strainer. Put the sugar in a non-corroding saucepan and pour in about 1 cup of the juice. Heat the mixture, stirring constantly, until the sugar has dissolved. Pour it back into the remaining juice, add the Champagne, and a few drops of lemon juice if it is needed to sharpen the flavor. Chill. Freeze according to the instructions with your ice cream maker.

We serve this sherbet in tall glasses with Champagne poured over, garnished with a section of the fruit and a sprig of mint. On the side we serve some of the peel, candied, and a White Chocolate Truffle flavored with Champagne.

LEMON TART

Makes 1¾ cups tart filling, enough for one 9-inch tart, which serves 8, or enough to serve as filling for a 3-layer cake: *One 9-inch pre-baked short crust tart shell (page 11) · 2 lemons · 2 eggs · 3 egg yolks · 6 tablespoons sugar · 2 tablespoons milk · ¼ teaspoon cornstarch · 3 tablespoons unsalted butter · 3 tablespoons salted butter*

Grate the peel from the lemons into a small non-corroding bowl. Juice the lemons and strain the juice into the same bowl. Strain out the seeds, but force as much pulp as possible through the strainer.

Beat the eggs and egg yolks with the sugar in a heavy non-corroding saucepan just until mixed. Gradually mix the milk into the cornstarch in a small cup, then add them to the egg mixture—the cornstarch is necessary if the filling is to brown properly when baking. If you do not want to brown the tart, the cornstarch can be omitted. Next stir in the juice mixture: it will look a bit curdled when the juice is added, but will smooth out later. Cut the butter in pieces and add to the mixture. Cook the mixture over low to medium heat, stirring constantly, until it just coats the spoon and is the thickness of crème anglaise. Let stand 5 minutes to thicken, then whisk slightly to smooth it.

At this point you can pour the filling into a container and keep it in the refrigerator for up to two weeks. In any case it is best to chill the filling before making a tart, but you may also pour it into the pre-baked tart shell without chilling it.

Preheat your oven to 375°F. Fill the slightly cooled pre-baked shell with the filling and bake for 30 to 35 minutes, or until the top is speckled with dark brown spots and the filling has puffed slightly. Remove from the oven and cool on a rack in its pan. You can also bake the tart just long enough to set the filling, about 15 to 20 minutes. This will make a smooth, shiny yellow tart.

This lemon tart is one of the most popular tarts we make at the restaurant. The filling can also be used as a cake filling or for lemon meringue pie.

MEYER LEMON MERINGUE PIE

For 6 to 8 servings: *One 9-inch pie shell (page 23)* · *1½ cups Meyer Lemon or Lemon Tart filling (above)* · *2 egg whites* · *¼ teaspoon cream of tartar* · *¼ cup sugar* · *½ teaspoon vanilla extract*

Bake the shell in a preheated 375°F oven for about 20 minutes, or until set and dry looking on the bottom, then turn heat down to 350°F and continue baking until the crust is golden brown. Cool slightly. Spread the lemon filling in the shell. Bake in the preheated oven for 10 to 15 minutes or until the filling is just set.

Make the meringue: Warm the egg whites slightly. Beat until frothy, then add the cream of tartar. Beat until they hold rounded peaks, and gradually beat in the sugar, then the vanilla. Carefully spread the meringue over the lemon filling, and press it against the edges of the pie shell to seal it. Make a pretty design in it with your knife or spatula. Bake at 375°F for about 10 minutes, or until the meringue is lightly browned. Cool thoroughly, 1 to 2 hours, but do not refrigerate.

This is a delicious lemon pie—fast, too, because you can make the filling any time since it will keep for two or three weeks. The pie shell can be made ahead also, and frozen.

If you prefer a cream topping on your pie, omit the meringue from the recipe. Spread the lemon filling in the cooled pre-baked shell. Bake as above and cool. Whip 1 cup whipping cream with sugar and vanilla to taste to soft peaks. Spread it on top of the lemon filling, or pipe it on through a decorative tip.

MEYER LEMON ICE CREAM

Makes about 1⅔ quarts: *3 Meyer lemons, about ¾ pound · 1 cup sugar · 1 cup half-and-half · 6 egg yolks · 3 cups whipping cream · Vanilla extract to taste*

Peel 1 lemon very thin with a vegetable peeler, taking care not to cut into the white pith, which is very bitter. Put the peel in a non-corroding saucepan with the sugar and the half-and-half. Heat the mixture to just under boiling, remove from the heat, and let steep for 10 to 15 minutes. Whisk the egg yolks in a bowl until just mixed and pour in some of the hot half-and-half mixture, stirring constantly. Pour it back into the pan and cook, stirring constantly, until the mixture coats the spoon.

Pour through a strainer into the bowl and add the finely grated peel of 2 lemons. Let stand in the warm mixture for 10 minutes and then add the cream. Juice the lemons, strain the juice, and add 9 tablespoons to the cream mixture. Taste and add more juice if you want more tartness, and a few drops of vanilla. Chill thoroughly. Freeze according to the instructions with your ice cream maker.

This ice cream can be served alone, garnished with a few shreds of lemon peel or a violet, or it can be used in a bombe with Blood Orange or Tangerine Sherbet. It can also be used to fill crêpes or buckwheat crêpes.

MEYER LEMON SHERBET

Makes about 1 quart: *3 good-sized Meyer lemons · 1 cup plus 3 tablespoons sugar · 4 cups water · Optional: 2 tablespoons Champagne or white wine*

Wash the lemons and grate the peel of 1 into a non-corroding bowl. Try to produce long 1/16-inch-wide shreds of the zest, being careful not to cut into the bitter white pith under the peel. Juice the lemons, measure ¾ cup of juice, and strain it into the bowl with the peel. Push as much of the pulp through the strainer as you can.

Heat the sugar with 1 cup of the water until it is completely dissolved, then add the remaining 3 cups of cold water. Add this to the juice and peel. Taste and add a little more juice if needed. Late in their season, Meyer lemons may be quite sweet and need some regular lemon juice added for tartness. Add the wine at this point if you are using it. The wine will make a creamier sherbet because its alcohol doesn't freeze. A softer sherbet can be made by adding an extra 2 tablespoons of sugar to the recipe, if you don't mind the extra sweetness. (I do.) Chill. Freeze according to the instructions with your ice cream maker.

Serve in a tall glass or a sherbet glass with a little Champagne poured over, and garnish with a sprig of mint.

MEYER LEMON SOUFFLÉ

For 4 servings: *1½ tablespoons sugar · 1 tablespoon plus 2 teaspoons flour · ½ cup milk · 5 egg yolks · 1 tablespoon unsalted butter (or substitute ¾ cup pastry cream, page 7, and 4 egg yolks for the preceding) · 3 Meyer lemons · 4 egg whites · ¼ teaspoon cream of tartar · 4 tablespoons sugar · Optional: 1 teaspoon candied Meyer lemon peel*

Mix the sugar and flour in a small, heavy, non-corroding saucepan. Stir in the milk gradually so as not to make lumps. When the mixture is smooth, cook over medium heat, stirring constantly, until it has boiled for a minute to cook the flour thoroughly. Whisk a little of the mixture into the egg yolks to warm them and whisk that back into the remaining milk mixture. Return to the heat and cook for another minute or two, just enough to cook the eggs. They will be cooked at 170°F. Add the butter to the egg mixture. When it is melted, grate the peel of the lemons into the mixture, using a fine grater. Cool.

Let stand an hour or two, or refrigerate, well covered, overnight. In the latter case you may want to use less lemon peel because the flavor intensifies on standing.

Half an hour before serving, heat the oven to 400°F. Butter a 1½-quart soufflé dish and coat it with sugar. Warm the egg whites slightly over hot water or swirl above a gas flame until barely warm. Beat the egg whites with the cream of tartar just until they hold a soft shape. Gradually beat in the sugar until the egg whites hold a soft shape and look smooth with very fine bubbles. Fold in the egg yolk mixture and the finely chopped candied peel, if you are using it. Or, if you prefer, wait and sprinkle the peel in a layer in the center of the soufflé. Fold only until just barely mixed and pour into the prepared soufflé dish. The mixture should hold a soft shape when you have folded everything together. If you want to make the traditional "high hat" on the soufflé, draw a circle with the tip of a table knife about an inch in from the side of the dish and an inch deep into the soufflé mixture. Squeeze a teaspoon or two of juice from one of the lemons, trail it over the top of the soufflé, and sprinkle the juice lightly with sugar.

Set the soufflé in the oven and bake about 20 minutes, or until it has puffed and is golden brown on top. If the soufflé seems to be browning too fast, turn down the heat to 375°F. It should still wobble a little when you take it from the oven, although you can bake it longer if you like it completely stiffened. I prefer mine soft and creamy in the center.

Serve immediately with very cold vanilla crème anglaise.

ORANGE AND ARMAGNAC SHERBET

Makes about a quart: *About 4 pounds oranges · 1 cup sugar · About 2 tablespoons Armagnac*

I use rather tart California Valencia oranges for this, but navels will work also. You might have to adjust the amount of Armagnac for the different varieties of oranges, but it should be added to your taste anyway.

Wash the oranges well and grate the rinds of 2 of them in fine shreds into a mixing bowl. Juice the oranges, measure 4 cups, and strain the juice into the bowl with the peel, pushing as much pulp through the strainer as you can.

Combine the sugar and about 1 cup of the juice in a non-corroding saucepan and heat, stirring constantly, until the sugar has dissolved. Return this mixture to the rest of the orange juice, stir well, and add the Armagnac. Chill thoroughly, taste, and add more Armagnac if necessary. If you are using very sweet oranges you may want to add a little lemon juice, too. Freeze according to the instructions with your ice cream maker.

Serve garnished with a sprig of mint, accompanied by crisp cookies or a strip or two of candied peel, perhaps dipping one end of each in dark chocolate.

BUCKWHEAT CRÊPES WITH
BLOOD ORANGE ICE CREAM

For 10 servings: *10 buckwheat crêpes (page 16) · 1 recipe Blood Orange Ice Cream (opposite) · 2 or 3 blood oranges · 6 tablespoons sugar · 1 or 2 tablespoons water · Powdered sugar for sprinkling*

Make the crêpe batter the day before you want to use it. You may also fry the crêpes and wrap them in plastic until you are ready to serve them. Make the ice cream and have it frozen the day before, too.

Make the sauce: Juice the blood oranges, strain, and measure ½ cup. Put the sugar and water in a heavy, light-colored saucepan and let stand until the water has moistened all the sugar. Put over medium to high heat and cook until the caramel turns light golden brown. Remove from the heat and carefully add the orange juice. I usually set the pan on the bottom of my sink so any spatters are contained. Return the pan to the heat and cook until smooth again. To test the consistency of the syrup, put a drop of it on a small plate that has been chilled in the freezer. When it makes a thin syrup on cooling, it has cooked enough. Chill.

When you are ready to serve the dessert, heat the oven to 375°F. Put some of the crêpes on a cooling rack over a baking sheet and heat them in the oven for a couple of minutes, or until they are getting crisp around the edges but are still supple enough to bend. Fold them in half and set on a rack to cool and finish crisping.

Fill each crêpe with the ice cream, using a soup spoon to shape it, and dust the top very lightly with powdered sugar, using a shaker. Lacking a shaker, put a little sugar in a wire strainer and tap the edge lightly. Spoon some of the sauce across the front of the crêpe. Serve immediately.

BLOOD ORANGE CURD

Makes about 1½ cups: *2 blood oranges (about 10 ounces) · 1 tablespoon lemon juice · ¼ teaspoon cornstarch · ¼ cup sugar · 1 egg · 4 egg yolks · 6 tablespoons unsalted butter*

Wash the oranges and finely grate the peel into a non-corroding bowl. Juice the oranges, strain 7 tablespoons of the juice into the bowl, and add the lemon juice. Mix the cornstarch and the sugar—this prevents lumps from forming when the cornstarch is mixed into the eggs. You may omit the cornstarch unless you are filling a tart that you want to brown. Put the egg and the yolks in a small non-corroding saucepan and whisk the sugar-cornstarch mixture into them. Stir in the juice-peel mixture. Don't be alarmed if it seems to curdle; it will smooth out later. Cut the butter into several pieces and add to the mixture.

Cook over low heat, stirring constantly, until the mixture coats the spoon as for crème anglaise. Remove from the heat and stir for a minute or two until the heat of the pan dissipates so the custard won't curdle on the bottom. Pour into a small container and chill.

This makes a good cake filling or a filling for little tartlets. You can also use it for a blood orange meringue pie (see the recipe for Meyer Lemon Meringue Pie, page 67).

BLOOD ORANGE ICE CREAM

Makes about 1⅓ quarts: *3 or 4 blood oranges, about 1 pound · ¾ cup half-and-half · 1 cup sugar · 6 egg yolks · 2½ cups whipping cream · Vanilla extract to taste*

Wash the oranges and cut very thin strips of peel from 1 of them, using a vegetable peeler. Try not to cut into the white pith under the peel. Put the peel in a non-corroding saucepan with the half-and-half and the sugar, and heat to just under boiling. Remove from the heat and let steep 15 minutes, then reheat.

Whisk the egg yolks and pour the hot mixture into them slowly, beating constantly so the eggs don't scramble. Pour back into the pan and set over low heat to cook, stirring constantly, until the mixture coats the spoon. Strain into a bowl. Grate fine shreds of the peel from the other oranges into the custard and let it stand 5 to 10 minutes. Add the cream. Juice the oranges and strain about ¾ cup of the juice into the mixture. Taste and add a little more juice, if you like, and then a few drops of vanilla extract. Freeze according to the instructions with your ice cream maker.

Serve with Macadamia Nut and Coconut Tart, or in crêpes or buckwheat crêpes with a little blood orange caramel sauce (page 72).

BLOOD ORANGE GRATIN

For 6 servings: *1 cup milk · ⅝ cup sugar · ¼ cup flour · 2 egg yolks · 4 blood oranges · 1⅛ cups whipping cream · 1 to 2 tablespoons kirsch · 2 tablespoons sliced almonds, lightly toasted and chopped, or pistachios, lightly toasted, skinned and chopped*

Heat the milk in a small saucepan to scalding. Mix the sugar and flour thoroughly in a small bowl. Beat the egg yolks until they are light and a little fluffy. Beat a little of the sugar mixture into the egg yolks (enough to make a thick batter). Beat in some of the warm milk to thin it, keeping the batter smooth. Add the rest of the sugar mixture and beat until very smooth. Mix in the rest of the milk, again beating until smooth. Return the mixture to the saucepan and cook, stirring constantly, until it boils for a minute or two. Chill. All the above can be done a day ahead.

Prepare the blood oranges: Slice off their peels, trying to cut just under the white pith. Keep the oranges nice and round, but trim off all bits of white pith. With a very sharp knife, cut the sections from the fruit by slicing against the membranes on each side of the sections down to the center. Drop the sections into a bowl as you free them. When you have removed all the sections from each orange, squeeze the juice from the membranes into the bowl. These can be prepared up to a few hours before serving time and reserved, covered with their juice; the bowl must be covered tightly with plastic and refrigerated.

74

Beat the cooked mixture to smooth it out and then beat in ⅛ cup of the cream to lighten the batter. Whip the rest of the cream with the kirsch until it holds a very soft shape, then fold it into the first mixture. Taste and adjust the kirsch flavor, if necessary. Beat the mixture slightly if it doesn't fold together smoothly, but be careful to beat only until smooth. This step too can be done several hours, or even a day, before serving.

Heat your broiler. Use individual gratin dishes, individual soufflé dishes, or a gratin dish that will hold six servings. Spread about half the mixture on the bottoms of the dishes. Arrange the orange sections on top and pour some of the juice over. Cover the oranges with the rest of the gratin mixture. The mixture will be thick, and difficult to spread over the wet orange sections. Cook under the broiler for about 2 minutes, or until the top is brown and bubbly.

Sprinkle the top lightly with the almonds or pistachios and serve immediately.

PUFF PASTRIES WITH BLOOD ORANGES

For 5 servings: 6 ounces puff pastry (page 25) · ⅔ cup pastry cream (page 7) · 1 egg yolk · 1 tablespoon whipping cream · 3 blood oranges · ⅓ cup whipping cream · Optional: ½ cup Champagne (flat Champagne is all right) · 1 to 2 teaspoons Cognac · 1 tablespoon water · 5 tablespoons sugar

These are pretty, individual puff pastries, split, with pastry cream and blood orange sections spilling out onto a pool of dark red caramel sauce.

Roll puff pastry ³/₁₆-inch thick and chill. With a sharp knife or a decorative cutter, cut into rectangles, squares, or flower shapes. The cutter must be sharp so it won't pinch the layers of puff pastry together and keep them from rising properly. Chill the pastry. Make a half recipe of pastry cream. The pastry cream can be made a day ahead, and the pastry can be rolled and shaped the day before serving also. Wrap the pastry very tight in plastic so it won't dry out.

The pastries should be baked within 2 hours of serving time. Put them on a baking sheet that is lightly moistened with water and brush them carefully with the egg yolk beaten with the 1 tablespoon cream. Be careful not to let any drip down the sides. If it does, it will keep the pastries from rising properly. You can cut tiny shapes from leftover scraps of very cold pastry and use them to decorate the tops; glaze their tops also. You can also make designs with a sharp knife, cutting about ⅟₁₆-inch into the cold pastry.

Set the pastries in a preheated 400°F oven. Bake for 10 minutes, reduce the heat to 350°F and bake until golden brown, 15 to 20 minutes. Remove from the oven and cool slightly, then carefully slice the pastry horizontally through the center to make a top and bottom layer. Return them to the oven for 5 minutes or so to dry out the center, if necessary.

Peel and section the oranges as for the Blood Orange Gratin above. If you cover them tight with plastic wrap and refrigerate them, you can do this earlier in the day. Whip the ⅓ cup cream so it holds a definite shape, but not until it looks grainy, and fold it into the pastry cream. If you are using Champagne, boil it in a small pan to reduce it to about 1 tablespoon. Cool slightly and stir into the pastry cream. Flavor with Cognac to taste.

Make the caramel sauce: Put the water in a small, heavy, light-colored saucepan and put the sugar over it. Let stand a few minutes to moisten the sugar, then cook over medium heat until it is light golden caramel. Pour 4 tablespoons of juice off the oranges and pour it very carefully into the caramel, standing back so it doesn't splatter you. Boil just until the caramel has dissolved, then remove from the heat. Stir in another table-spoon of orange juice and set aside.

To serve, set each bottom pastry layer on a plate and spoon some of the pastry cream mixture over it, letting it fall over one edge. Arrange five or six orange sections over the pastry cream and set the top pastry layer over it. Pour a little of the blood orange caramel around the pastry and serve immediately.

This recipe may seem complicated, but much of the work can be done ahead, leaving final assembly of the dessert for the last minute.

BLOOD ORANGE SHERBET

Makes 1 quart: *Approximately 6 pounds blood oranges · 1 cup sugar · A few drops of lemon juice*

Wash the oranges and grate the peel of 3 of them into a non-corroding bowl, pulling the oranges across the grater to make shreds as long and fine as possible. Juice the oranges and strain 4 cups of juice into the same bowl, pushing as much pulp through the strainer as you can. Put the sugar in a non-corroding saucepan and pour in about ¾ cup of the juice. Heat, stirring constantly, until the sugar has melted completely and you can feel no sugar crystals when you rub some juice between your fingers. Pour the sugar mixture back into the remaining juice and add a few drops of lemon juice if the sherbet needs more tartness. Chill. Freeze according to the instructions with your ice cream maker.

Serve garnished with a sprig of mint with crisp cookies, make a bombe with Meyer Lemon Mousse, or serve in combination with Pineapple, Kiwi, or Passion Fruit Sherbet.

BLOOD ORANGE TART

For 8 servings: *One 9-inch tart shell, short crust (page 11), or puff pastry (page 25) · 1 to 2 tablespoons unsalted pistachio nuts · About 5 blood oranges · 3 tablespoons sugar · 1 tablespoon water · Optional: Armagnac, Cognac, or brandy to taste · ½ recipe pastry cream (page 7)*

Bake the tart shell as directed in the recipe. Shell the pistachios and toast them in a preheated 350°F oven for about 5 minutes, just long enough to bring out their flavor but not so long that they lose their green color. Cool them slightly, rub off their skins, chop them into ¹⁄₁₆-inch to ⅛-inch pieces, and set them aside for the garnish. Section the blood oranges (see Blood Orange Gratin, page 74) into a small bowl, cover with their juice, cover tight and refrigerate if you are not making the tart immediately.

When you are ready to put the tart together, preferably just before serving, put the sugar and water into a small, light-colored saucepan and cook over medium heat until it becomes a light golden caramel. Pour it quickly into the bottom of the tart shell and swirl it over the bottom. It probably won't cover the bottom completely, but try to get an even covering by pouring the caramel in circles. This caramel makes a nice crunchy texture contrast in the tart.

Stir a little Armagnac, Cognac, or brandy into the pastry cream. Be careful not to beat it too much because it will thin out if it is overbeaten. Spread the pastry cream in a layer over the caramel in the bottom of the shell. Dry the orange sections on a towel or a paper towel, then arrange them over the pastry cream, overlapping the sections slightly. Begin from the outside of the tart and turn the sections in opposite directions in each successive ring. If the center is too small to make a final circle, fill it with small sections, perhaps in the form of a rose, an open flower, or a spray of sections side by side. Sprinkle pistachios around the outside edge or around the center row of sections, or wherever you think they will look best. I like to see the red-orange sections against the creamy color of the pastry cream with accents of green pistachio nuts.

The tart shell and the pastry cream can be made in advance. All you really need to do the day of serving is bake the shell, prepare the nuts and caramel, section the oranges, and put the tart together. You can substitute navel oranges, readily available for a much longer season than the blood oranges.

BLOOD ORANGE AND MEYER LEMON BOMBE

For 10 to 12 servings: *1 quart Blood Orange Sherbet (page 77)* · *One recipe frozen mousse (page 9)* · *2 or 3 Meyer lemons*

Chill the mold in the freezer. Line the bottom and sides with the slightly softened sherbet, and return to the freezer to freeze hard.

Make the mousse. Flavor it to taste with Meyer lemon peel grated in shreds as long as you can make them. Taste the mousse with a little of the sherbet—the lemon flavor will get stronger as it sits. One flavor should not overwhelm the other. Fill the center of the bombe with the flavored mousse and freeze again until you can spread the remaining sherbet over the top. Freeze hard, unmold onto a chilled serving plate, and cover with plastic. Keep in the freezer until you are ready to serve.

Serve in slices, garnished with a sprig of mint, and accompanied by a plate of crisp Ladyfingers.

POMELO ICE CREAM

Makes 1 quart: *1 pomelo, 2½ to 2¾ pounds · ⅔ cup sugar · ½ cup half-and-half · 4 egg yolks · 1½ cups whipping cream · A few drops of lemon juice*

Remove about a quarter of the peel of the pomelo in a very thin layer with a vegetable peeler, being careful not to take any of the white pith. Put it in a non-corroding saucepan with the sugar and the half-and-half and heat to just under boiling. Remove from the heat and let steep for about 15 minutes.

Whisk the egg yolks in a small bowl just enough to mix them; stir in the warm half-and-half mixture. Return the mixture to the pan and cook, stirring constantly, until the custard coats the spoon. Strain into a bowl. Grate fine the rest of the peel from the pomelo and add to the warm custard. Let stand 5 to 10 minutes while you juice the pomelo. I have had to cut the fruit into eighths and trim off its inch-thick skin before it would fit into my juicer. Strain the juice—you should have about ½ cup. Mix the cream into the custard and then mix in the juice to taste. Add a few drops of lemon juice if you want more tartness. Chill. Freeze according to the instructions with your ice cream maker.

Serve with crisp cookies.

CARAMEL TANGERINES

For 4 to 8 servings: *4 to 8 tangerines · 2 cups sugar · 6 tablespoons water · Butter for the plate · Mint or tangerine leaves · Crème anglaise (page 5)*

You can prepare the tangerines several hours before serving time: Peel them carefully, trying not to dig into the fruit or break it apart. When you have removed all the peel, dip the tangerine in a bowl of cold water and scrape it gently with a paring knife to remove as much as possible of the white pith remaining on the outside. You may have to dip the tangerine repeatedly. As you finish each tangerine, set it on a rack to dry, preferably for a few hours. The caramel sticks to them properly only if they are dry when you dip them.

Put the sugar in a heavy, deep, light-colored pot. Pour the water over it and let stand until it has moistened all the sugar, then set on the stove over medium heat. Have ready a pan of ice water to set the pot into if you need to stop the caramel cooking. Cook until the syrup becomes a light gold, somewhat lighter than you will want it finally, then take it off the heat. It will continue to darken slightly. If it begins to look reddish brown, set it into the pan of ice water immediately to cool it and stop the cooking.

Butter a plate or a baking sheet to set the tangerines on after dipping, and have two buttered forks ready. The caramel should be a nice golden color. Keep it as hot as possible without coloring it further, rewarming as necessary, so that it will make a thin, crisp coating on the fruit. If the caramel cools too much you will have a thick gloppy coating—not pretty, and hard to eat.

Drop a tangerine into the caramel and roll it quickly with the fork. Coat it completely with the caramel, then lift it out with the fork and set it on the buttered plate quickly, pushing it off one fork with the other. Be quick, or the caramel may stick to your fork and pull away from the tangerine as you set it on the plate. If you are careful to lift it by the part that will be on the bottom there is no harm done; it won't show anyway.

This process is tricky. You may want to practice it a bit with some small fruits, strawberries, for example, to get the feel.

Serve within an hour on a pretty plate. Decorate the tops with mint sprigs or tangerine leaves, which can be attached by first dipping their stems in the caramel. Surround the fruits with a pool of crème anglaise. You can also serve a bowl of lightly sugared strawberries on the side. Serve with Langues de Chat or Lace Cookies.

TANGERINE ICE CREAM

Makes 1 quart: *3 or 4 tangerines · ⅔ cup sugar · ½ cup half-and-half · 4 egg yolks · 2 cups whipping cream · A few drops of vanilla extract*

Wash the tangerines. Remove the peel from 1 tangerine with a vegetable peeler, being very careful not to take any of the white pith. Put it with the sugar and half-and-half into a non-corroding saucepan and heat just to boiling. Remove from the heat and let steep for 5 to 10 minutes. Whisk the egg yolks to break them up and pour the warm half-and-half mixture into them, whisking constantly. Return to the pan and cook over low heat, stirring constantly, until the custard coats the spoon. Pour through a strainer into a bowl and grate the rind of 2 more tangerines into the custard. Grate as fine as possible and let stand in the warm custard a few minutes. Juice the tangerines, and measure 5 to 6 tablespoons.

Add the cream, the tangerine juice, and vanilla to taste to the custard. Chill. This can all be done a day before you want to freeze the ice cream. Freeze according to the instructions with your ice cream maker, pack into an airtight container, and freeze.

Serve with Lace Cookies drizzled with chocolate, or other chocolate cookies, or with Macadamia Nut and Coconut Tart.

TANGERINE OEUFS À LA NEIGE

For 6 to 8 servings: *For the custard: 2 cups milk · ¼ cup sugar · 4 egg yolks · ½ teaspoon grated tangerine, Meyer lemon, or lemon peel*

Heat the milk and the sugar in a non-corroding saucepan. Whisk the egg yolks just enough to break them up and whisk in some of the hot milk mixture to warm them. Return to the pan and cook over low heat, stirring constantly, until the custard coats the spoon. Strain, add the finely grated peel, and chill.

For the meringues: *3 egg whites* · *¼ teaspoon cream of tartar* · *6 tablespoons sugar* · *A few drops of vanilla extract*

Make the meringues: Heat about 1 inch of water in a shallow non-corroding sauté pan to 170°F and keep the water at that temperature. Warm the egg whites slightly over the hot water. Beat them with the cream of tartar until they hold straight peaks when you withdraw the beater. Gradually beat in the sugar and beat until they hold stiff peaks again. Beat in a few drops of vanilla until they are stiff. Shape them by scooping a rounded tablespoonful of the meringue and pushing it into the hot water. You can also use an oval or round ice cream scoop. Leave plenty of room for them to expand while they cook and let them cook for 3 to 4 minutes. Turn them gently and cook 3 to 4 more minutes. Be sure that the temperature of the water does not go above 170°F, which is the temperature at which egg proteins coagulate; higher temperatures will toughen them. Remove from the pan with a slotted spoon and drain on a pan lined with a towel or a paper towel. Repeat until all the meringues are cooked. You might prefer to make slightly smaller meringues and serve two to each person. Cool them but don't refrigerate. They will keep for several hours until you are ready to serve them.

At serving time put the custard into a bowl and arrange the meringues over it. Drizzle with caramel syrup, or make the following caramel garnish:

4 tablespoons sugar · *1½ tablespoons water*

Make the caramel (see page 34) and cool it until you can drizzle thin threads of it over the islands.

Serve immediately. Serve an island and some custard to each person, grate some long fine shreds of tangerine or lemon peel over the top, and accompany with crisp cookies.

TANGERINE MOUSSE

Makes 1¼ to 1½ quarts: *¾ to 1 pound tangerines, preferably tangy ones: Minneola or other tangelos · 3 tablespoons cold water · 1½ teaspoons gelatin · 3 eggs · ¼ cup plus 1 tablespoon sugar · 1 cup whipping cream · Lemon juice*

Wash the tangerines well and grate the peel in fine shreds into a bowl. Juice the tangerines and strain ⅔ cup of their juice into the same bowl, saving any extra juice. Put the cold water in a small pan and sprinkle the gelatin into it. Beat the eggs with the sugar until they hold a slight shape when you lift the beater. It is much easier to do this with an electric mixer or a hand-held electric beater. Whip the cream until it holds a soft shape. Dissolve the gelatin over low heat. It melts between 105°F and 115°F, so don't let it get hot. Slowly add the juice and peel mixture to the gelatin mixture, stirring constantly.

Fold the whipped cream into the egg and sugar mixture. Pour the gelatin-juice mixture into the cream mixture, whisking briskly where the juice goes in to keep it from jelling before it is thoroughly mixed. It will tend to jell and make little lumps when it hits the cold mixture unless you whisk briskly while you add it.

Taste and add some of the reserved juice or a little lemon juice if you would like more tartness or a stronger flavor. Chill for several hours or overnight, whisking occasionally during the first hour to prevent it from separating.

Serve in a glass, garnished with a few shreds of tangerine peel, accompanied by Lace Cookies dipped in chocolate or Langues de Chat.

To make a Meyer Lemon Mousse: Follow the above directions, using the grated peel of 3 Meyer lemons, ½ cup of juice, and 5½ tablespoons sugar. This will take just under a pound of lemons. Serve garnished with shreds of lemon peel.

To make a Lime Mousse: Follow the above directions, substituting the grated peel of 1½ limes and ⅜ cup lime juice for the tangerine peel and juice.

TANGERINE SHERBET

Makes about 1 quart: *About 4 or 5 pounds tangerines, preferably tangy ones: Minneola, Fairchild, Kinnow, or Honey · 1 cup less 1 tablespoon sugar · Cognac, brandy, or curaçao to taste*

Grate the peel of 1 washed tangerine. A small flat grater with about 1/16-inch holes works well. Pull the tangerine along the grater to make long shreds, which will show up a bright orange in the paler orange sherbet. Juice the tangerines and strain out the seeds, but keep as much pulp in the juice as you can. Put the sugar in a non-corroding saucepan and pour in about 1 cup of the juice. Heat the mixture over medium heat to melt the sugar, stirring constantly. Rub a little of the juice between your fingers; when the sugar is melted and you can no longer feel any graininess, stir the warm mixture into the reserved juice. Stir in a little Cognac, brandy, or curaçao to taste. Chill and freeze according to the instructions with your ice cream maker.

Serve this sherbet garnished with a fresh violet, a candied violet, or a sprig of mint. Accompany it with a plate of assorted cookies or with Tangerine or Vanilla Ice Cream. It is also refreshing served between dinner courses.

The texture of this tart sherbet is nice soon after it is made. It will be quite hard the day after if you store it in a 0°F freezer. If you want it to keep, or to use it in a bombe or other composed ice cream dessert, add another tablespoon of sugar to the mixture for a creamier texture.

The sherbets in this book use as little sugar as possible and are often quite hard at 0°. Warm them to 5° to 7° to serve. If you are in a hurry you can usually serve them by scraping a spoon across the top.

TANGERINE SHERBET IN TANGERINE CUPS

For 6 to 8 servings: *½ recipe Tangerine Sherbet (above) · 6 to 8 neatly cut tangerine halves · Mint or violets for garnish*

This is a very beautiful and refreshing dessert, though a very simple one, and can be made well ahead of serving time.

84

Make the sherbet and freeze it in your ice cream maker. Meanwhile, clean all the pulp from the insides of the tangerine halves. It usually tears out easily after the tangerines have been juiced. Set the skins on a plate or tray in the freezer for 20 minutes, or until frozen hard. When the sherbet is frozen, remove it from the machine and quickly fill the tangerine halves with it, rounding the sherbet on their tops to make them look like whole tangerines. Freeze until firm.

Serve on a pretty plate, with a doily if you like, and garnish the top with a sprig of mint or, preferably, lay a violet (with its stem) across the top. Serve with Lace Cookies or other thin crisp cookies.

TANGERINE SOUFFLÉ

For 4 to 5 servings: *1½ tablespoons sugar · 1 tablespoon plus 2 teaspoons flour · ½ cup milk · 5 egg yolks (or substitute ¾ cup pastry cream, page 7, and 4 egg yolks for all of the above) · 1 tablespoon unsalted butter · 1 or 2 tangerines · Optional: 1 teaspoon finely chopped candied tangerine peel, soaked in 1 teaspoon Cognac, brandy, Grand Marnier, or curaçao · 5 egg whites · ¼ teaspoon cream of tartar · 4 tablespoons sugar*

Mix the 1½ tablespoons sugar and the flour in a heavy non-corroding saucepan and gradually stir in the milk. Set on the heat and cook, stirring constantly, until it has boiled at least 2 minutes, in order to cook the flour. Remove from the heat. Lightly beat the egg yolks, then beat some of the hot mixture into them. Return to the pan and cook, whisking constantly, until the mixture has thickened again and is smooth. It should reach 170°F.

Remove from the heat and stir in the butter. Grate in fine shreds of the tangerine peel to taste. The flavor will get stronger when the soufflé is baked. Cover the mixture and let it cool to lukewarm, stirring occasionally. Heat the oven to 400°F. Butter a 1½-quart soufflé dish and shake sugar in it to coat it.

Stir the candied peel into the lukewarm egg yolk mixture. (You can add the candied peel mixture later, when you fill the baking dish. Sprinkle it on top of the soufflé mixture after you have half filled the dish, then cover it with the rest of the mixture.)

Warm the egg whites slightly over hot water or swirl above a gas flame until barely warm, then beat them with the cream of tartar until they hold rounded peaks. Gradually beat in the 4 tablespoons sugar and continue beating until the whites hold a rounded peak and you can no longer feel the grains of sugar between your fingers. Fold about a quarter of the egg whites into the egg yolk mixture to lighten it. Fold in the remaining whites just until evenly mixed. Pour into the prepared baking dish, sprinkle the top with a little sugar, and squeeze a little tangerine juice over it. Place in the 400°F oven and bake for 20 to 25 minutes, depending on how soft you like the center of your soufflé. If the soufflé seems to be browning too fast, turn the heat down to 375°F.

Serve with cold crème anglaise that has had a little tangerine caramel swirled into it, or with a small pitcher of the caramel and a larger pitcher of crème anglaise on the side.

4

TROPICAL FRUITS

Tropical fruits begin to arrive in early spring, when we need a respite from winter's apples, pears, and citrus fruits. They reach the height of their season in summer, when hot weather demands light, refreshing meals and cooling desserts.

Pineapples are particularly refreshing at the end of a long rich meal, and for me need no enhancement—though a slight sprinkling of kirsch is traditional and will help a less than perfect pineapple. Homemade pineapple sherbet or ice cream will be a revelation if you have never eaten any but the supermarket product. And a plate of various tropical sherbets is a bright color and taste accent for a quiet-colored meal, especially if it is garnished with a few slices of kiwi fruit and pineapple. A winter compote made with slices of pineapple, kiwi fruit, mango, and papaya, with a little passion fruit flesh and a few of its dark seeds for contrast, needs only a

88

grating of lime peel and a sprinkling of rum or kirsch. Accompanied by coconut macaroons, it would be perfect after a Brazilian feijoada or a South American rice or bean dish.

Passion fruit is very beautiful, with its leathery dark purple skin enclosing black seeds mixed with yellow-green flesh in a red-lined case. The flavor is very penetrating—very little of its pulp is needed to flavor a sherbet or ice cream. In combination with orange or tangerine juice, with a splash of champagne, it makes a most refreshing winter sherbet. Kiwi fruit is invaluable, both for its taste of mixed strawberries and bananas and for its sparkling black seeds and bright apple green color. Not long ago it was available only imported from New Zealand or home grown. Now that there is commercially grown kiwi fruit from California, there is a steadier supply. At the restaurant we often make kiwi sherbet to serve in an array of sherbets and fruit. Mango sherbets and occasional mango tarts with their rich, peachlike flavor, so nicely enhanced by rum or Sauternes, are favorites. We also make delicious papaya sherbet when ripe, sweet ones are available.

Coconut, since it is a true nut, makes richer desserts than other tropical fruits. Coconut ice cream is thus a good foil for the lighter tropical fruit sherbets. Macadamia Nut and Coconut Tart is a perfect ending for a light supper with a tropical feeling, or a satisfying treat with an afternoon espresso.

Tropical fruits are still exotic newcomers and it will take time to learn how to integrate them into menus, so these desserts are still a sideline at Chez Panisse. Besides, most tropical fruits don't ripen properly once shipped, and therefore never achieve their full promise.

COCONUT BLANCMANGE

Makes 1 quart, for 8 to 10 servings: *1½ cups flaked unsweetened coconut* · *2 cups plus 2 tablespoons milk* · *5 tablespoons sugar* · *1 tablespoon gelatin* · *¼ cup cold water* · *1½ cups whipping cream* · *A few drops of vanilla extract*

Toast the coconut in a preheated 325°F oven for 5 to 10 minutes, or until it is golden brown. Stir it often to keep it browning evenly. Put it in a non-corroding saucepan with the milk and heat almost to boiling. Steep for 20 to 25 minutes, keeping it hot. Strain through a very fine strainer, pressing well to extract all the milk from the coconut. Measure the coconut milk and add enough milk to make 1¼ cups. Stir in the sugar until it is dissolved.

Sprinkle the gelatin over the water in a small saucepan and let it stand a few minutes to soften. Heat until the gelatin dissolves (115°F). Stir into the milk and sugar mixture. Whip the cream until it mounds very slightly on its surface when you drop some from the beater. Set the coconut milk mixture over a bowl of ice water and stir it constantly with a rubber spatula, always scraping the sides of the bowl so the gelatin won't harden there in lumps. Stir until it begins to thicken and remove it from the ice water. Quickly pour it into the whipped cream, whisking constantly. Fold the cream and milk mixtures together completely and flavor with a few drops of vanilla extract.

Lightly oil a 1-quart mold with sweet almond oil or other flavorless oil, rubbing it on with a paper towel so there is only a very thin film. Pour the blancmange into the prepared mold, cover tightly with plastic wrap, and chill for at least 6 hours before serving.

Serve ungarnished, or in a pool of tangerine crème anglaise or orange crème anglaise, accompanied by Langues de Chat.

COCONUT ICE CREAM

Makes 1 quart: *1⅛ cups flaked unsweetened coconut · 2¼ cups milk · ¾ cup sugar · 6 egg yolks · 1½ cups whipping cream · A few drops of vanilla extract*

Toast the coconut in a preheated 325°F oven for 5 to 7 minutes, or until it is golden, stirring occasionally to keep it browning evenly. Heat it in a non-corroding saucepan with the milk almost to boiling and let steep for 20 minutes. Press through a very fine strainer to extract the coconut milk. Measure the coconut milk and add enough milk to make 1½ cups. Return to the cleaned saucepan and heat with the sugar, stirring to dissolve it. Whisk the egg yolks just enough to break them up and whisk in some of the hot coconut milk to warm them. Return to the pan and cook the custard over low heat, stirring constantly, until it coats the spoon. Strain into a container, stir in the cream, and a few drops of vanilla to taste. Cover and chill. Freeze according to the instructions with your ice cream maker.

Serve with Pineapple, Passion Fruit, Mango, Blood Orange, or Orange Sherbet. Or use in bombes with any of those sherbets. Like all ice creams, this is nice accompanied by crisp cookies.

MARY JO'S COCONUT MACAROONS

Makes 4 to 4½ dozen: *2 cups flaked unsweetened coconut · ¾ cup macadamia nuts · 2 egg whites · ¼ teaspoon cream of tartar · A pinch of salt · ¾ cup sugar*

Toast the coconut in a 325°F oven until it is pale golden brown. Stir it often to keep it toasting evenly. This should take 5 to 10 minutes. Toast the macadamias also until they just begin to color, then cool and chop them fine by hand. Warm the egg whites slightly over hot water or swirl above a gas flame until barely warm. Beat them with the cream of tartar and salt until they hold stiff peaks. Beat in the sugar until they hold stiff peaks again. Fold in the nuts and coconut (don't worry if it does not quite hold together).

Butter and flour a baking sheet or cover it with parchment. Take tea-spoonfuls of dough, press into 1-inch balls, and set them an inch apart on the baking sheet. Bake in a preheated 325°F oven for about 10 minutes, or until they are lightly browned.

MACADAMIA NUT AND COCONUT TART

For 8 servings: *One 9-inch almond-flavored short crust tart shell (page 12), baked · ½ cup flaked unsweetened coconut · 1¼ cups macadamia nuts · 6 tablespoons unsalted butter · 3 tablespoons honey · 3 tablespoons whipping cream · 3 egg yolks · ⅝ cup light brown sugar · Vanilla extract to taste*

Toast the coconut in a preheated 325°F oven just until light golden brown, stirring occasionally to toast it evenly—it will take 5 to 10 minutes. Turn the oven up to 350°F and toast the nuts 5 to 6 minutes until lightly browned. Melt the butter with the honey, stir in the cream, and combine with the egg yolks and sugar, whisking just until thoroughly mixed. When the nuts are cool enough to handle, chop them into ¼-inch to ⅜-inch chunks. Shake them in a strainer to remove the dusty particles. Stir the nuts and coconut into the sugar mixture, and add a little vanilla to taste. Pour into the pre-baked shell and bake in a preheated 375°F oven about 20 minutes, or until set and golden brown.

Serve with Blood Orange or Tangerine Ice Cream, or crème Chantilly.

KIWI SHERBET

Makes 1 quart: *2 pounds kiwi fruit · ¾ cup sugar · Optional: kirsch to taste*

Be sure you have ripe kiwis: they should give slightly when you press them, and feel a little soft. Peel the kiwis and pull out the hard core at the end. Cut them in half and purée. You can leave the seeds in if you like the way they look, or you can strain them out. Sometimes I strain them all out, and sometimes I strain only half the mixture so the sherbet will be speckled, rather than peppered, with the seeds.

Heat about 1 cup of the purée in a small saucepan with the sugar, stirring until the sugar has dissolved. Add this to the rest of the purée and chill. Flavor with a few drops of kirsch, if you like, and freeze according to the instructions with your ice cream maker.

Serve alone or as part of a plate of several sherbets. The light apple-green color of this sherbet is invaluable, and the flavor is like a mixture of strawberry and banana. For both these reasons, this goes well with many other fruits or fruit sherbets: Pineapple, Strawberry, Orange, or Tangerine.

MANGO SHERBET

Makes a generous quart: *3 pounds very ripe, perfumed mangoes · ¾ cup sugar · ½ cup water · Juice of 2 limes · 2 teaspoons rum, to taste*

Slice the mangoes off their pits and peel them. Scrape as much pulp off the fibrous pits as you can and purée all the pulp; measure 3½ cups and set aside. Cook the sugar and water together for 5 minutes. Cool the syrup, then add it to the mango purée with lime juice and rum to taste. Chill thoroughly; then freeze according to the directions for your ice cream maker.

Serve with crisp cookies or Mary Jo's Coconut Macaroons, or serve with other sherbets such as Pineapple or papaya, or with Coconut Ice Cream.

To make Mango Sherbet with Sauternes: Follow the above recipe but omit the rum and serve the sherbet in parfait glasses. Pour a little Sauternes over the sherbet when you serve it and accompany with Langues de Chat.

PASSION FRUIT ICE CREAM

Makes 1 quart: *1 cup less 2 tablespoons sugar · 1 cup plus 2 tablespoons half-and-half · 6 egg yolks · 2¼ cups whipping cream · 4 to 6 passion fruits*

Warm the sugar with the half-and-half in a non-corroding saucepan until it has dissolved. Whisk the yolks in a small bowl just enough to break them up, then add the hot half-and-half mixture, whisking constantly. Return to the pan and cook until it coats the spoon.

Strain into a bowl and add the cream. Juice the passion fruits: slice them in half and scoop out the seeds and pulp into a strainer, working it until you can't press out any more juice. You will need ¼ to ⅓ cup. Add it to the cream mixture, using the larger amount if you want the flavor stronger. Passion fruits have a very intense flavor, and it will grow stronger after the mixture stands for a while. Chill the mixture. Freeze according to the instructions with your ice cream maker.

Serve with crisp cookies or Mary Jo's Coconut Macaroons, or as part of a plate with sliced fruits of various kinds, such as strawberries, kiwis, or pineapple, accompanied by a little strawberry sauce.

PASSION FRUIT MOUSSE

Makes 1½ quarts, for about 6 servings: *3 eggs · ⅓ cup sugar · 1½ teaspoons gelatin · 4 tablespoons cold water · 1 cup whipping cream · 6 passion fruits*

Beat the eggs with the sugar until they are thick and hold a mound that slowly sinks back into the mixture. It takes me about 10 minutes to do this with my electric hand mixer. In a small pan sprinkle the gelatin over 3 tablespoons of the water and let stand for a few minutes. Whip the cream so it holds soft peaks, but don't let it get stiff and grainy.

Juice the passion fruits by halving them and scooping out the insides into a strainer set over a bowl. Press them with a rubber spatula until you have extracted all the juice. You will want about ⅓ cup. Fold the whipped cream into the beaten egg mixture and whisk in the passion fruit juice.

Dissolve the gelatin over low heat. When completely dissolved the liquid will feel warm to your finger. Don't let it go over 115°F. Add the remaining tablespoon of cold water to the gelatin, stirring carefully, and whisk this quickly into the mousse. Be careful to whisk where the gelatin is going in so you don't get strings of it when it hits the cool mousse mixture. Chill thoroughly in a covered bowl. Whisk it once or twice while it chills to keep it from separating.

Serve garnished with a sprig of mint or a few strawberries or fraises des bois, accompanied by crisp cookies such as Langues de Chat or Mary Jo's Coconut Macaroons. You may also serve it with a lightly sweetened strawberry purée.

PASSION FRUIT SHERBET

Makes 1 quart: *¾ cup sugar · 1 cup water · 8 passion fruits · About ⅔ pound oranges · 3 small bananas*

Passion fruit has a very penetrating flavor. You can use less than this amount and still have enough passion fruit perfume. Substitute orange juice for any passion fruit juice you omit.

Boil the sugar and water together for 5 minutes and let cool. Juice the passion fruits by halving them and rubbing them over a small juicer. Then put the juice, seeds, and pulp into a strainer and press and scrape thoroughly with a rubber spatula until you can't get any more juice. Measure ½ cup.

Add the cool syrup to the passion fruit juice. Juice the oranges and measure ⅔ cup. Peel the bananas and purée them, mixing in the orange juice as you go to keep them from turning brown. Mix the purée with the passion fruit mixture and chill. Freeze according to the instructions with your ice cream maker.

Serve in combination with Pineapple, Kiwi, or Strawberry sherbets, or with Coconut Ice Cream, and accompany with crisp cookies.

ANOTHER PASSION FRUIT SHERBET

Makes about 1 quart: *About 4 pounds oranges · 1 cup plus 2 tablespoons sugar · About 10 passion fruits*

Juice the oranges, strain the juice, and measure 4 cups into a bowl. Press and scrape the oranges to get as much pulp as possible through the strainer. Pour about 1 cup into a non-corroding saucepan. Add the sugar and heat, stirring occasionally, until the sugar has dissolved. Pour into the bowl with the remaining juice and cool.

Juice the passion fruits. Use a small juicer or scoop them out with a stainless steel spoon. Pour into a strainer and press and scrape with a rubber spatula until you have separated as much juice and pulp from the seeds as you can. Add the passion fruit juice to the orange juice mixture and chill. Freeze according to the instructions with your ice cream maker.

Serve garnished with a sprig of mint. This is a really refreshing sherbet that we serve with Mary Jo's Coconut Macaroons.

PINEAPPLE SHERBET BOMBE
WITH KIRSCH MOUSSE

For 10 to 12 servings: *1 recipe Pineapple Sherbet (opposite)* · *1 recipe frozen mousse (page 9)* · *Kirsch to taste* · *Mint or strawberries for garnish*

Chill a 1½-quart to 1¾-quart bombe mold in the freezer and line the bottom and sides with an even layer of softened pineapple sherbet, using about two-thirds of it. Return to the freezer and let harden while you make the mousse. Flavor the mousse with kirsch and taste some with the sherbet to be sure the flavors are in balance. Fill the center of the bombe to within about an inch of the top with the mousse and freeze. Spread the rest of the sherbet evenly over the top of the bombe and wrap tightly in plastic, then with foil. Freeze hard.

Serve unmolded, garnished with sprigs of mint or with strawberries, accompanied by Mary Jo's Coconut Macaroons or by Langues de Chat.

96

PINEAPPLE ICE CREAM

Makes about 1 quart: *1 ripe pineapple weighing about 1 pound · 1⅛ cups whipping cream · ⅝ cup sugar · 4 egg yolks · Vanilla extract to taste · Optional: kirsch to taste*

Slice the peel thin from the pineapple and cut off the top. Pull out the eyes, using the tip of a vegetable peeler, and then cut the pineapple lengthwise into quarters. Cut out all the core and chop the pineapple into coarse chunks. Heat the chunks in a non-corroding saucepan just to a boil. Chop coarsely in a food processor or blender, using all the juice, and measure out 1¼ cups of the purée.

Warm the cream with the sugar until the sugar has dissolved. Whisk the egg yolks just enough to mix them and stir in a little of the hot cream mixture. Return to the pan and cook until the custard coats the spoon. Add to the pineapple and flavor it with a few drops of vanilla and kirsch. Chill. Freeze according to the instructions with your ice cream maker.

This is delicious served with Coconut Ice Cream, or with Tangerine or Passion Fruit Sherbet.

You can plant the top of the pineapple in a pot to make a nice house plant. We grew a very sweet-tasting pineapple this way in a western window near the kitchen porch.

PINEAPPLE SHERBET

Makes a generous quart: *1 ripe pineapple weighing about 2½ pounds · ½ cup plus 1 tablespoon sugar · Optional: kirsch to taste*

Cut the stem off the pineapple and slice off the skin in thin strips. Pull out the eyes with a vegetable peeler and cut the fruit lengthwise into quarters. Cut the core out completely—it has long dry fibers that are unpleasant in the sherbet. Slice the pineapple into chunks and purée them in your blender or food processor; you should have 3 cups. If you have more, or less, adjust the amount of sugar accordingly, using 3 tablespoons of sugar for each cup of purée.

Dissolve the sugar with about a quarter of the purée in a non-corroding saucepan over low heat, then mix in the remaining purée. Add a few drops of kirsch to heighten the flavor, if you like, then chill the mixture. Freeze according to the directions with your ice cream maker.

Serve garnished with a sprig of mint, or serve in a bombe, or in combination with any of the following sherbets: Strawberry, Raspberry, Orange, Tangerine, Kiwi, Passion Fruit, blackberry or Boysenberry, Blood Orange, Mango, or papaya.

A TROPICAL SHERBET

Makes a scant quart: *About 2½ pounds tangerines · 1 or 2 lemons · 3 ripe bananas · ⅞ cup sugar · Optional: kirsch to taste*

Juice the tangerines and strain, pushing as much pulp through the strainer as you can. Measure 2¼ cups. Juice the lemons and measure 4 to 5 tablespoons. Peel the bananas and purée in a blender or food processor with the lemon juice, which will keep the bananas from turning brown. Or you can push the bananas through a strainer after slicing them and tossing them with the lemon juice.

Heat about 1 cup of the tangerine juice with the sugar in a small pan just until dissolved. Mix with the rest of the tangerine juice and the banana purée, and chill. Add a few drops of kirsch, if you like, and freeze according to the directions with your ice cream maker.

Serve with Mary Jo's Coconut Macaroons or any crisp cookie.

5

FLOWERS, HERBS, AND SPICES

GARDENING AND COOKING are two of my greatest pleasures; I love to use herbs and flowers from the garden in my cooking. I remember my Italian-born Aunt Victoria's zucchini blossom fritters. Later, I discovered that nasturtium blossoms added a peppery accent to a tossed salad. When I began making desserts, it was only natural to use flowers and herbs for flavoring.

At the restaurant we begin in late winter with the first violets. Their perfume brings the promise of spring to desserts. We use fresh violets to garnish citrus sherbets or we make candies with them. By late January or early February the pink flowering plums are in full bloom and the first flower-scented ice creams are being made. The acacias and mimosas quickly follow with their sprays of tiny yellow or white blossoms against gray-green ferny foliage; when they burst into flower, it is time to make crêpes with mimosa blossom ice cream and buttered honey. By March we are

100

cooking with scented geraniums, and looking forward to the first roses and jasmine blossoms in April and May. When the first berries arrive, we take our fill of them in tarts and shortcakes and ice creams; but then we begin making rose geranium custards to accompany them. By this time the summer fruits are ripening and we use herbs to accent them. Angelica, basil, cinnamon basil, lavender, and lemon thyme take their places as the seasons advance, to flavor custards and poaching syrups.

I use the petals of old rose varieties to flavor ice creams and to candy for garnishes—they generally have a stronger scent than the newer hybrids. In my front yard I have a hedge of rugosas—a very hardy rose that has a particularly powerful perfume. I like to candy the petals of my climbing Joseph's Coat because they are delicate rather than fleshy, and their variegated sunset colors shine through the sugar beautifully to mark the dinner's and the day's end. Since desserts are made in large quantities at the restaurant and we can get only limited amounts of flowers, we usually make infusions to flavor custards and ice creams. At home you can be more lavish and try many different kinds of flowers—almond-scented broom, clove-scented carnations, hawthorn, orange and lemon blossoms, elderflowers and their ripe berries, lilacs, orchids, lily of the valley, peach blossoms . . .

Angelica is one of the most versatile herbs. The leaves and stems can be used to flavor custards and the stems can be candied to flavor cakes and cookies, or for a garnish. Commercial candied angelica bears little resemblance in flavor to what can be made at home. The combined herb and spice scent of cinnamon basil suits ripe peaches, pears, and figs beautifully. Rose geranium is meant for ripe blackberries or boysenberries—or simply bake the leaves into a pound cake. There are dozens of other scented geraniums to experiment with—some recall citrus fruits, others apples or spices.

Do take care that the plant you decide to use is edible. Sometimes the flowers are edible though other parts of the plant are not. And be sure the plants have not been treated with any poisonous insecticide. Be adventurous—the herbs and flowers around you offer unlimited possibilities.

ALMOND BLOSSOM ICE CREAM

Makes a generous quart: *1½ cups new almond blossoms · ¾ cup sugar · ¾ cup milk · 2¼ cups whipping cream · 3 egg yolks · Optional: almond extract to taste*

Pick over the blossoms, break off any bits of stem, and put them into a small non-corroding saucepan. You may include any unopened buds. Add the sugar, milk, and cream, and heat to just under boiling, stirring occasionally. Let steep for 30 minutes to an hour, reheating as necessary to keep the mixture hot, until you like the strength of the blossom flavor. Whisk the egg yolks slightly to break them up and whisk in a little of the hot blossom milk to warm them. Return to the pan and cook over low heat, stirring constantly, until the custard coats the spoon. Strain into a container, cover, and chill. Taste and add a little almond extract if you want a stronger flavor; then freeze according to the instructions with your ice cream maker.

This ice cream has the taste of bitter almonds and flowers—it is really special. Serve it with Lace Cookies.

HONEY MOUSSE

Makes 3¼ cups: *1 egg · 1 teaspoon gelatin · 1 tablespoon cold water · 1⅓ cups whipping cream · ¼ cup good honey · 1½ teaspoons Grand Marnier, to taste*

The flavor of this mousse depends on the honey you choose: use the nicest you can find.

Beat the egg in a small bowl until it mounds slightly. Sprinkle the gelatin over the cold water in a small saucepan and let it stand a few minutes. Whip the cream until it makes a soft shape when some is dropped from the beaters. Heat the gelatin over very low heat, stirring constantly until it dissolves, and stir in the honey. Continue to stir the honey mixture over very low heat until it is smooth. Set aside or stir over ice water to cool until it begins to thicken. Whisk the beaten egg into the whipped cream. Whisk the honey mixture quickly into the cream mixture and flavor to taste with Grand Marnier. Chill.

Serve with figs, raspberries, or peaches, or garnished simply with lightly toasted sliced almonds. If it is too thick, whisk lightly to soften it.

JASMINE ICE CREAM

Makes about 1½ pints: *1 cup jasmine flowers and buds · ½ cup milk · 1½ cups whipping cream · ½ cup less 1 tablespoon sugar · 2 egg yolks*

I use only *Jasminum polyanthum* for this recipe. The *Cestrum* species, variously called day-blooming, night-blooming, or willow-leaved jessamine, and the *Gelsemium* species, called yellow or Carolina jessamine, are all poisonous.

Strip the jasmine flowers from the stems. You may use the buds as well as the flowers, but avoid the stems. Put the flowers in a non-corroding saucepan with the milk, cream, and sugar, and heat to about 200°F or just under boiling. Steep until you like the flavor—about 45 minutes—keeping the temperature around 200°F. Whisk the egg yolks in a small bowl to break them up and stir in some of the hot milk mixture. Return to the saucepan and cook over low heat, stirring constantly, until the mixture coats the spoon. Strain into a bowl, pressing the flowers to extract their juices. Taste for flavor: if it seems too strong you can add more cream and sugar, maintaining the proportion of ¼ cup sugar for every 1 cup of cream. Melt the sugar in a little of the heated cream before adding it. Chill the mixture; then freeze according to the instructions with your ice cream maker.

This is good served with Langues de Chat.

MIMOSA ICE CREAM CRÊPES
WITH BUTTERED HONEY

Makes 1½ pints, for approximately 6 servings: *Mimosa blossoms · ½ cup milk · 1½ cups whipping cream · ½ cup less 1 tablespoon sugar · 2 egg yolks · 6 crêpes, about ⅕ recipe of crêpe batter (page 14)*

Strip the mimosa blossoms from their stems and leaves. You will need 1 cup of blossoms. Put them in a non-corroding saucepan with the milk, cream, and sugar, and heat to 200°F, or just under boiling. Let steep for about 30 minutes, keeping the temperature at 190°F–200°F. Whisk the egg yolks slightly in a small bowl and pour in some of the hot milk mixture, stirring constantly. Return the mixture to the pan and cook over low heat, stirring constantly, until the custard coats the spoon. Strain into a bowl, pressing the flowers to extract their flavor. Chill thoroughly. Freeze according to the instructions with your ice cream maker.

Serve in crêpes that have been crisped according to the instructions on page 16. Sprinkle a few mimosa blossoms on the ice cream and drizzle buttered honey—½ cup light flower honey warmed with ¼ cup sweet butter—over and around the crêpes.

WHITE PLUM BLOSSOM ICE CREAM

Makes about ¾ quart: *1 cup white plum blossoms · ¾ cup milk · 2¼ cups whipping cream · ¾ cup sugar · 3 egg yolks · A few drops of almond extract*

The blossoms—but not the bark or leaves—of any cultivated fruiting or flowering plum of the *Prunus* species can be used for this recipe. Don't use wild "plums" unless you are sure they are *Prunus*; some blossoms may be poisonous.

Put the blossoms in a small non-corroding saucepan with the milk, cream, and sugar, and heat to just under boiling. Steep for about 1 hour, reheating as necessary to keep the mixture hot. Taste occasionally; when you like the flavor, continue with the recipe.

Whisk the egg yolks slightly and stir in the plum blossom mixture. Return to the pan and cook over low heat, stirring constantly, until the custard coats the spoon. Strain into a bowl, pressing the flowers to extract their flavor. Chill. Taste and add a few drops of almond extract, if necessary, to enhance the flavor. Freeze according to the instructions with your ice cream maker.

Serve garnished with plum blossoms and accompanied by Langues de Chat, or serve in a cookie cup. The flavor is unusual and is to be savored.

SUGARED ROSE PETALS

For at least 50 petals: *1 egg white · 1 teaspoon water · Sugar · Freshly picked roses, kept in water until ready for use*

If you must pick the roses a while before making this dessert, keep them in lukewarm water until use. Don't let the petals get wet.

Beat the egg white with the water in a small bowl until it is frothy and well broken up. You don't want to take the whole egg white with you when you dip your brush into it. Choose a plate or a flat pan large enough to dry the rose petals in a single layer, and sprinkle it with a thin layer of sugar. Have ready a small bowl of sugar, too.

Gently pull the petals off a rose, taking care not to bruise them. Using a small pastry brush, paint each side of the petals completely with a thin coat of the egg white mixture. Sprinkle each side with sugar from the bowl to coat it and set the petal on the sugared plate to dry. Continue, being careful not to use too much egg white or you will have thick globs that won't dry properly. You want to be able to see the rose's color through a veil of sugar one grain thick. Let dry for an hour or two or perhaps longer, depending on the humidity—in the San Francisco Bay Area the humidity is usually low; I can't say how long this might take in other parts of the country.

Use these rose petals to garnish ice cream desserts, floating islands, or whatever seems appropriate.

To candy other flowers: it is important to be absolutely sure that the flowers you want to candy are edible. At the restaurant, we have used violets, jasmine, acacia blossoms, almond, plum, and peach blossoms, elderflowers, lavender, and citrus blossoms.

Pick perfect flowers, put only their stems in water, and keep in a cool place until you are ready for them. Proceed as in the above recipe. For best color use within a few hours. Once dry, the petals or flowers may be stored in a tightly covered glass jar to be used for flavoring.

CRÊPES WITH
ROSE PETAL ICE CREAM AND STRAWBERRIES

For 10 servings: *10 crêpes, about ⅓ recipe of crêpe batter (page 14) · 1 quart Rose Petal Ice Cream (below) · Sugared Rose Petals · 1 to 2 pints strawberries or fraises des bois · Sugar to taste · Kirsch to taste · Powdered sugar*

Make the crêpe batter a day or two ahead and fry the crêpes the day before you plan to use them, or early the same day. Wrap in plastic and refrigerate. Make the ice cream at least a day ahead of serving. You may sugar the rose petals ahead of time too: leave them out until they are dry, then store in a tightly closed jar at room temperature.

When ready to serve the dessert, wash, dry, and hull the strawberries. Save the prettiest ones and purée about a third of the others for the sauce. Add sugar and a few drops of kirsch to taste, or sweeten the purée with cold sugar syrup if you have it. Slice the rest of the berries—fraises des bois won't need slicing, of course—and sugar them lightly. Crisp the crêpes in a preheated 375°F oven for a few minutes, until they are crisp around the edges but will still bend in half. Cool briefly, then set them on your dessert plates. Fill with oval scoops of the ice cream. Spoon a little of the sauce across the plate in front of the crêpe and put the sliced berries or the fraises des bois around it. Shake powdered sugar very lightly over the top of the crêpe, and for color accent sprinkle on a few torn rose petals. Serve immediately.

ROSE PETAL ICE CREAM

Makes 1½ pints: *2 highly scented roses · ½ cup milk · 1½ cups whipping cream · ½ cup sugar · 2 egg yolks*

I use rugosa roses from my garden border for this recipe—and I don't use treated roses.

Take the petals off a rose and warm them in a small noncorroding saucepan with the milk, cream, and sugar to about 200°F (just under boiling). Steep the mixture until you like the flavor.

Whisk the egg yolks slightly and stir in some of the milk mixture to warm them. Return to the pan and cook over low to medium heat, stirring constantly, until the custard coats the spoon. Strain into a small bowl and chill. Freeze according to the instructions with your ice cream maker. While the ice cream is freezing, pull the petals off another fresh-picked rose. When the ice cream has finished freezing, tear the petals into small pieces and fold them into the mixture before you pack it into the freezing container.

Serve alone, garnished with Sugared Rose Petals, with strawberries or fraises des bois, with blackberries or boysenberries, accompanied by Langues de Chat or Lace Cookies.

VIOLET CANDIES

For 2 dozen candies: *24 fresh sweet aromatic violets · Paper bonbon cases measuring 1 inch in diameter · Optional: tiny pieces of gold leaf · 2 ounces white chocolate*

Take the violets off their stems and arrange them in the bottoms of the paper cases, face down—if you double the cases they will hold their shape better. Or use chocolate molds if you have them. Tear off little pieces of gold leaf and put them around the violets in the bottoms of the cases or molds. I find three pieces is quite enough. The gold leaf will tend either to stick to you or to fly away, but if you just tear off pieces with tweezers and drop them directly into the cases, you should have no trouble.

Chop the chocolate into small pieces, put it in the top of a small double boiler, and set it over warm water. Stir the chocolate constantly and don't let it get more than slightly warm. As soon as the melted chocolate is smooth, drop it by half spoonfuls into the cases. You may also put the chocolate into a pastry bag with a plain round tip and pipe it into the cases. There should be just enough to make a layer ³⁄₁₆-inch to ¼-inch thick. If necessary, use a toothpick or the tip of a knife to swirl the chocolate gently into an even layer, taking care not to disturb the violet.

There should be just enough chocolate to barely cover the flower. Set the cases in a cool place to firm, or put in the refrigerator or freezer for just a few minutes. Unmold by gently pulling the sides away from the chocolate and turn the violet side up.

Serve within a few hours or the violet will begin to wilt since it is not completely covered with the chocolate. Serve after dinner (but before coffee), or any time you would like a very beautiful, simple candy with an unusual taste.

ANGELICA ICE CREAM

Makes 1¼ quarts: *1 cup half-and-half · 2 cups whipping cream · ⅔ cup sugar · 1 stalk of fresh angelica, about a foot long · 6 egg yolks*

Angelica archangelica is indigenous to all continents of the Northern Hemisphere and to New Zealand. It has a very distinct herbal flavor and is an important flavoring in many liqueurs. Unfortunately, it isn't available in the markets: you have to grow it yourself, or get it from someone who does, or find it growing wild (but be sure what you find is really angelica). Plant and seed suppliers are listed in the sources (page 295).

Put the half-and-half, cream, and sugar in a non-corroding saucepan. Wash the angelica and slice it in half lengthwise to be sure the hollow stalks are clean inside, then cut it into lengths that will fit in the pan. Include the leaves in the mixture. Heat to just under boiling and keep hot for 30 minutes, or until you like the flavor. Whisk the egg yolks just enough to mix them and stir in some of the hot cream mixture. Return to the pan with the angelica and cook over low to medium heat, stirring constantly, until the custard coats the spoon. Strain into a bowl, pressing out the angelica. Taste for flavor: if it seems too strong, add a little more cream heated with sugar—1 tablespoon of sugar for every 4 tablespoons of cream. Chill; then freeze according to the directions with your ice cream maker.

Since angelica is a flavor you don't often taste, serve this ice cream alone, with a simple cookie like Langues de Chat.

108

NUTMEG GERANIUM ICE CREAM

Makes about 1 quart: *¾ cup sugar · ¾ cup milk · 2¼ cups whipping cream · 6 sprigs of nutmeg geranium leaves (25 to 30 small leaves) · 3 egg yolks*

Mix sugar, milk, and cream in a non-corroding saucepan. Rinse the geranium leaves and add them. Heat to just under boiling and let steep for about 30 minutes, reheating if the mixture cools. Steep the mixture until you like the flavor. Whisk the egg yolks in a small bowl just to break them up, pour in some of the warm cream mixture to warm the eggs, and return the mixture to the pan. Cook over low to medium heat, stirring constantly, until it coats the spoon lightly. Strain into a bowl, pressing the leaves to get their flavor. Chill thoroughly. Freeze according to the directions with your ice cream maker.

This ice cream will have a delicious flavor of nutmeg with a hint of rose behind it. It is good served with an equal portion of Meyer Lemon Ice Cream.

ROSE GERANIUM POUND CAKE

Makes a 9-inch cake, for 12 servings: *15 to 18 small rose geranium leaves · 1¼ cups unsalted butter, softened · 1⅓ cups sugar · ¾ teaspoon vanilla extract · ¾ teaspoon rose water · 1 tablespoon plus 1 teaspoon Cognac · 6 eggs · ⅛ teaspoon mace · ½ teaspoon salt · ½ teaspoon cream of tartar · 2⅔ cups unsifted cake flour · Vanilla powdered sugar (page 4) to sprinkle on the cake*

If you are in a hurry and the butter and eggs are cold, cut the butter into a stainless steel mixing bowl, melt it partly, and let it stand until the rest softens. Warm the eggs by covering them with hot water and letting them stand a few minutes. Butter and flour a 9-inch springform pan or a 10-inch bundt or tube pan. Rinse and dry the rose geranium leaves and arrange a dozen of them in a ring around the bottom of the pan, undersides up. Arrange the rest in the center. Set aside.

109

Cream the butter until very light and fluffy. Beat in the sugar and continue beating until the mixture is fluffy again. Beat in the vanilla, rose water, and Cognac. Add the eggs one by one, beating to incorporate each one thoroughly before adding the next one. Beat until the mixture is smooth. Mix the mace, salt, and cream of tartar into the flour and sift the flour over the butter mixture in four portions, beating just until each one is mixed in. Carefully spoon some of the batter into the pan to anchor the leaves in place. Pour the rest of the batter into the pan and smooth it. Tap the pan on the counter to force out any air bubbles.

Bake in the center of a preheated 325°F oven for about an hour and a quarter, or until a toothpick inserted in the center comes out clean. Cool. Turn out of the pan and dust lightly with powdered vanilla sugar. Accompany with tea, coffee, or a glass of wine. The cake is also spectacular when baked in a tube pan and served with its center filled with Sugared Rose Petals—in which case you will want to omit the leaf design from the bottom of the cake pan.

ROSE GERANIUM ICE CREAM

Makes a generous quart: *1¼ cups half-and-half* · *2½ cups whipping cream* · *1 cup less 1 tablespoon sugar* · *8 to 10 rose geranium leaves* · *5 egg yolks*

Warm the half-and-half, cream, sugar, and the rinsed rose geranium leaves in a non-corroding saucepan. Keep the temperature at 180°F to 200°F and steep for about 15 minutes, or until you like the strength of the flavor. Whisk the egg yolks in a small bowl to break them up but don't let them foam. Pour a little of the steeped mixture in, stirring constantly. Return to the pan and cook over low heat, stirring constantly, until the custard coats the spoon. Strain into a container and chill. Freeze according to the directions with your ice cream maker.

This is perfect with wild blackberries, olallieberries, or boysenberries. You can also serve it in cookie cups with a sauce made from any of those berries, perhaps with Langues de Chat alongside.

LAVENDER HONEY ICE CREAM

Makes 1 quart: *¾ cup honey · 1 sprig fresh or dry lavender (the blossom end only) · 1 cup half-and-half · 2 cups whipping cream · 6 egg yolks*

Warm the honey with the lavender in a non-corroding saucepan. Taste after 5 minutes to check the strength of the lavender flavor and leave a little longer, if necessary, until the flavor pleases you. Be careful: lavender is a very strong flavor. Heat the half-and-half and the cream in a non-corroding saucepan and whisk the egg yolks in a bowl until they are just broken up. Whisk in some of the hot cream and return to the pan. Cook over low heat, stirring constantly, until the mixture coats the spoon. Strain into a container and stir in the flavored honey. Chill thoroughly. Freeze according to the instructions with your ice cream maker.

Lavender honey from Provence is the inspiration for this dessert. This is good served with a warm Fig Tart, and makes an especially nice dessert after a pork dinner.

PAIN D'ÉPICE

Makes one 4-inch by 8-inch loaf and one 3-inch by 5-inch loaf: *1 cup hot water · 1 cup honey · 1 tablespoon sugar · ¼ teaspoon salt · 2 teaspoons baking soda · 1 teaspoon baking powder · ¼ cup rum · 1 teaspoon aniseed, ground · 1 teaspoon cinnamon · ¾ teaspoon ground ginger · ¼ teaspoon ground cloves · 3 or 4 twists of white pepper from the mill, or ¼ teaspoon · 2 cups rye flour · 1½ cups unbleached flour · 3 tablespoons chopped candied clementine, tangerine, or orange peel · Optional: 1½ tablespoons chopped candied angelica · 1 cup lightly toasted unblanched almonds, coarsely chopped*

The honey should be smooth and liquid. If your honey has crystallized, heat to dissolve the crystals, then cool to lukewarm. Pour the hot water over the honey in a bowl and stir to mix well. Stir in sugar, salt, baking soda, and baking powder. Add rum, then the spices. Mix a cup each of the rye flour and the unbleached flour in another large bowl. Make a well in the flour, and gradually whisk the honey mixture in, taking care that no lumps form. Whisk in the rest of the flours just until the batter is smooth. Stir in the candied peel and angelica just until mixed. At this point you may set the mixture aside in a cool place, covered, for it to age five days to a week. This aging will help to marry the flavors and smooth the texture—in Dijon it is the custom to age part of the batter several months before baking—but it isn't necessary.

Just before baking, add the chopped almonds, stirring just until completely mixed. Scrape the batter into well-buttered loaf pans, filling them three-quarters full. Bake in a preheated 400°F oven for 10 minutes, then reduce the heat to 350°F and bake until done—from 50 minutes to 1½ hours depending on the size and shape of your pans. A toothpick will come out of the center clean when the cake is done.

Remove the loaves from the pans and cool on a rack. The tops will have cracked while baking. Glaze them, if you like, by brushing them with honey that has been brought just to a boil. Decorate, perhaps along the cracks, with designs made with very lightly toasted blanched almond halves. Then wrap the loaves in plastic and age for at least a day or two before serving.

Pains d'Épice will keep up to several weeks if refrigerated, in which case they should be wrapped in foil as well as plastic; they make nice gifts. They can be served in thin slices, buttered or not, accompanied by a glass of fragrant red wine like Rhône or Zinfandel, or by a cup of tea.

CINNAMON ICE CREAM

Makes a generous quart: *1¼ cups half-and-half · 2½ cups whipping cream · 1 cup less 1 tablespoon sugar · 1 stick cinnamon · ½ teaspoon ground cinnamon · 6 egg yolks*

Warm the half-and-half, cream, sugar, and both kinds of cinnamon in a non-corroding saucepan. Steep for about 15 minutes, always keeping the temperature below boiling. Taste once or twice to be sure it is not getting too strong for you, remembering that the flavor will grow stronger even after the ice cream is frozen. Whisk the egg yolks just enough to break them up and pour in some of the hot mixture, stirring constantly. Return to the pan and cook over low heat, stirring constantly, until the custard coats the spoon. Strain into a container, put the cinnamon stick into it if you want the flavor stronger, and chill thoroughly. Remove the cinnamon stick and freeze according to the instructions with your ice cream maker.

We serve this with apple or plum tarts, but it is also nice by itself with Langues de Chat, Lace Cookies, or Hazelnut Logs.

CLOVE ICE CREAM

Makes 1 quart: *⅔ cup sugar · 1 cup half-and-half · 2 cups whipping cream · 12 whole cloves · 6 egg yolks · Optional: ⅟₁₆ to ⅛ teaspoon ground cloves*

Warm the sugar, half-and-half, and cream with the whole cloves in a small pan to just under boiling and keep hot for 30 minutes or so. Taste the mixture to see how strong the flavor is; proceed when it is about as strong as you like it. Whisk the egg yolks just enough to break them up. Stir some of the hot mixture into them to warm them and return to the pan. Cook over low to medium heat, stirring constantly, until the custard coats the spoon. Strain into a bowl and chill thoroughly, preferably overnight, to let the clove flavor develop. Taste again just before freezing and add a little ground clove if you like. Freeze according to the instructions with your ice cream maker.

We serve this with a Rhubarb Tart—it is a very nice combination. It is also good served with Lemon Ice Cream. You will want to make the clove flavor stronger if you are serving it with rhubarb, more delicate if it is going to be served alone or with another ice cream.

113

VARIATIONS ON COFFEE ICE CREAM

Makes a generous quart: *1 cup half-and-half · 2 cups whipping cream · ¾ cup sugar · 6 tablespoons coffee beans (I use mocha-java) · 6 egg yolks · 1 to 2 teaspoons vanilla extract*

Warm the half-and-half, cream, sugar, and coffee beans in a non-corroding saucepan. Let it steep for 30 to 45 minutes, or until the coffee flavor is strong enough for you. Don't let the mixture boil or it will curdle, but do rewarm it if necessary to bring out the coffee flavor. When steeped to your satisfaction, whisk the egg yolks just enough to break them up, then stir in a little of the coffee mixture to warm them. Return to the pan and cook over low heat, stirring constantly, until the mixture coats the spoon. Strain and chill. Flavor with vanilla to taste and freeze according to the instructions with your ice cream maker.

COFFEE CARAMEL ICE CREAM

This is a more richly flavored variation of coffee ice cream. Follow the above recipe, but omit the sugar from the steeping mixture of half-and-half, cream, and coffee beans. Instead, caramelize 1 cup sugar in a heavy, light-colored saucepan with 3 tablespoons water. Cook it over high heat until it has turned a light caramel color. Working quickly so the caramel doesn't burn, remove it from the heat, set it down in your sink where it won't spatter you, and add ¼ cup warm water. Cook to dissolve the caramel, adding a little more water if necessary, and add this to the half-and-half mixture; then proceed as above.

COFFEE CARAMEL SWIRL ICE CREAM

This variation of coffee ice cream is also richer, but with the caramel swirled into it rather than incorporated.

Make 1 recipe of the basic coffee ice cream mixture. While it is chilling, make the caramel swirl mixture:

2 tablespoons water · *½ cup sugar* · *2 tablespoons unsalted butter* · *¼ cup cream*

Put 1 tablespoon of the water with the sugar in a heavy, light-colored saucepan and cook until it is a light caramel color. Remove from the heat and carefully add another tablespoon of water to cool it. Immediately stir in the butter and cream and bring to a boil. Remove from the heat, put a drop on a cold plate, and set this in your freezer to check the texture: it should remain creamy when it has chilled completely. If it is too hard, add a little more cream; if too soft, boil a little longer. When the caramel is the right texture, chill it until cold. Using a rubber spatula, swirl it into the soft ice cream as you take it from the ice cream maker. Pack into a container and freeze.

COFFEE ICE CREAM WITH CHOCOLATE TRUFFLES

This ice cream has the added interest of creamy chocolate candies.

Make 1 recipe of the basic ice cream mixture. While it is chilling, make the chocolate truffle mixture:

4 ounces semisweet chocolate · *1 ounce unsweetened chocolate* · *5 tablespoons unsalted butter* · *½ cup plus 2 tablespoons whipping cream* · *1 to 2 teaspoons brandy or Cognac or other liqueur to taste*

Melt the chocolates with the butter and cream in a small heavy saucepan over very low heat or over hot water, stirring constantly. Pour into a small bowl and chill thoroughly. When the chocolate is cold, shape small truffles by dipping a ½-teaspoon measuring spoon in water and quickly scooping out a truffle. Lay on a sheet pan in a single layer. When you have shaped all of the truffles, chill them thoroughly. Freeze the ice cream mixture according to the instructions with your ice cream maker and fold the truffles into the soft ice cream when it comes from the machine. Freeze.

Serve with Lace Cookies, Bow Ties, or Langues de Chat, and a good cup of coffee.

BLACK CURRANT TEA ICE CREAM

Makes a generous quart: *1 cup boiling water · 2 tablespoons black currant tea leaves · 2¼ cups whipping cream · ¾ cup sugar · 3 egg yolks · Optional: black currant syrup (cassis)*

Pour the water over the tea leaves in a stainless steel or glass bowl and let steep for 5 minutes. Filter or strain through a fine strainer to remove all bits of tea leaves and set aside. Warm 1 cup of the cream with the sugar in a heavy saucepan until the sugar has dissolved, stirring occasionally. Whisk the egg yolks in a bowl just enough to mix them. Stir in some of the hot cream mixture to warm them, then return to the pan and cook over low heat, stirring constantly, until the mixture coats the spoon. Strain through a medium-fine strainer into a container and add the rest of the cream and the tea. Chill. Taste and add a drop or two of cassis if you think it is needed to heighten the flavor, and freeze according to the directions with your ice cream maker.

This is good served with chocolate cookies.

MAPLE CUSTARD

Makes 6 half-cup custards: *2 cups cream · ½ cup maple syrup · 6 egg yolks*

I use a dark grade C maple syrup, but you could also use about ½ cup of maple sugar to taste.

Warm the cream. Stir the syrup or sugar into the egg yolks. Mix in a little of the warm cream, then mix in the rest of the cream, stirring constantly. Strain into a pitcher and pour into custard cups or pots de crème. Bake in a hot water bath in a preheated 325°F oven, lightly covered with foil—just lay a sheet of foil on top. Bake for about 40 minutes or until the custards are set in a ring about ½-inch wide around the outside edge. They should still be soft in the center.

Serve, warm or chilled, with Walnut Drops.

BERRIES

IN CALIFORNIA we are lucky to have a long berry season. From March to November some variety is always obtainable, starting with strawberries, including the tiny wild fraises des bois, then continuing with raspberries, olallieberries, boysenberries, black raspberries, loganberries, blueberries, gooseberries, and red and black currants.

Strawberry tarts and shortcakes are among the most popular of all Chez Panisse desserts—people can't resist them. It is very difficult to get flavorful, ripe strawberries from conventional suppliers; we have to pick and choose carefully. As often as possible, we use a softer, more perishable variety that is grown for us, the Quinalt. They can't be shipped, but are easily grown in home gardens. We also put strawberries into little nests of spun sugar with cream or into Timbales Élysées, which, with its lacy caramel cap, is one of the loveliest of desserts.

118

Fraises des bois, with their scent and flavor of roses, are good garnishes for many desserts. Served in crêpes with Rose Petal Ice Cream they produce a perfect marriage of flavors, and just a few added to a mixed berry compote will spark the whole thing. These, too, can be grown at home; in fact, they are easier to cultivate than larger strawberry varieties. They also grow wild in many parts of the country.

The raspberry season begins in June, and after a short hiatus in midsummer's heat, is with us again until the frost or rains put an end to it in November or even December. When the boysenberries, most luscious of all, arrive in early summer, we begin to mix the flavors and colors of all these berries in compotes, cobblers, and pies, adding the very special perfume of black raspberries when we get them. The dusky purples and blues of the various blackberries, accented by the dark red raspberries and bright red strawberries, make one of the most beautiful of all summer compotes. When occasionally we can buy gooseberries, or red or black currants, we make curds to fill tarts, or we purée them and fold them into sweetened whipped cream for fools.

All berries make wonderful tarts, pies, ice creams, sherbets, shortcakes, or cobblers, as well as garnishes or sauces for other summer fruits. Their flavors combine well with one another as well as with apricots, peaches, plums, and nectarines. Berry ice creams and sherbets can be layered in bombes in endless combinations for festive but easy party desserts, since they can, and indeed must, be made well in advance of serving. One of the best ways to use imperfect berries is in fools or curds. But perhaps the best dessert of all is just a bowl of berries with heavy cream, crème fraîche, crème anglaise, or Champagne sabayon. Because they are delicate and fragile and so distinctively flavored, perfect ripe berries seem to me to resist complicated preparations, needing very little beyond their own innate goodness.

More than any other fruit, berries are worth growing yourself. Because of their delicacy, they don't market well. Ripe ones are so soft that they can't be handled very much, and once picked, quickly lose much of their perfume, especially if refrigerated. Raspberries are the easiest to grow, and many kinds are available, including black and golden ones. Blackberries, too, are available in much wider variety to the gardener. If you don't have the space to grow your own berries, look for them in country produce stands—better yet, find a farm that will allow you to pick them yourself.

BERRY COBBLER

For 4 to 6 servings: *2 pint baskets boysenberries · ½ pint basket blueberries · ½ half-pint basket raspberries · ⅓ cup sugar · 1 to 1½ tablespoons flour Cobbler dough: 1½ cups flour · ⅜ teaspoon salt · 1½ tablespoons sugar · 2 ¼ teaspoons baking powder · 6 tablespoons unsalted butter · ¾ cup whipping cream*

You may use a mixture of any berries available to you—except strawberries. Blackberries or boysenberries are nice for the bulk; a few raspberries or black raspberries add a delicious perfume.

Measure 4½ cups of mixed berries and toss them with the sugar and flour. Use the larger amount of flour if the berries are very juicy. Let stand while you make the dough. Mix the dry ingredients for the dough, leaving out the salt if you are using salted butter. Cut in the butter until the mixture looks like coarse cornmeal. Add the cream and mix lightly, until the dry ingredients are just moistened. The dry ingredients for the topping can be prepared ahead—even several days ahead—and kept refrigerated. The cream can then be added when you are ready to bake the cobbler.

Put the berry mixture into a 1½ quart gratin or baking dish. Make patties of the dough, 2 to 2½ inches in diameter and ½-inch thick. Arrange them over the top of the berries. Bake in a preheated 375°F oven for 35 to 40 minutes, or until the topping is brown and the berry juices bubble thickly around it.

Serve warm with cream to pour over. People who don't ordinarily like dessert will often eat this.

BERRY COMPOTE

For 6 servings: *1 pint basket strawberries · A handful each of several other kinds of berries: boysenberries, blueberries, blackberries, raspberries, olallieberries, fraises des bois, or whatever you can get · 4 to 6 teaspoons sugar · ½ teaspoon kirsch, to taste*

As close as possible to serving time, wash the strawberries, dry in a towel, and hull. Put them in a bowl with the rest of the berries and sprinkle with the sugar and the kirsch to taste. Toss quickly and gently and put the mixed berries in your prettiest bowl.

Serve with a pitcher of cream to pour over if you like, and a few crisp cookies. This is satisfying far beyond its simplicity—a perfect dessert for a sun-warmed summer lunch.

WILD BLACKBERRY CURD

Makes 2 cups: *3 cups wild blackberries (some should be tart) · 6 tablespoons unsalted butter · 3 tablespoons sugar, to taste · 2 tablespoons lemon juice · 3 eggs · 2 egg yolks*

Purée the blackberries and pass through a fine strainer to remove their seeds. Measure 1½ cups into a non-corroding saucepan. Add the butter and heat, stirring constantly, until the butter has melted. Add the sugar and lemon juice, tasting carefully because the flavor of wild blackberries varies considerably. Put the eggs and egg yolks in a bowl and whisk just enough to mix them, then stir in some of the hot purée. Return to the pan and cook, stirring constantly, until the mixture reaches 170°F, or is thick enough to leave a shape on the top when some of it is dropped from a spoon. Chill.

This will keep at least a week, and is good for filling cakes or as a tart filling. Lisa Goines, one of our pastry assistants, uses it with lemon tart filling to make tarts with beautiful designs, spooning the heaviest filling in first in whatever design she wants, then filling the spaces with the thinner filling. If the curds are about the same consistency, she pipes them separately into the baked tart shell with a pastry bag.

To make a Wild Blackberry Curd Tart: Fill a 9-inch pre-baked short crust tart shell (page 11) with the Wild Blackberry Curd. Bake in a preheated 350°F oven until the filling has set, 20 to 25 minutes. Serve garnished with crème Chantilly.

WILD BLACKBERRY ICE CREAM

Makes a generous quart: *3 cups wild blackberries* · *¾ cup sugar* · *2 cups whipping cream* · *Vanilla extract to taste*

Purée the blackberries in a food processor or a food mill and strain through a fine sieve to remove the seeds. Measure out 1 cup and set aside. Heat the sugar with 1 cup of the cream in a non-corroding saucepan until the sugar has dissolved. Stir in the remaining cream and the purée. Taste and add a few drops of vanilla. Chill thoroughly; then freeze according to the instructions with your ice cream maker.

Serve with crisp cookies.

WILD BLACKBERRY MOUSSE

Makes a generous quart: *2 cups wild blackberries, or 2 half-pint baskets very ripe, fragrant blackberries* · *1 teaspoon gelatin* · *2 tablespoons cold water* · *⅜ cup sugar, to taste* · *1½ cups whipping cream* · *Vanilla extract to taste* · *Optional: kirsch to taste*

Purée the blackberries in a food processor or food mill and put them through a sieve fine enough to remove their seeds. You will have 1 cup or slightly more after straining. Sprinkle the gelatin over the cold water in a small pan and let stand 5 minutes. Measure ¾ cup of the purée and stir in the sugar. When the gelatin has softened, set it over low heat and warm it to 105°F to 115°F, swirling it until you can no longer see undissolved specks of gelatin.

Quickly stir in the purée and sugar mixture. Whip the cream so it just barely holds a shape when a little is dropped from the beater. Don't overwhip it—there must be no hint of graininess. Quickly whisk in the

122

blackberry gelatin mixture along with a few drops of vanilla and the kirsch if you are using it. Be careful not to overmix at this point. You are actually continuing to whip the cream as you mix in the purée. If for some reason the result is too thin, you can whisk it slightly to thicken it again. You may also add a little more purée and sugar at this point if you wish. When finished, the mousse should be the texture of very softly whipped cream. Chill.

Serve garnished with blackberries or drizzled with a little of the leftover purée, sweetened to taste. Or serve the mousse with an equal portion of White Chocolate Mousse. Accompany either presentation with crisp cookies—Langues de Chat or Lace Cookies.

WILD BLACKBERRY SAUCE

Makes about ¾ cup: *1 cup wild blackberries · ¼ cup sugar · ¼ cup water · Lemon juice to taste · Kirsch to taste*

Purée the blackberries in a blender, food processor, or food mill, and press them through a strainer that is fine enough to remove their seeds. Measure ½ cup purée and set aside. Boil the sugar and water together for 5 minutes and cool. Add it to the ½ cup blackberry purée and season to taste with a few drops of lemon juice, if the berries are not tart enough, and a few drops of kirsch.

Serve with assortments of berry sherbets and ice creams, or with crêpes that have been crisped and filled with Vanilla Ice Cream or other berry ice creams.

BLUEBERRY ICE CREAM

Makes a generous quart: *1 pint basket blueberries · 2 tablespoons water · ¾ cup sugar · 2 cups whipping cream · Vanilla extract to taste · Grated lemon peel to taste*

Rinse the blueberries and put them in a non-corroding saucepan with the water. Cook over low to medium heat for 10 to 15 minutes, or until they have released their juice and are tender. Purée and strain through a very fine strainer if you want to remove the seeds. They are like strawberry seeds, so you can leave them in the ice cream if you like. Measure out 1 cup of the warm purée and stir the sugar into it until it has dissolved. Stir in the cream and a few drops of vanilla and a few shreds of grated lemon peel. Chill thoroughly; then freeze according to the instructions with your ice cream maker.

Serve with Langues de Chat or other crisp cookies.

BLUEBERRY SHERBET

Makes a scant quart: *3 pint baskets blueberries · ½ cup plus 2 tablespoons water · ¾ cup plus 1 tablespoon sugar · Grated lemon peel to taste · Lemon juice to taste · Kirsch to taste*

Rinse the berries and pick out any bad ones. Put them in a non-corroding saucepan with the 2 tablespoons water and cook over low heat until tender. Purée in a blender, food processor, or food mill. You will want 3 cups. Boil the ½ cup water and sugar together for 5 minutes and add to the purée. Grate a little lemon peel very fine and add about ¼ teaspoon. Squeeze in a few drops of lemon juice and add a few drops of kirsch if you like. Chill thoroughly; then freeze according to the instructions with your ice cream maker.

Serve with other berry sherbets or with Vanilla Ice Cream, or alone with crisp cookies.

BLUEBERRY TART WITH MEYER LEMON CREAM

For 8 servings: *1 cup pastry cream (page 7) · 1 or 2 Meyer lemons · One 9-inch short crust tart shell (page 11) · 1 pint basket blueberries · 2 to 3 tablespoons strained raspberry, red currant, or blueberry jam · ½ teaspoon kirsch*

Make the pastry cream, omitting the vanilla from the recipe. While it is hot, finely grate in the Meyer lemon peel to taste. Chill.

124

Bake the tart shell according to the directions in the recipe. When you are ready to assemble the tart, beat the pastry cream just enough to smooth it and spread evenly in the cooled tart shell. Pick over the blueberries, removing any stems, leaves, or bad berries. Put the jam in a non-corroding sauté pan large enough to hold the berries in one or two layers. If the mixture is runny, cook it briefly to thicken it. Add the berries and kirsch and cook over high heat very briefly, tossing the berries. They should be just coated with the jam and barely warm—their juices should not start to run or the berries will not glaze. Distribute them evenly over the top of the pastry cream with a slotted spoon and serve immediately.

BOYSENBERRY ICE CREAM

Makes 1¼ quarts: *2½ pint baskets boysenberries · 1 cup sugar · 2 cups whipping cream · Vanilla extract to taste*

Purée the boysenberries in a blender, food processor, or food mill, and put them through a strainer fine enough to remove the seeds. Measure out 2 cups and set aside. Warm the sugar with 1 cup of the cream until it has dissolved, and add the remaining cream. Mix in the reserved purée, flavor it to taste with a little vanilla, and chill. Freeze according to the instructions with your ice cream maker.

Serve with a little of the sugared purée drizzled over, or serve in a crisped crêpe garnished with berries and some of the purée.

BOYSENBERRY PIE

For 8 servings: *Pie pastry for a 2-crust 9-inch pie (page 23) · 2 pint baskets boysenberries (or 4 cups wild blackberries) · 3 tablespoons flour · ⅓ cup sugar · Optional: a few drops of kirsch · 1 egg yolk · 2 teaspoons milk or whipping cream*

Roll out the pastry, line a 9-inch pie pan with it, and chill. Roll out a piece for the top, lay it on a baking sheet, and chill it, too.

Make the filling: Pick over the berries to be sure none are moldy or spoiled. Toss them in a bowl with the flour, sugar, and kirsch if you are using it (use only 2 tablespoons flour if you are using wild blackberries.) Let stand until the sugar and flour are moistened and then pour the mixture into the pie shell. Brush the rim of the bottom crust with water and lay the top crust on it. As soon as the top crust is pliable, press it lightly around the edge to seal, then trim it about ½ inch beyond the edge of the bottom crust. Fold it under the edge of the bottom crust and make a fluted edge. Beat the egg yolk and milk or cream with a fork and brush the mixture on top of the pie. Prick the top with a fork in several places, or cut a decorative design into it, using the tip of a paring knife and cutting about ⅟16-inch deep or about halfway through the crust. Pierce the design in a few places so steam can escape during baking.

Bake on the lower shelf of a preheated 400°F oven for about 1 hour, or until the bottom is brown and the juice bubbles thickly from the vents. If the edges brown too fast, cover them with a strip of foil while the pie finishes baking—I usually do this after about half an hour. The bottom will usually be brown after an hour if you are using a foil or colored pie pan, but it may take longer if the pie is baking in a glass pan. Cool for an hour or two before serving. The pie can be warmed in a 400°F oven for 5 to 10 minutes before serving.

Serve with Vanilla Ice Cream. This pie may serve only four. When I made one for my father's eightieth birthday party, one of the guests took a bite, smiled, and said, "That's the kind of thing you can sit down to the whole thing."

BOYSENBERRY SHERBET

Makes a scant quart: *3 pint baskets boysenberries · ¾ cup plus 1 tablespoon sugar · ½ cup water · Optional: kirsch and lemon juice to taste*

Purée the berries through a food mill. Or purée them in a blender or food processor, straining afterward to remove the seeds. Meanwhile, bring the sugar and water to a boil and set it aside to cool. Measure out 2¼ cups of the berry purée and add the slightly cooled sugar syrup to it. Taste and add a few drops of kirsch or lemon juice, or both, if you like. Chill, taste again, and adjust the flavoring if necessary. Freeze according to the directions with your ice cream maker.

Serve with other berry sherbets or ice creams, or with Vanilla Ice Cream, or with summer fruits arranged around it. It is also nice with Black Raspberry and Strawberry sherbets, garnished with strawberries or fraises des bois.

BOYSENBERRY TART WITH ROSE GERANIUM CREAM

For 8 servings: *1 cup rose geranium pastry cream (page 7) · One 9-inch short crust tart shell (page 11), baked · 2 pint baskets boysenberries · 2 tablespoons strained raspberry jam · ½ teaspoon kirsch*

Make half the pastry cream recipe but steep 8 to 10 rose geranium leaves in the milk while you heat it, leaving them in for about 15 minutes. Reheat it if necessary until you like the strength of flavor. Strain the milk and make the pastry cream with it. Chill thoroughly. When ready to assemble the tart, spread the pastry cream evenly in the shell. Spread the boysenberries on a flat surface and pick out any that are moldy or overripe. Pick out the largest ones and stand them around the edge of the tart, pushing them as close together as you can. Continue making rings of berries, using the smaller ones toward the center. Heat the jam to bubbling and stir in the kirsch. Brush the berries with this, covering them evenly with a thin coating. If the jam thickens too much while you work, rewarm it.

Move the tart to a serving dish, garnish with a sprig of rose geranium leaves and flowers, and serve as soon as possible.

127

BLACK CURRANT ICE CREAM

Makes about 1 quart: *1 half-pint basket black currants · ½ cup half-and-half · ½ cup sugar · 3 egg yolks · 1¼ cups whipping cream · A few drops of kirsch and vanilla extract*

Strip the currants from their stems with a fork. Put them in a non-corroding saucepan with a few teaspoons of water to keep them moist until they release their own juice. Cook 5 to 10 minutes, until tender, then purée through a food mill. Strain out the seeds and measure 5 tablespoons purée.

Warm the half-and-half with the sugar until the sugar dissolves. Whisk the egg yolks in a small bowl until just mixed. Add the warm half-and-half, stirring constantly. Return the mixture to the pan and cook over low heat, stirring constantly, until the custard coats the spoon. Strain into a bowl and stir in the cream and the currant purée. Add a few drops of kirsch and vanilla to taste. Chill thoroughly. Freeze according to the instructions with your ice cream maker.

Serve with black currant sauce, or in a crêpe with black currant sauce (shake a little powdered sugar on the crêpe). Or serve in a cookie cup with the sauce drizzled over the ice cream.

BLACK CURRANT SHERBET

Makes 1 quart: *4 half-pint baskets black currants · 1 cup sugar · 3½ cups cold water · Kirsch and lemon juice to taste*

Strip the currants from their stems with a fork. Rinse and put in a non-corroding saucepan with a few teaspoons of water. Cook over low heat 5 to 10 minutes, or until tender. Purée through a food mill and strain out the seeds. Boil the sugar with 1½ cups of the water for 5 minutes. Add the remaining cold water and about ¾ cup of the black currant purée to the sugar syrup. Flavor to taste with a few drops of kirsch and lemon juice if needed. Chill. Freeze according to the instructions with your ice cream maker.

Serve garnished with a sprig of mint.

RED CURRANT CURD

Makes a scant pint, enough for a 9-inch tart: *2 half-pint baskets red currants · 4 tablespoons water · ⅜ cup sugar · 2 tablespoons unsalted butter · 2 eggs · 1 egg yolk*

Pull the currants off their stems. Put them in a strainer and rinse. Cook with the water in a non-corroding saucepan over low heat for about 10 minutes, or until very soft. Strain through a food mill or strainer. You should have about 1⅛ cups purée. Stir in the sugar and butter and cook over low heat until the sugar is dissolved. Whisk the eggs and egg yolk just enough to blend them; then whisk in some of the hot purée to heat the eggs. Return to the pan and cook until thickened. The mixture should reach a temperature of 170°F.

Spoon this into pre-baked tartlet or tart shells and garnish with crème Chantilly, or use it to fill cakes.

RED CURRANT SAUCE

Makes about ¾ cup: *1 half-pint basket red currants · ¼ cup plus 2 tablespoons water · ¼ cup sugar · Kirsch to taste*

Strip the currants from their stems with a fork or by hand, dropping them into a strainer. Rinse, and put them in a small, heavy non-corroding saucepan with the 2 tablespoons water. Cook over low heat for 10 to 15 minutes, or until they are soft. Purée through a food mill or in a food processor. Strain to remove the seeds. You should have about ½ cup of purée. Add ¼ cup of water to the purée, then the sugar, and cook gently for 5 minutes. Taste and adjust the sugar if necessary, leaving the purée somewhat tart. Put through a very fine strainer if you want a perfectly clear sauce. Chill; then flavor with a few drops of kirsch, if you like.

This is especially good served with Hot Apple Charlotte.

ELDERBERRY ICE CREAM

Makes 1 quart: *2 half-pint baskets elderberries · 3 tablespoons water · ¾ cup sugar · 2 cups whipping cream · Vanilla extract to taste*

Strip the elderberries from their stems, dropping them into a colander, then rinse and drain. Cook over low to medium heat in a non-corroding saucepan with the water for about 5 minutes. Purée, then put through a fine enough strainer to remove the seeds. Measure out 1 cup and stir in the sugar while the purée is still hot. When the sugar has dissolved, add the cream. Chill. Add a few drops of vanilla. Freeze according to the instructions with your ice cream maker.

Serve with crisp cookies. If you have a little purée left over, stir a bit of sugar into it until it dissolves, and use it as a sauce to drizzle over the ice cream.

CORNUCOPIA OF FRAISES DES BOIS

For about 10 servings: *1 recipe cookie cups (page 13) · 1 cup whipping cream · Sugar to taste · ½ teaspoon vanilla extract · 3 to 4 cups fraises des bois, or mixed strawberries and fraises des bois · Kirsch to taste*

Bake the cookie cups and mold them around a cone shape—one of the metal forms used for making puff pastry cream horns, for example. Store them in an airtight container until serving time. Whip the cream and flavor it to taste with sugar and vanilla. When you are ready to serve the dessert, toss the fraises des bois (and the cleaned, sliced strawberries if you are using them) with a few drops of kirsch. Spoon 2 or 3 tablespoons of the cream gently into each cornucopia and fill with ¼ to ⅓ cup of berries, letting them spill out the end.

Serve immediately with a little sweetened strawberry purée around the cornucopia.

FRAISES DES BOIS ICE CREAM

Makes about 1½ pints: *1 cup whipping cream* · *½ cup sugar* · *2 egg yolks* · *½ pound fraises des bois* · *Vanilla extract to taste* · *Optional: kirsch*

Warm the cream with the sugar until the sugar has dissolved. Whisk the egg yolks just enough to mix them and stir in the warm cream mixture. Return to the pan and cook, stirring constantly, until the mixture coats the spoon. Strain into a bowl. Crush the berries or purée them in a food mill or, briefly, in a food processor. The berries should not be a smooth purée, just broken up slightly. You should have about 1 cup of purée. Add it to the warm custard. Flavor with a few drops of vanilla to heighten the flavor and a few drops of kirsch, if you like. Chill. Freeze according to the instructions with your ice cream maker.

Serve alone, with Langues de Chat or other crisp cookies, in a cookie cup, or in crêpes.

FRAISES DES BOIS SHERBET

Makes 1½ pints: *1 pound fraises des bois* · *¾ cup sugar* · *½ cup water* · *Optional: kirsch to taste*

Purée the berries in a food mill or briefly in a food processor and measure out 2 cups. Boil the sugar and water for 5 minutes. Cool the syrup and add to the berry purée. Put through a fine strainer to remove the seeds; they will turn bitter in the sherbet after it is frozen. Add a few drops of kirsch to taste and chill thoroughly. Freeze according to the instructions with your ice cream maker.

Serve with Fraises des Bois or Rose Petal Ice Cream, or with Kiwi or Tangerine Sherbet, and accompany with crisp cookies like Lace Cookies.

GOOSEBERRY CURD

Makes 1⅔ cups, enough to fill a 9-inch tart: *2 half-pint baskets goose-berries* · *2 tablespoons water* · *½ cup sugar* · *2 tablespoons unsalted butter* · *2 eggs* · *1 egg yolk*

Rinse the gooseberries and put them in a non-corroding saucepan with the water. Cover and cook over low to medium heat, stirring occasionally, for about 20 minutes, or until the gooseberries are very mushy. Purée them through a food mill or a strainer. You should have about 1¼ cups of purée.

Stir the sugar and butter into the warm purée and heat, stirring constantly. Whisk the eggs and the egg yolk just until mixed, then whisk in a little of the hot gooseberry mixture to heat the eggs. Return to the pan and cook over low heat, stirring constantly, until the mixture is well thickened and has reached a temperature of 170°F. Pour into a container, cover, and chill.

Use this to fill small tartlets, garnishing them with rosettes of crème Chantilly; or fill a 9-inch pre-baked tart shell with the curd and pipe rosettes of crème Chantilly over the top, leaving a small spot uncovered in the center so the curd will show. This also makes a delicious filling for cakes. Like most high-acid fruit curds, this will keep at least two weeks in the refrigerator.

GOOSEBERRY FOOL

Makes a generous pint, serving 4: *1 half-pint basket gooseberries* · *⅓ cup water* · *⅛ cup sugar* · *¾ cup cream* · *A few drops of vanilla extract*

The fool is a dessert dating from the Middle Ages—coarsely puréed or crushed fruit of various kinds that is mixed with sweetened whipped cream.

Top and tail the gooseberries, pulling off the little stem and blossom ends. You can save time and skip this step by putting the berries through a food mill, but the fine purée that results will give you a smooth fool.

It tastes just as good, but I prefer the fool's texture when it contains little pieces of gooseberry.

Cook the gooseberries, puréed or not, with the water for about 10 minutes, or until the berries are tender or the purée is heated through. Add the sugar and chill the mixture. You can do this several days ahead of serving time if you keep the mixture tightly covered. On the day you want to serve the fool, whip the cream to soft peaks and fold in the gooseberry mixture and a few drops of vanilla. Taste and add a little more sugar or vanilla, if you like.

Serve with crisp plain cookies of some sort. With its slight hint of rhubarb flavor, this is a surprisingly delicious yet very simple dessert.

HUCKLEBERRY ICE CREAM

Makes 1 quart: *1½ half-pint baskets huckleberries · ¼ cup water · 3¼ cups whipping cream · 1 cup sugar · A few drops of vanilla extract*

Cover yourself well and avoid spattering while you work with these berries. They have a formidable dye—they even turned the metal of my food mill blue when I put them through it.

Put the huckleberries into a strainer, a handful at a time, and rinse thoroughly with cool water, picking out any leaves or bad berries. Put the berries in a non-corroding saucepan. Add the water, cover, and bring to a simmer. Cook about 10 minutes, or until the berries are soft. Purée through a food mill and then put through a very fine strainer to remove seeds and stems. I wouldn't suggest puréeing them in a blender or food processor because you might grind up the stems. Measure out ¾ cup and set aside. Warm 2 cups of the cream with the sugar in a non-corroding saucepan, stirring occasionally, until the sugar has dissolved. Add the remaining cream and the huckleberry purée. Add a few drops of vanilla to taste and chill. Freeze according to the instructions with your ice cream maker.

This is a beautiful mauve ice cream and a real treat when you have a chance to get huckleberries. Serve it in parfait or sherbet glasses with Vanilla Ice Cream, or in cookie cups or crêpes with huckleberry sauce.

LOGANBERRY CURD

Makes a generous pint: *2 half-pint baskets loganberries* · *⅜ cup sugar* · *4 tablespoons unsalted butter* · *2 eggs* · *2 egg yolks*

Purée the berries in a blender, food processor, or food mill. Put through a fine strainer to remove the seeds. You should have about 1½ cups purée. Heat the purée and add the sugar and butter, stirring until the sugar is dissolved. Whisk the eggs and egg yolks just enough to mix them, then whisk in some of the hot purée. Return to the pan and cook over low heat until well thickened. The mixture should reach a temperature of 170°F. Chill.

Use as a cake filling, or to fill small tartlets or a 9-inch tart. Pre-bake the shells, then fill them when you are ready to serve and garnish with crème Chantilly in rosettes or spooned alongside. You might also combine this curd with lemon curd to make half-and-half, striped, or dotted tarts.

RASPBERRY BOMBE WITH PRALINE

For 10 to 12 servings: *A scant quart Raspberry Sherbet (page 137)* · *One recipe frozen mousse, flavored with vanilla (page 9)* · *A few tablespoons of almond praline (page 34)*

Please read about making and serving bombes on page 9. Chill a 1½-quart bombe mold in the freezer and line the bottom and sides with an even layer of about two-thirds of the raspberry sherbet. Freeze this hard while you make the mousse and the praline. Hand chop the praline into ⅛-inch chunks. When the mousse is ready, pour half of it into the lined mold and sprinkle it lightly with the praline. Leave a little of the mousse showing between bits of praline or the bombe will tend to pull apart where the praline layer is. Pour the rest of the mousse over the praline and freeze hard. Cover with the remaining sherbet and freeze again. Unmold onto a chilled plate and cover with plastic. Return to the freezer to reharden the surface.

Serve on chilled plates, garnished with a sprig of mint, for an unusual red and creamy white dessert.

134

RASPBERRY BOMBE
WITH VANILLA AND COFFEE ICE CREAMS

For 8 to 10 servings: *2 cups Coffee Ice Cream (page 114)* · *2 cups Vanilla Ice Cream (page 6)* · *2 cups Raspberry Sherbet (page 137)*

Please read about making and serving bombes on page 9. Chill a 1½-quart mold or loaf pan in the freezer. Measure 2 cups of slightly softened coffee ice cream and line the bottom of the mold smoothly with it. Freeze until firm, then put a layer of 2 cups of vanilla ice cream smoothly over the coffee layer. Freeze again and add a layer of raspberry sherbet to the top. Freeze until firm, turn out, and slice to serve.

Garnish with a sprinkling of hazelnut praline or a very fine tracery of melted chocolate, and serve with Lace Cookies.

RASPBERRY CURD

Makes about 2 cups, enough to fill one 9-inch tart: *3 half-pint baskets raspberries* · *About ½ cup sugar* · *4 tablespoons unsalted butter* · *1½ teaspoons lemon juice, to taste* · *2 eggs* · *2 egg yolks*

Purée the raspberries and put them through a fine strainer to remove the seeds. Measure 1½ cups purée, heat it in a non-corroding saucepan, and stir in the sugar and butter. Taste and add the lemon juice to taste. Whisk the eggs and egg yolks just enough to mix them, then stir in some of the hot purée to warm them. Return to the pan and cook over low heat, stirring constantly, until the mixture is thick—it should reach a temperature of 170°F. Chill.

This can be used as a cake filling, or to fill a tart or tartlets. Garnish with a little crème Chantilly.

RASPBERRY ICE CREAM

Makes about 1 quart: *1¼ cups whipping cream · ⅞ cup sugar · 4 egg yolks · 2½ to 3 half-pint baskets of raspberries · A few drops of vanilla extract · Optional: a few drops of kirsch*

Warm ¾ cup of the cream with the sugar in a non-corroding saucepan until the sugar has dissolved. Whisk the egg yolks lightly and pour in some of the warmed cream mixture, stirring constantly. Return to the pan and cook over low heat, stirring constantly, until the custard coats the spoon. Strain through a medium-fine strainer into a container and add the remaining cream. Chill while you prepare the raspberries. Purée the raspberries through a food mill or in a food processor and put through a fine strainer to remove the seeds. Measure 1⅛ cups and add with the vanilla and kirsch to the custard. Taste and add a little more purée if you wish, then chill thoroughly. Freeze according to the directions with your ice cream maker.

Serve in cookie cups drizzled with Warm Chocolate Sauce or some slightly sweetened raspberry purée; or serve accompanied by Lace Cookies.

RASPBERRY MOUSSE

Makes 1 quart: *2 half-pint baskets of raspberries · 2 cups whipping cream · ¼ cup sugar · Kirsch and vanilla extract to taste*

Purée the raspberries in a blender, food processor, or food mill and put through a strainer fine enough to remove the seeds. Measure out ¾ cup purée. Whip the cream with the sugar until it is just beginning to hold a shape. Fold the ¾ cup purée into the cream using as few strokes as possible, so the mousse doesn't become stiff. Add a little kirsch and vanilla to taste while folding the mixtures. Measure ¼ cup more of raspberry purée and stir in just enough sugar to sweeten it slightly. Stir until the sugar dissolves. Swirl into the mousse, leaving the mixture marbled.

Serve chilled, with Lace Cookies drizzled with chocolate.

136

RASPBERRY CARAMEL SAUCE

Makes about ¾ cup: *1 half-pint basket raspberries · ¾ cup sugar · ½ cup water · 2 teaspoons lemon juice · A few drops of kirsch*

Purée the raspberries and strain them through a fine enough strainer to remove the seeds. You will have about ½ cup. Put the sugar and 2 tablespoons of the water in a heavy, light-colored saucepan and let stand until the sugar is moistened. Cook over medium to high heat until the sugar is a light golden caramel, swirling it gently to keep it cooking evenly. Remove from the heat to check the color. When it is light gold, set the pan in the sink and carefully pour in the remaining 6 tablespoons water so the caramel doesn't spatter you. Set the pan back on medium heat and cook, stirring, until the caramel has dissolved. Remove from the heat and stir in 6 to 8 tablespoons of raspberry purée. Add the lemon juice to taste and a little kirsch, and chill. Taste and adjust the flavoring.

Even though this sauce is sweet, I often prefer to use it rather than raspberry purée, whose strong flavor can overwhelm whatever it is served with.

RASPBERRY SHERBET

Makes about 1 quart: *⅞ cup sugar · ⅔ cup water · 5 half-pint baskets raspberries · Kirsch to taste*

Boil the sugar and water together, then chill. Purée the raspberries through a food mill or in a food processor and put through a fine strainer to remove the seeds. Measure 2⅝ cups purée and add it to the chilled syrup. Taste and add a few drops of kirsch if you like. Chill thoroughly; then freeze according to the directions with your ice cream maker.

Use this to make various bombes, or serve it in combination with other berry sherbets, or as part of an assortment of fresh fruits and sherbets. Or serve it with Vanilla Ice Cream, accompanied by Lace Cookies or other crisp cookies.

RASPBERRY SOUFFLÉS

For 6 individual soufflés: *3 tablespoons pastry cream (page 7)* · *4 tablespoons sugar* · *3 egg yolks* · *1¼ teaspoons kirsch, to taste* · *¾ cup raspberries* · *3 egg whites* · *¼ teaspoon cream of tartar* · *Vanilla crème anglaise (page 5)*

Butter and sugar the insides of six 5-ounce soufflé dishes. Heat your oven to 400°F. Whisk together the pastry cream, 1 tablespoon of the sugar, the egg yolks, and the kirsch. Unless the raspberries are tiny, break them in half, but don't crush them. Warm the egg whites over hot water or swirl them above a gas flame until they are barely warm. Beat the egg whites with the cream of tartar until they hold soft peaks. Gradually sprinkle in the remaining 3 tablespoons sugar while you continue beating until the whites hold soft peaks again. Quickly fold in the egg yolk mixture, but before it is completely folded together, sprinkle the raspberries over the mixture so they will fold in as you finish. Be careful to stop as soon as the two mixtures are blended—or even a little before. Overmixing will cause the egg whites to deflate.

Pour the mixture into the prepared soufflé dishes to within ½ inch of the tops and bake 8 to 10 minutes, or until they are golden brown on top but still shake a little when you jiggle them. If you like them firm in the center, bake a minute or two longer.

Serve immediately on a pretty plate with a doily, accompanied by a pitcher of very cold crème anglaise to pour into the soufflés.

RASPBERRY TART

For 8 servings: *One 9-inch pre-baked short crust tart shell (page 11)* · *½ cup strained raspberry jam or red currant jelly (or a mixture of the two)* · *2 half-pint baskets raspberries* · *½ teaspoon kirsch*

Warm the jam and brush a very thin layer on the bottom of the pre-baked tart shell: this will keep the raspberries from rolling around as you arrange them in the shell. Spread the berries out gently on a flat surface so you can see their condition and size. Pick out handfuls, starting with the largest ones, and arrange them in circles in the tart shell, pushing each one firmly against its neighbor. Fill the shell with one tight layer and put the tart into a preheated 375°F oven for 5 minutes only. This brings out the perfume of the raspberries without softening them and making them mushy. Heat the jam again until it boils, stirring. Remove from the heat and add the kirsch. Brush the raspberries as lightly as you can with this glaze. Don't use too much or the tart will be too sweet.

Serve as soon as possible. You may prepare the tart up to the warming and glazing an hour or two before serving, but it is best served soon after it is glazed. Serve the tart garnished with crème fraîche or crème Chantilly, if you like.

BLACK RASPBERRY ICE CREAM

Makes a generous quart: *1 half-pint basket black raspberries · 3 cups cream · ⅞ cup sugar · 3 egg yolks · A few drops of vanilla extract*

Purée two-thirds of the berries in a food processor or through a food mill. Strain to remove the seeds. You should have 6 to 8 tablespoons. The purée will be very thick and lumpy, as if it were jelling. Warm 1½ cups of the cream with the sugar until the sugar is dissolved. Whisk the egg yolks in a bowl just enough to mix them and pour in some of the hot cream mixture, stirring constantly. Return to the pan and cook over low heat, still stirring constantly, until the custard coats the spoon. Remove from the heat and strain into a bowl. Add the remaining cream and raspberry purée to taste. Add the vanilla and chill the mixture. Taste again and add more vanilla if you wish. Freeze according to the directions with your ice cream maker.

Serve in a cookie cup with a little black raspberry purée thinned with some sugar syrup, or simply accompanied by crisp cookies such as Langues de Chat or Lace Cookies. I find this a really special flavor, with a lingering perfume. Have a glass of port afterward—the port will be improved!

BLACK RASPBERRY SHERBET

Makes 1 quart: *3 half-pint baskets black raspberries · 1 cup plus 2 tablespoons sugar · 2½ cups water · Lemon juice to taste · Optional: kirsch to taste*

Purée the berries in a food processor or through a food mill, and strain to remove the seeds. You should have 2 cups of purée. Boil the sugar and water for 5 minutes, then cool. Add the purée to the cooled syrup and season to taste with lemon juice and a few drops of kirsch, if you like. Chill thoroughly. Freeze according to the instructions with your ice cream maker.

Serve alone, with Langues de Chat or Lace Cookies, or with any berry sherbets, or with Peach or Nectarine Sherbet.

STRAWBERRY SPRING CAKE

For 12 servings: *One 9-inch sponge cake (page 16) · 2 pint baskets straw-berries or 2 half-pint baskets fraises des bois · Sugar and kirsch to taste · ¼ cup strained raspberry jam or red currant jelly · 1 to 1½ cups crème Chantilly*

Slice the cake into two layers. Rinse, dry, and hull the strawberries; fraises des bois don't need this step. Save about 2 cups of the nicest and smallest berries for the top. Slice the rest and toss them in a bowl with a few tablespoons of sugar and some kirsch to taste. Spread the sliced berries evenly on the cut edge of the bottom layer of the cake. There should be a reasonably thick layer. Press the berries down firmly, then cover with the top layer. Melt the jam or jelly and brush a thin coating on the top of the cake. Arrange the reserved whole strawberries in circles, starting at the center of the cake and covering as much of the top as they will. Brush the berries with the glaze. Ice the sides with the crème Chantilly and use a pastry bag to pipe a design around the edges of the circle of strawberries on top.

Serve immediately, or keep chilled until you can serve it—in which case let it warm at room temperature for 15 to 30 minutes before serving.

140

EASTER NESTS

For 8 servings: For the angel hair: *¾ cup sugar · 3 tablespoons water · 3 tablespoons corn syrup*
For the filling: *2 pint baskets ripe strawberries · A few drops of kirsch · 1 cup whipping cream · Sugar to taste · Vanilla extract to taste*

First prepare a place to spin the angel hair: Using light vegetable oil, oil a broomstick and set it between two chairs with newspapers underneath. Or lightly oil a 3-foot wide area of your kitchen counter if it has a hard finish like stainless steel, tile, or formica—this won't work on a wood counter.

Make the angel hair: Put the sugar in a small heavy saucepan and pour the water over it. When the sugar is completely moistened, add the corn syrup and set over high heat. When it comes to a boil, cover the pan and let simmer for 5 minutes to wash down any crystals that might have formed on the side of the pan. Uncover and continue cooking, swirling the pan occasionally, until the syrup is pale gold. Remove from the heat, set into a pan of ice water, and stir with a fork until the temperature is reduced to about 250°F and the caramel runs off the fork in threads. Make the angel hair by dipping the fork in the caramel and waving it back and forth quickly over the broomstick or counter top. Try to pull the threads out about two feet long. Gather it up occasionally, pushing it together lightly, and put it into an airtight container. Be careful not to compress it too much. Handle it gingerly: it can be sharp. Continue until you have at least two quarts of loosely packed angel hair.

When you are ready to serve the dessert, wash and dry the berries and slice them unless they are small. Toss with a few drops of kirsch. Whip the cream into soft mounds and flavor to taste with a little sugar and vanilla. Carefully take handfuls of the angel hair and arrange about a cup on each serving plate. Make it round and then push some of the caramel out to the sides from the center to make a nest shape. Fill the center hole with whipped cream and scatter about ⅓ cup strawberries over it.

Serve immediately and eat carefully—the caramel can be sharp.

STRAWBERRY ICE CREAM

Makes a generous quart: *1½ cups whipping cream · ¾ cup sugar · 3 egg yolks · 1 to 1½ pint baskets strawberries · Vanilla extract to taste*

Make the custard a day ahead so it can be thoroughly chilled (or chill it over ice if you are in a hurry). Heat the cream with ½ cup of the sugar in a non-corroding saucepan until the sugar dissolves. Whisk the egg yolks just enough to mix them and stir in some of the hot cream mixture to warm them. Return to the pan and cook, stirring constantly, until the custard coats the spoon. Strain and chill.

About an hour before you want to freeze the ice cream, rinse, dry, and hull the strawberries. Crush them fine with a potato masher and stir in the remaining ¼ cup sugar. You should have about 1½ cups of crushed berries. Let stand for an hour or so, stirring occasionally, to let the sugar dissolve, then mix with the custard. Flavor to taste with a few drops of vanilla and chill thoroughly. Freeze according to the directions with your ice cream maker.

Serve with crisp cookies such as Langues de Chat.

STRAWBERRY SHERBET

Makes 1 quart: *⅔ cup sugar · ½ cup water · 2 pint baskets strawberries · Optional: kirsch or framboise to taste*

Boil the sugar and water together in a small pan for 5 minutes, then chill the syrup. Wash the strawberries, then drain and hull them. I use a vegetable peeler, inserting the tip beside the hull, putting my thumb on the hull and pulling up—I find that the hull and core come out perfectly. Purée the berries in your food processer, blender, or food mill, or by pushing them through a strainer. Stir the cold syrup into the purée and flavor it, if you like, with a few drops of kirsch or framboise. Chill thoroughly. Freeze according to the instructions with your ice cream maker.

As always, the flavor of this sherbet depends completely on the flavor of the fruit. If you buy berries that aren't perfectly ripe, you can leave

142

them at room temperature overnight and they will ripen some. Strawberries should be red and fragrant. If they show any signs of beginning to mold or of losing their juice, refrigerate and use them as soon as possible. If any berries show even a tiny spot of mold, throw them away because the flavor of the mold permeates the whole berry and possibly even the berry it was touching.

Serve the sherbet alone, or with an ice cream of your choice—Rose Petal, Vanilla, or Strawberry come to mind—or as part of a mixed sherbet plate with Kiwi and Tangerine, Pineapple and Kiwi. Let your imagination and your sense of color and taste be your guide.

STRAWBERRY SHORTCAKE

For 12 servings: *2 cups flour · ½ teaspoon salt · 1 tablespoon baking powder · 2 tablespoons sugar · ½ cup unsalted butter · ¾ cup plus 2 tablespoons whipping cream · 4 pint baskets strawberries · Sugar to taste · 3 cups whipping cream for crème Chantilly*

Mix the flour, salt (unless you are using salted butter), baking powder, and sugar. Cut in the butter until the mixture looks like cornmeal with a few larger pieces of butter in it. Use a pastry blender or two knives, if you like; I just rub the mixture quickly between my fingers. Mix in ¾ cup cream, just until most of the dry mixture has been moistened. Turn out on a board and knead a few times until the dough just comes together. Roll ½-inch thick and cut into squares or circles, or whatever shape you like. This recipe will make 12 individual shortcakes.

Place on an unbuttered baking sheet. Knead together lightly any scraps and roll once more and cut. Brush the tops with the remaining 2 tablespoons cream and bake in a preheated 450°F oven for 10 to 12 minutes or until the tops are lightly browned and the dough is set. Cool on a rack and serve while warm.

Wash, dry, and hull the berries. Crush about one-quarter of the berries and slice the rest in with them. Toss with sugar to taste—a tablespoon or so per basket—and chill until serving time. The strawberry mixture should be very juicy.

To serve: Warm the shortcakes if necessary, split them, and spoon the berries liberally over the bottom halves. Set the tops back on and spoon some crème Chantilly over them. There should be lots of berries and lots of cream.

STRAWBERRY TART

For 8 servings: *One 9-inch pastry shell, short crust (page 11), or puff pastry (page 25)* · *1 cup pastry cream (page 7)* · *1 or 2 pint baskets strawberries* · *2 to 4 tablespoons strawberry, raspberry, or red currant jam* · *Optional: a few drops of kirsch*

Bake the shell according to directions for the pastry you use. The pastry cream can be made several days ahead. Wash the berries if they need it and set them on a towel. Pat them dry and hull them. Spread the pastry cream in the cooled shell. Arrange the berries in circles in the shell, standing them close together if you use whole ones, overlapping them slightly if you slice them. You will need the larger amount of berries if you use them whole. Warm the jam to melt it, add a few drops of kirsch, if you like, and brush the berries with a thin layer of jam, reheating as necessary to keep it liquid.

TIMBALES ÉLYSÉES

For 10 servings: *One recipe cookie cups (page 13)* · *1½ to 2 cups Vanilla Ice Cream (page 6)*
For the caramel: *½ cup sugar* · *2 tablespoons water* · *2 tablespoons corn syrup*
For the filling: *2 to 3 cups mixed strawberries and fraises des bois, or 2 large peaches poached in vanilla syrup and chilled* · *¼ cup red currant jelly or seedless raspberry jam* · *½ teaspoon kirsch* · *½ cup whipping cream* · *Sugar to taste* · *Vanilla extract to taste* · *3 or 4 candied violets*

Make the cookie cups and store them in an airtight container until serving time. Make the ice cream ahead as well.

144

Make the caramel cages as close to serving time as possible: Butter the outside of a ladle that is about 3 inches in diameter, and butter a baking sheet. Put the sugar and water in a heavy saucepan and let stand until the sugar is moistened. Add the corn syrup and cook over medium heat until light golden brown. Remove from the heat and set into a pan of ice water briefly to cool the caramel to about 250°F; you will be able to spin a thread with it at this temperature. Working quickly, dip a fork into the caramel and crisscross the ladle with threads of it, building up a few layers to make a strong cage. With a pair of scissors, clip off the threads that extend beyond the edge of the ladle. Cool the caramel, sliding it gently on the ladle to be sure it doesn't stick. As soon as it has cooled enough to hold its shape, slide it carefully off the ladle and stand it on the buttered baking sheet. The cages are thin and delicate; handle them gently so as not to break them. Make nine more, reheating the caramel as necessary to keep it at the right temperature and consistency. Store them carefully in an airtight container until serving time, putting parchment or waxed paper between the layers.

When ready to serve, slice the strawberries and mix them with the fraises des bois. The peaches should be sliced thin if you are using them. Melt the jelly or jam and stir in the kirsch. Whip the cream until it is stiff enough to pipe a soft shape from a pastry bag and flavor it to taste with sugar and vanilla. To assemble, put a small scoop of ice cream in each cookie cup and sprinkle about ¼ cup of berries over it, or arrange a few peach slices over the ice cream. Drizzle about a teaspoon of the warmed jelly or jam over that. Pipe a ring of small whipped cream rosettes around the edge of the fruit and the ice cream and set a caramel cage over the top. Pipe a small rosette of cream on top of the caramel cage and put a small piece of candied violet on it.

Serve immediately. Eat this carefully: the caramel is sharp. This is a lovely combination of flavors and textures, well worth the effort it takes.

7

SUMMER
FRUITS

SUMMER BEGINS for us with the first cherries late in May. In the upstairs café we bake them into puff pastry tarts in the wood oven. The apricot season follows very quickly and is so short that we try to get our fill of them right away. The two combine naturally in tarts of burgundy Bing cherries and bright orange apricots. Intense apricot purées are the base for several delicious soufflés. Sour cherries, all too rare in our part of the country, have a rich almond pit flavor that makes irresistible pies.

Very soon the first nectarines are in the markets: May Grands, Spring Grands, Early Sun Grands, Ruby Grands—all Grand nectarines taste good. Rose nectarines and Fantasias arrive in June, and some variety is always in the market until the end of September. Nectarines have slightly firmer flesh and a tarter, spicier flavor than that of their peach relatives. We make

148

tarts and pies with them or stuff and bake them. They are delicious with wine-flavored ice creams or sabayons, or bitter almond ice cream with a little bright red strawberry purée spreading around them. All summer we make crisps from nectarines or in combination with different berries, or with plums. Crisps are one of the most popular desserts in the upstairs café, more popular by far even than chocolate cake.

Early in June the first Babcock peaches arrive, with their sweet white flesh. They are the most richly perfumed of all peaches, perfect sliced into sweetened red wine. The First Ladies follow, and then the Red Haven, Empress, Hale, Suncrest, Regina, Elberta, Fayette, Cal Red, and O'Henry. In your area you may find different varieties. We make them into tarts, cobblers, crisps, and everybody's favorite, it seems, fresh peach ice cream. We also poach peaches to serve with Champagne sabayon and raspberry sauce, and we make Escoffier's Peaches Rose-Chéri, veiled with multicolored sugared rose petals.

The first plums arrive at the same time as the first peaches—it is almost too much to keep up with. We combine plums with peaches in desserts, or we splurge and serve three different plum sherbets together, taking advantage of the great variation of flavor and texture among different varieties. With Santa Rosa plums we bake some of the most beautiful of our tarts, bright red plum slices edged with dark skin that shine with raspberry glaze.

All these summer fruits are stone fruits, and taste especially good with bitter almond ice cream, which has the taste of their pits. Kirsch and other spirits distilled from unstoned fruit also enhance them, as do raspberries and strawberries, as much with their contrasting colors as with their flavors.

I have been very lucky to be able to buy produce for the restaurant from a man who will let me taste and choose the best. You may not be able to do this, but at least do try to find a reliable greengrocer who selects produce carefully. It is important to buy all fruits picked as nearly ripe as possible. You may have better luck at farmer's markets or roadside stands where locally grown produce is available. Once you have tasted tree-ripened fruit, it is very hard to settle for anything less. If you have room in your garden for a tree or two, so much the better; your nursery will have varieties suited to your climate.

SUNSET BOMBE

For 10 to 12 servings: *1½ cups Peach Sherbet (page 170)* · *1½ cups Nectarine Sherbet (page 170)* · *1½ cups Santa Rosa Plum Sherbet (page 174)* · *1½ cups Vanilla Ice Cream (page 6)*

Chill a 1½-quart bombe mold in the freezer. (See page 9 about making, molding, and unmolding bombes.) Spread an even layer of the slightly softened peach sherbet in the bottom of the mold and freeze until hard enough to spread the next layer over. Spread with the slightly softened nectarine sherbet and continue freezing and layering with the plum sherbet and then the vanilla ice cream. Freeze the completed bombe until thoroughly hardened, then unmold onto a serving plate if you are presenting it whole. Cover well with plastic and return to the freezer to harden until serving time.

Serve whole at the table, or serve slices on plates that have been chilled in the freezer. Garnish with a few fraises des bois or a drizzle of strawberry purée or a sprig of mint, and accompany with Lace Cookies.

APRICOT SHERBET BOMBE WITH ALMOND MOUSSE

For 8 to 10 servings: *3 cups Apricot Sherbet (page 152)* · *¼ cup unblanched whole almonds* · *1 recipe frozen mousse (page 9)* · *Kirsch to taste*

Use a 1½-quart mold, a stainless steel loaf pan, or a bombe mold. Make and freeze the sherbet. Put the mold in the freezer to chill. Toast the almonds in a preheated 350°F oven for 5 to 7 minutes, or until they smell nutty, then cool them. Line the bottom and sides of the mold with an even layer of the apricot sherbet, using about three-fourths of it. It is easier to do this before the sherbet is completely firm. Put the mold back in the freezer.

Make the mousse, flavoring it with kirsch to taste. When it is finished, chop the almonds fine and fold them in. Fill the center of the bombe with the almond mousse mixture and freeze until it is hard enough to spread the rest of the apricot sherbet over the top. Freeze again until firm. At this point you can put the bombe back into the freezer, covered well with plastic, and let it wait several hours until ready to serve.

Serve unmolded onto a chilled tray, or slice it with a sharp knife, sprinkling the slices with chopped almonds or garnishing them with a mint sprig and drizzling with a very little bit of raspberry purée—raspberry purée is very strong and will easily overwhelm the other flavors. You could also garnish this bombe with a sprinkling of fraises des bois or drizzle it with strawberry purée. Accompany the bombe with Langues de Chat or other crisp cookies.

APRICOT CURD

Makes 2½ cups: *About ⅔ pound ripe apricots · 2 or 3 tablespoons water · ⅜ cup sugar · 4 tablespoons unsalted butter · 1 tablespoon plus 1 teaspoon lemon juice, to taste · 2 eggs · 1 egg yolk*

Wash, pit, and cut the apricots into sixths or eighths. Cook in a non-corroding saucepan with the water (the water keeps the apricots from sticking until they release their own juices). Cook slowly until tender. Purée them through a food mill or in a food processor and strain the purée. Measure out 1 cup, and while it is still warm dissolve the sugar in it. Cut the butter into little pieces and melt it in the purée also. Add the lemon juice. Whisk the eggs and the yolk together, then whisk in a little of the warm purée to warm the eggs. Return to the pan and cook, stirring constantly, until the temperature reaches 170°F and the curd is quite thick. Cool. This keeps in the refrigerator for at least a week.

Use apricot curd for tarts or tartlets (garnish with a little whipped cream), as a cake filling, or mixed with whipped cream as a filling for cream puffs.

APRICOT ICE CREAM

Makes 1 quart: *⅔ pound apricots · 2 tablespoons water · 1⅓ cups whipping cream · 1 cup sugar · 4 egg yolks · Vanilla extract and kirsch to taste*

Wash the apricots, pit them, and cut in rough slices into a non-corroding saucepan. Add the water, cover, and cook until tender. Purée in a blender, food processor, or food mill. Strain. Warm the cream with the sugar in a non-corroding saucepan until the sugar is dissolved. Whisk the egg yolks just enough to mix them and add the warm cream mixture, stirring constantly. Return to the pan and cook over low heat, stirring constantly, until the mixture coats the spoon. Strain into a bowl and stir in the apricot purée. Adjust the flavoring to your taste with a little vanilla and kirsch. Chill thoroughly; then freeze according to the instructions with your ice cream maker.

Serve in cookie cups with some sauce made from a little apricot purée flavored with sugar and kirsch, and garnish with a few raspberries, fraises des bois, or sliced strawberries.

APRICOT SHERBET

Makes about 1¼ quarts: *1¾ to 2 pounds ripe apricots · 1 cup sugar · 1 cup water · Optional: 1 teaspoon kirsch*

Wash the apricots and halve them, saving one of the pits. Cut the apricots in rough slices and put them in a non-corroding saucepan with ¼ cup water. Crack the reserved pit to get the kernel, and add it to the apricots. Cover and cook over low heat, stirring occasionally to keep the fruit from burning, until the apricots are tender. Purée them in a blender or food processor, or put them through a food mill, then strain them through a wire strainer. Some apricots are very fibrous; the blender and processor won't cut up the fibers. You should have 3 cups of purée. Boil the sugar with 1 cup water, then cool it. Add the purée to the cooled sugar syrup, flavor with a few drops of kirsch, if you like, and chill. Freeze according to the instructions with your ice cream maker.

Serve alone, or with crisp cookies, or with a compote of seasonal fruits.

APRICOT AND CHERRY PIE

For 8 servings: *Pastry for a 2-crust 9-inch pie (page 23)* · *1½ pounds firm ripe apricots* · *15 to 20 large ripe Bing cherries, or about ¼ cup pitted sour cherries* · *1½ tablespoons flour* · *½ cup sugar* · *Optional: kirsch to taste* · *1 egg yolk* · *2 teaspoons whipping cream or milk*

Roll out half the pie crust about ⅛-inch thick and line a 9-inch pie plate with it. Freeze or chill it. Wash the apricots and cut them in half to remove the pits. Slice them about ¾-inch thick and measure. Wash the cherries, pit them, and cut them in half. You should have at least 4 cups of fruit in all. Toss it with the flour and sugar, and a little kirsch, if you like, until the sugar and flour are moistened. Spread the fruit in the chilled pie shell. Roll out the remaining crust to a circle at least 12 inches in diameter.

Brush the rim of the bottom shell with water and lay the top crust over the pie. Press gently around the moistened edge to seal it. Trim the top pastry off about ½ inch beyond the bottom crust and fold it under the edge of the bottom crust, pressing together and crimping the edge decoratively. Brush the top with a glaze made by beating the egg yolk and cream together with a fork. Decorate the top crust as you like, tracing designs about 1/16-inch deep into the pastry with a paring knife. Avoid cutting all the way through the pastry, but pierce the shell in four or five places to let steam escape.

Bake in a preheated 400°F oven for about an hour, or until the crust is golden brown, the fruit is tender, and the juices bubble thick from the vents. The edge of the pie may be brown long before the rest is baked; if so, make a 2-inch or 3-inch-wide strip of aluminum foil and fold it over the edge to cover it. A glass pie plate will slow the baking. Allow the pie to cool at least an hour before serving.

This pie is especially good made with sour cherries, but delicious also with Bings. Serve it warm, with Vanilla, Bitter Almond, or Noyau Ice Cream.

APRICOT SOUFFLÉS

For 6 individual soufflés: *About ⅓ pound apricots · ¼ cup water · 3 tablespoons sugar · Kirsch to taste · ¼ cup pastry cream (page 7) · 5 egg whites · ¼ teaspoon cream of tartar · Crème anglaise (page 5)*

Wash and pit the apricots. Cut them into quarters and put them in a non-corroding saucepan with the water. Cook, covered, over low heat for about 15 minutes, or until tender, stirring occasionally. Purée in a blender or food processor or through a food mill. Pass through a medium-fine strainer: some apricots are very fibrous and will not make a fine purée unless they are strained. Cook the puree over low to medium heat, stirring constantly, until it is reduced to ¼ cup. Stir in 1 tablespoon of the sugar and a few drops of kirsch. Cool.

Heat your oven to 400°F. Butter and sugar the insides of six 4-ounce or 5-ounce soufflé dishes. Whisk together the cooled apricot purée and the pastry cream. Warm the egg whites over hot water, or swirl them above a gas flame until they are barely warm. Beat them with the cream of tartar until they hold soft peaks, then beat in the remaining 2 tablespoons sugar until they hold soft peaks again. Quickly fold the egg whites into the apricot mixture and pour into the prepared dishes to within ½ inch of the tops.

Bake for 7 to 8 minutes, or until the tops are golden brown but the soufflés still wiggle a little when you shake them—unless you like the center firm, in which case you should bake them a minute or two longer. If they are baked longer you risk drying them out.

Serve immediately on doilies on pretty plates, with a pitcher of very cold crème anglaise to pour into them.

This soufflé is a creamy, classic version. The following one has a more pronounced apricot flavor.

ANOTHER APRICOT SOUFFLÉ

For 6 individual soufflés: *⅔ pound ripe apricots · ¼ cup water · 4 table-spoons sugar · A few drops of kirsch · 2 egg yolks · 4 egg whites · ¼ teaspoon cream of tartar*

Prepare the purée as above but cook it down until you have a scant ½ cup. Cool slightly and whisk in 2 tablespoons of sugar, the kirsch, and then the egg yolks. Butter and sugar the insides of six 4-ounce or 5-ounce soufflé dishes. Heat the oven to 400°F. Warm the egg whites slightly, then beat them with the cream of tartar until they hold soft peaks, and then gradually beat in the remaining 2 tablespoons sugar until they hold soft peaks again. Fold the egg whites into the apricot mixture and fill the soufflé dishes to within ½ inch of the tops. Bake for 7 to 8 minutes, or until the tops are golden but the soufflés still wiggle a little.

Serve immediately with very cold crème anglaise.

APRICOT TART

For 8 servings: *One 9-inch short crust shell, baked (page 11) · 2 cups water · ⅔ cup sugar · 1-inch piece of vanilla bean · 1½ pounds firm ripe apricots · 1 cup frangipane cream (page 7) · 3 or 4 tablespoons apricot jam · ½ teaspoon kirsch · 2 tablespoons pistachio nuts*

Make a syrup of the water, sugar, and vanilla bean. Wash the apricots, halve them along their natural divisions, and pit them. Put the halves into the simmering syrup and cook, without letting them boil, until they are barely tender. The apricots will continue to cook from their own heat a short while after you remove them from the syrup, so be sure to take them out before they are soft. Cool on a plate in the refrigerator and chill the syrup separately. If you are not to make the tart immediately, store the apricot halves, covered tightly, in the cooled syrup. They will keep for several days. You may also make the frangipane cream well ahead of serving time.

When ready to serve the tart, bake the tart shell and cool it. Fill it with a smooth layer of the frangipane cream. Drain the apricot halves on a paper towel and blot them so they have no excess juice. Arrange them in tight circles over the pastry cream, rounded side up. Warm the apricot jam in a small non-corroding saucepan until it boils, remove from the heat, and stir in the kirsch. Brush the apricots with the glaze, reheating it briefly if it thickens too much while you are working. Sprinkle the very edge of the tart with a rim of the finely chopped pistachio nuts that have been skinned and then crisped in a preheated 200°F oven for 10 to 30 minutes. Serve immediately.

APRICOT AND CHERRY TART

For a 9-inch tart, serving 8: *One 9-inch puff pastry shell (page 25), frozen · ¾ pound dark sweet cherries · About ¾ pound firm ripe apricots · 1 egg yolk · 2 teaspoons whipping cream · 4 Italian macaroons, crushed · ½ to 2 tablespoons sugar · Optional: 1 teaspoon kirsch · 2 to 3 tablespoons apricot jam*

Preheat your oven to 400°F. If using a baking stone, preheat it too. A stone gives the crust a special texture, but you can also bake this tart on a metal baking sheet. In any case, put the frozen tart shell on a lightly floured baking sheet while filling it. Wash the cherries, dry them, stem and pit them. Wash and dry the apricots, slice them in half, and stone them.

Beat the egg yolk and cream together and brush the mixture all around the edge of the frozen tart shell. Quickly sprinkle the crushed macaroons over the bottom of the shell. Arrange a circle of cherries around the edge of the shell, pressing them together as tight as possible. Next arrange a circle of apricot halves, pitted side down, and pressed tight together. The fruit loses some volume as it bakes; if it is not pressed tight, gaps will appear. Continue to fill in the shell in whatever design you like. When the apricots are all arranged, fill the large spaces among them with cherries. Work quickly so the shell doesn't defrost or it will be very difficult to slide it onto the stone. If the pastry does defrost while you are working, set it back in the freezer to harden.

Sprinkle the top with sugar—use the lesser amount if the fruit is sweet, more if it is tart. Bake the tart for 30 to 35 minutes, or until the bottom of the shell is golden brown and the fruit is tender. If the edge browns too fast, lay a sheet of foil loosely over the tart while it finishes baking. Let the tart cool on a rack. Add the kirsch to the apricot jam, warm it over low heat, and brush the resulting glaze on the fruit.

Serve warm, with Vanilla Ice Cream or kirsch ice cream.

ALICE'S CHERRY COMPOTE
WITH BALSAMIC VINEGAR

For 6 servings: *2 pounds black cherries · ¼ cup sugar · 1 teaspoon kirsch · 2 to 3 teaspoons balsamic vinegar*

When Alice was trying to cook some underripe cherries early in the season, she discovered that balsamic vinegar magically brings out their flavor.

Put the cherries in a colander, pick out any bad ones, rinse and stem. Put them in one layer in a heavy-bottomed non-corroding sauté pan. If you haven't a pan big enough, cook the cherries in two or more batches. Sprinkle the fruit with the sugar and shake the pan over high heat for about 5 minutes, or until the sugar melts and the cherries feel a little soft when you press them. The sugar will make little white crystals on the cherries before it melts.

Sprinkle the cherries with the kirsch and vinegar and shake them for about 30 seconds longer. Scrape them with their juice into a container and chill or cool to room temperature, then let stand at least an hour or two.

Serve in a sherbet glass with crisp cookies or Sarah's Macaroons.

CHERRY COMPOTE WITH
LEMON-MACAROON CREAM

For 3 or 4 servings: *1 pound ripe Bing cherries · 2 tablespoons sugar · 1 teaspoon brandy · 1 teaspoon kirsch*

Wash the cherries and stem them. Put them in a non-corroding sauté pan large enough to hold them one layer deep and sprinkle with the sugar.

157

Put on high heat and shake occasionally to turn the cherries. Cook about 5 minutes, or until they look glazed and feel tender when you press them. They should not get mushy. They will continue to cook from their own heat after you take them off the fire. Add the brandy and kirsch and toss the cherries briefly when they are done.

Pour the cherries into a container and scrape in any thick, jellylike juices they have left in the pan. After the cherries sit for a while they will release their own juices to make a little syrup: you will probably have about ½ cup from a pound of cherries.

Serve, at room temperature or chilled, over the following cream, accompanied by Langues de Chat.

For the Lemon-Macaroon Cream: *½ cup whipping cream · 1 lemon · 4 Italian macaroons · Optional: sugar to taste*

Whip the cream to very soft peaks and grate the peel into it—use a fine grater so it will flavor the cream quickly. Crush the macaroons and stir them into the cream mixture. Taste to see if any sugar is needed, adding it if necessary. Let the cream stand for a couple of hours, if possible, to allow the lemon flavor to develop.

You can use the macaroons without incorporating them in the lemon cream. Sprinkle the crushed macaroons in the bottom of a dessert glass, then add a layer of cherries and top with the lemon cream. This preparation has a nicer texture because you have a little crunch from the macaroons to complement the soft cherries and cream. If you make the lemon cream without the macaroons, you will need to sweeten it with a little sugar.

CHERRY ICE CREAM

Makes a generous quart: *1 pound very ripe Bing or other full-flavored cherries · 2 tablespoons water · 1¼ cups whipping cream · ⅝ cup sugar · 3 egg yolks · Kirsch to taste · Vanilla extract to taste*

Wash and pit the cherries and cook them with the water in a non-corroding saucepan for about ½ hour, or until they are tender, stirring occasionally. Cool slightly and purée them through a food mill or in a blender or food processor. You should have about 1¼ cups purée. Warm the cream and sugar in a non-corroding saucepan until the sugar dissolves. Whisk the egg yolks in a small bowl just enough to mix them, and pour in some of the hot cream mixture, stirring constantly. Return to the pan and cook over low heat until the custard coats the spoon. Strain into a bowl and add the cherry purée. Chill. Taste and flavor with a few drops of kirsch and vanilla. Freeze according to the instructions with your ice cream maker.

Serve with Lace Cookies or Langues de Chat.

NOYAU ICE CREAM

Makes a scant quart: *40 or 50 cherry stones or 20 apricot pits · ¾ cup sugar · ¾ cup milk · 2¼ cups whipping cream · 4 egg yolks · Optional: almond extract*

Break open the cherry or apricot pits to get the kernels from inside. The cherry stones can be hit with a hammer or mallet to crack them; apricot pits can usually be cracked with a nutcracker. Crush the kernels in a mortar with a pestle until well broken up. Put them with the sugar in a non-corroding saucepan, add the milk and cream, and heat to just under boiling, about 180°F. Let steep about 30 minutes, reheating once or twice and tasting occasionally to see how strong the flavor is. It should not get bitter, but just taste of almonds. When you like the flavor, whisk the egg yolks just enough to mix them and pour in some of the hot mixture, stirring. Return to the pan and cook until it coats the spoon. Chill thoroughly; then taste and add a few drops of almond extract if you like. Strain into the ice cream can and freeze according to the instructions with your ice cream maker.

This is delicious with Apricot, Apricot and Cherry, Sour Cherry, or Peach Pie, or tarts, or in combination with Peach and Raspberry sherbets.

Noyau is the French word for fruit stone, hence the name of this ice cream.

SOUR CHERRY PIE

For 8 servings: *Pastry for a 2-crust 9-inch pie (page 23)* · *2 pounds sour cherries* · *⅔ cup sugar* · *2 tablespoons flour* · *1 teaspoon kirsch* · *1 egg yolk* · *2 teaspoons milk or cream*

Roll out the pastry ⅛-inch thick and line the pie pan. Roll out the top crust and lay it on a baking sheet. Chill both crusts while you make the filling. Wash the cherries, stem and pit them. You should have about 4 cups. Toss them with the sugar, flour, and kirsch, and let them stand until the dry ingredients are moistened. Mix again and put into the pie shell. Brush the rim of the bottom crust with water and lay the top crust over it. When the top crust is pliable, press it lightly to seal the two layers and trim the top crust, allowing about ½-inch overlap beyond the bottom crust. Fold it under the bottom crust and make a fluted edge.

Beat the egg yolk and the milk or cream with a fork and, using a pastry brush, brush the mixture on top of the pie. Prick the top with a fork in several places, or incise a decorative design into the top using the tip of a paring knife and cutting about ¹⁄₁₆-inch deep. Cut only halfway through the crust for the design, but pierce it in a few places so steam can escape while baking.

Bake in a preheated 400°F oven on the lower shelf for about 1 hour, or until the bottom is brown and the juice bubbles thickly from the vents. If the edges brown too fast, cover them with a strip of foil while the pie finishes baking. I usually do this after about 30 minutes. The bottom will usually be brown after an hour if you use a foil or colored pie pan, but it may take longer if the pie is baking in glass. Cool an hour or two before serving. The pie can be rewarmed in a 400°F oven for 5 to 10 minutes before serving.

Serve with Vanilla Ice Cream.

CHERRY SHERBET

Makes a scant quart: *3 pounds Bing or other ripe, full-flavored cherries* · *¼ cup water* · *¾ cup sugar* · *Kirsch to taste* · *A few drops of balsamic vinegar (to bring out the cherry flavor)*

Wash and pit the cherries and cook them with the water in a non-corroding saucepan for about 30 minutes, or until they are tender, stirring occasionally. Cool slightly and purée them through a food mill or in a blender or food processor. You should have about 3 cups. The purée will not be perfectly smooth but will still have tiny chunks of fruit. While the purée is still hot, stir in the sugar until it dissolves. Chill. Taste and flavor the mixture with a few drops of kirsch and vinegar to taste. Freeze according to the instructions with your ice cream maker.

Serve with sliced peaches or with white peach sherbet or Apricot Sherbet.

CHERRY TART

For 8 servings: *One 9-inch puff pastry shell, frozen (page 25)* · *1½ pounds ripe Bing cherries* · *1 egg yolk* · *2 teaspoons milk or cream* · *3 to 4 tablespoons sweet or sour cherry jam or raspberry or red currant jam* · *Optional: ½ teaspoon kirsch*

Wash the cherries, dry them, stem and stone them. Brush the edge of the tart shell with a glaze made of the egg yolk and milk or cream beaten together with a fork. Toss the cherries with all but 1 tablespoon of the jam and put them into the prepared shell. Spread them evenly but don't worry if a few sit on top of the others; you can push them into a single layer later when they have shrunk a bit.

Bake in a preheated 400°F oven about 35 minutes, or until the sides and bottom of the tart are brown and the cherries are tender when pierced with the tip of a knife. If the sides should brown too quickly, lay a piece of foil loosely on top of the tart while it finishes baking. When done, remove the tart to a rack to cool for a few minutes. Heat the rest of the jam quickly with the kirsch, if you are using it, and brush the cherries with it.

Serve warm with Vanilla, Bitter Almond, or kirsch ice cream.

CHERRY JAM

Makes about ¼ cup: *About ¼ pound cherries, stoned · 3 tablespoons sugar · A few drops of lemon juice*

Warm the cherries and crush them with a potato masher or a slotted spoon. Bring them to a boil and add the sugar and the lemon juice if you are using sweet cherries. Cook over high heat, stirring often, until the juice thickens to a jam consistency when you put it on a plate in the freezer for a few minutes.

BAKED STUFFED NECTARINES

For 8 servings: *Almond stuffing (from Stuffed Baked Pears, page 48) · 1½ pounds firm ripe nectarines · 1 or 2 tablespoons unsalted butter*

Make the stuffing. Wash the nectarines, dry them, and slice in half along their natural division. Separate the fruit from the pit by twisting the halves in opposite directions. Remove the pits and scoop out a little bit of the flesh, if necessary, to make a hole deep enough to fill with a rounded tablespoon of the filling. Arrange them in a buttered baking dish just large enough to hold them. Brush the tops of the fruit with the melted butter and bake in a preheated 375°F oven for about 15 minutes, or until the filling has browned and the nectarines are cooked through and tender when pierced with the tip of a knife, but still hold their shape. Let stand for 10 minutes or so; then slip off their skins when they are cool enough to handle. They will have a beautiful red blush wherever their skins were red.

Serve while still warm with sabayon garnished with a few strawberries or raspberries, or with Bitter Almond, Beaumes-de-Venise, or Sauternes Ice Cream, or with Frozen Zabaglione.

162

NECTARINE COUPE WITH
RASPBERRY ICE CREAM AND ANISE CREAM

For about 8 servings: *One recipe Raspberry Ice Cream (page 136)* · *¾ cup cream* · *Sugar to taste* · *Pernod to taste* · *3 or 4 very ripe, flavorful nectarines (¼ to ½ per person, depending on size)*

Make the ice cream. Whip the cream with sugar and Pernod to taste to a soft, lightly mounding consistency. Wash and dry the nectarines and cut them into slices ¼-inch to ⅓-inch thick. Sprinkle with a little sugar if you think they need it. Serve each person a sherbet glass or plate of ice cream with a few slices of nectarine around it. Serve a bowl of the cream for people to spoon over the ice cream, and accompany with a crisp cookie on the side.

This is a very pretty dessert with its gold nectarine blushed red around the deep pink ice cream and the white cream over it.

NECTARINE AND BERRY CRISP

For 8 servings: *1 recipe crisp topping with almonds (page 42)* · *About 2 pounds nectarines* · *1 or 2 cups boysenberries, raspberries, or olallieberries* · *1 tablespoon flour* · *About ½ cup sugar*

Make the topping. Wash the nectarines, slice them about ½-inch thick, and measure 4 to 5 cups into a bowl. Measure the berries and add them to the nectarines. Toss the fruit with the flour and sugar. Use less sugar at first if you think the fruit is very sweet, then taste to see if more is needed. Turn into a 9-inch pie pan or a gratin dish of similar size. Smooth the top and sprinkle an even layer of the topping over the fruit. Bake in a preheated 375°F oven about 35 minutes, or until the top is golden brown, the fruit is tender, and the juices bubble thick around the edges.

Serve with heavy cream to pour over, or with Vanilla Ice Cream.

NECTARINE AND RASPBERRY CRISP

For 6 to 8 servings: *1 recipe crisp topping with almonds (page 42)* · *3 or 4 pounds ripe nectarines* · *1 half-pint basket raspberries* · *2 to 4 tablespoons sugar* · *1½ tablespoons flour*

Make the topping. Wash the nectarines, pit them, and slice about ⅓-inch thick. You should have about 6 cups. Add the raspberries, sugar to taste, and flour, and toss together. Remember when adding the sugar that the topping is sweet. Put the mixed fruit in a 6-cup gratin dish or pie plate. Smooth the top and sprinkle with an even layer of the topping no more than ¼-inch thick. Bake in a preheated 375°F oven about 45 minutes, or until the top has browned evenly and the juices bubble thickly around the edges. If the top browns too fast, lay a piece of foil loosely over it while the crisp finishes baking, but remove the foil for the last 5 minutes to let the top crisp again.

Serve with cream to pour over the crisp.

NECTARINE ICE CREAM

Makes a scant quart: *1½ pounds ripe nectarines* · *¼ cup water* · *1⅔ cups whipping cream* · *⅞ cup sugar* · *5 egg yolks* · *Vanilla extract to taste* · *Optional: kirsch*

Wash and pit the nectarines but do not peel them. Cut them in rough slices into a non-corroding saucepan, add the water, and cook over low heat until tender. Purée through a food mill or in a blender or food processor. Measure out 1¾ cups and set aside to cool.

Heat the cream and sugar together until the sugar has dissolved, stirring occasionally. Whisk the egg yolks just enough to mix them and pour in some of the hot cream mixture, whisking constantly. Return to the pan and cook over low heat, stirring constantly, until the mixture coats the spoon. Strain into the nectarine purée and stir to mix well. Taste and add a few drops of vanilla and kirsch to heighten the flavor, if you like, and chill. Then taste again, add more flavoring if necessary, and freeze according to the instructions with your ice cream maker.

Serve as an accompaniment to a Pecan Torte, with other ice creams such as Strawberry or Beaumes-de-Venise, with Plum or Peach Sherbet, or in cookie cups.

NECTARINE PIE

For 8 servings: *Pastry for a 2-crust 9-inch pie (page 23)* · *3¾ pounds firm ripe nectarines* · *5 tablespoons sugar* · *1½ tablespoons flour* · *½ teaspoon kirsch* · *1 egg yolk* · *2 teaspoons cream or milk*

Roll out the pastry about ⅛-inch thick, line a 9-inch pie plate with it, and chill. Roll out a piece for the top, lay it on a baking sheet, and chill that also while you make the filling. Wash and dry the nectarines, cut them in half and pit them. Cut into slices about ⅓-inch thick and measure out 4 cups. Toss them with the sugar, flour, and kirsch and turn them into the prepared pie shell. Brush the rim of the bottom crust with water and lay the top crust on it. When the top crust is pliable, press it lightly around the edge to seal, then trim it about half an inch beyond the edge of the bottom crust. Fold it under the bottom crust and make a fluted edge.

Beat the egg yolk and cream or milk with a fork and brush the mixture on top of the pie. Prick the top with a fork in several places, or incise a decorative design in the top using the tip of a paring knife and cutting about ¹⁄₁₆-inch deep. Pierce the pastry in a few places to let steam escape.

Bake in a preheated 400°F oven on the lower shelf for about 1 hour, or until the juice bubbles thickly from the vents and the crust is baked. If the edges brown too fast, cover them with a strip of foil.

Cool for about an hour before serving. Serve warm with Vanilla or Bitter Almond Ice Cream.

NECTARINE TART

For 8 servings: *One 9-inch puff pastry tart shell (page 25), chilled or frozen, or one 9-inch short crust tart shell (page 11), pre-baked · 1 pound firm ripe nectarines · 1 tablespoon sugar · 2 tablespoons cooked-down fruit poaching liquid or apricot jam · ½ teaspoon kirsch*

Wash and dry the nectarines, slice them in half, and pit them. Cut into slices about ⅓-inch thick and arrange in circles in the tart shell, with the slices just barely overlapping one another. Sprinkle with the sugar. If you are using the puff pastry shell, bake in a preheated 400°F oven for about 35 minutes, or until the nectarines are cooked and the bottom of the shell is well browned. You may need to lay a piece of foil over the top if the pastry browns too quickly on the top.

For the short crust shell, bake at 375°F for about 30 minutes, or until the nectarines are tender.

Cool the puff pastry tart on a rack, the short crust tart in its pan. Brush either one with the heated poaching liquid or apricot jam mixed with the kirsch.

Serve with a little crème Chantilly or Vanilla Ice Cream.

PEACH AND ALMOND STRIPED BAVARIAN

For 8 to 10 servings: *1 recipe Blancmange (page 198) · ¾ pound very ripe, flavorful freestone peaches · 1 tablespoon water · 2 tablespoons sugar, to taste · Optional: a few drops of lemon juice · 1½ teaspoons gelatin · ¼ cup cold water · ½ cup whipping cream · Kirsch · Vanilla extract*

Make the blancmange mixture. Peel the peaches, cut them in half, and remove the pits. Slice thin into a non-corroding saucepan and cook with the water over low heat until cooked through. Purée them in a blender or food processor, or through a fine strainer, then return to the pan and cook over low heat, stirring often, until reduced to 1 cup. Stir in the sugar, and a few drops of lemon juice if the peaches aren't tart enough for you. Strain through a very fine strainer.

166

Sprinkle the gelatin over the cold water in a small pan and let stand 5 minutes. Heat gently to dissolve the gelatin—to between 105°F and 115°F. Don't overheat it. Stir this into the peach purée. Whip the cream until it leaves a very slight shape when some is dropped from the beater. Put the bowl of peach purée over a bowl of ice water and stir constantly with a rubber spatula, carefully scraping the sides of the bowl, until the purée begins to thicken and the spatula leaves a trail in it. Remove from the ice water and quickly whisk into the whipped cream until just mixed. Flavor to taste with a few drops each of kirsch and vanilla.

Lightly oil a 1½-quart mold with sweet almond or other neutral-tasting oil by rubbing it on with a paper towel. Measure out 2 cups of the blancmange mixture and spread evenly into the mold. Chill 10 to 15 minutes, or until just barely firm enough to hold another layer.

Spread 2 cups of the peach bavarian mixture evenly over the first layer and chill again briefly, until set just enough to hold the next layer. If you wait too long to add successive layers they will separate when you unmold the bavarian. Add one more layer of 2 cups of the blancmange and smooth the top. Chill thoroughly.

To unmold, slip a stainless steel knife gently between the bavarian and the mold and run it around the mold to break the vacuum. Set the serving plate on top of the mold and turn both over to let the bavarian slide out onto the serving plate. If it still won't slip out of the mold, lift the mold at one end, slip the knife back in to break the vacuum again, and the bavarian should slide out.

Serve with a few fraises des bois sprinkled around it, or with a little lightly sweetened peach purée.

PEACH COBBLER

For 6 servings: *1¾ pounds firm ripe peaches · 2 tablespoons sugar, to taste · 3 tablespoons flour · ⅔ recipe cobbler dough (page 120) · 2 tablespoons whipping cream*

Wash, peel, and pit the peaches. Slice them thin into a bowl: you should have 3 or 4 cups. Toss with the sugar and flour. Divide among 6 custard cups or individual soufflé dishes, filling each almost to the top. Make the cobbler dough and roll it out ¼-inch to ⅓-inch thick. Cut pieces with a cookie cutter to fit the tops of the baking dishes, leaving ¼ inch of the fruit exposed around the edges. (At the restaurant we have a daisy-shaped cutter that we use, but any cutter that makes a pretty shape will work. You can also cut the dough with a knife.) Set the biscuits on top of the fruit and brush their tops with cream. Bake in the lower third of a preheated 400°F oven for 15 minutes.

Serve with a pitcher of cream to pour over.

To make a Peach and Raspberry Cobbler or a Peach and Blueberry Cobbler: Add about ¾ cup raspberries or blueberries to the peach mixture before tossing with the sugar and flour.

PEACH CRISP

For 6 to 8 servings: *1 recipe crisp topping with pecans or almonds, or without nuts (page 42)* · *4 pounds firm ripe peaches* · *1½ tablespoons flour* · *1 tablespoon sugar, to taste*

Make the crisp topping. Halve, peel, and pit the peaches and cut them into slices about ⅓-inch thick. You should have about 8 cups. Toss them with the flour and the sugar—you will need the sugar only if the peaches are tart. (Remember that the topping is sweet.) Spread the peaches in a 2-quart gratin dish or pie plate and sprinkle evenly with topping. You may not need the full amount; use your own judgment. Bake in a preheated 375°F oven for about 40 minutes, or until the topping is evenly brown and the peach juices bubble thickly around the edges. If the topping is brown before the peaches are cooked through, lay a piece of foil loosely over the top while the crisp finishes baking.

Serve warm with a pitcher of heavy cream to pour over.

168

FRESH PEACH ICE CREAM

Makes a generous quart: *1½ cups whipping cream · ¾ cup sugar · 3 egg yolks · 1 pound very ripe, good-flavored peaches · Vanilla extract to taste*

Make the custard a day ahead so it can chill. Warm the cream and ½ cup of the sugar in a non-corroding saucepan until the sugar dissolves, stirring occasionally. Whisk the egg yolks just enough to mix them and stir in some of the hot cream mixture to heat them. Return to the pan and cook until the custard coats the spoon. Strain into a container and chill.

When you are ready to freeze the ice cream, peel and pit the peaches and cut in thin slices into a bowl. Toss them with the remaining ¼ cup sugar and let stand an hour or so until the sugar is dissolved. Crush the peaches with a potato masher or something that will crush them fine, but don't purée them. You don't want large chunks of peach, which will freeze like pieces of gravel in your ice cream, but you do want tiny pieces of peach, not a smooth purée. You should have about 1½ cups of peaches and juice. Mix this with the custard and add a few drops of vanilla to taste. Freeze according to the directions with your ice cream maker.

This is delicious served with a few Lace Cookies or Langues de Chat.

BABCOCK PEACHES IN ZINFANDEL

For 1 serving: *2¼ tablespoons sugar · ⅜ cup Zinfandel, or other full-bodied fruity red wine · 1 to 1½ ripe Babcock peaches, depending on their size*

Stir the sugar in the wine until dissolved. Pit, peel, and slice the peaches about ⅜-inch thick into the wine. Let stand a few hours and serve in wine glasses with enough wine to cover. Serve with crisp cookies—Langues de Chat or Lace Cookies. This idea came from Judy Rodgers and is one of those perfect marriages, deceptively simple—like fraises des bois in a glass of Zinfandel or Rhone. Such ideas inspire recipes like the following.

ELBERTA PEACHES POACHED IN RED WINE
WITH CINNAMON BASIL

For 6 to 8 servings: *1½ cups water · 1½ cups sugar · 3 cups Zinfandel or other full-bodied fruity red wine · 3 sprigs of cinnamon basil, each having 6 to 8 leaves · 3 pounds ripe Elberta peaches*

You can use other varieties of good-tasting freestone peaches as long as they are ripe and firm fleshed.

Simmer the water, sugar, Zinfandel, and basil in a non-corroding saucepan for 5 minutes. Slice the peaches in half, pit, and peel. Cut them in slices about ¾-inch thick and cook briefly in the wine syrup. This should take no more than 10 minutes if you have ripe peaches—you just want to heat them through.

Chill in their syrup and serve cold with some of the wine syrup, accompanied by Langues de Chat.

PEACH SHERBET

Makes about 1 quart: *1¾ pounds very ripe peaches · 2 tablespoons water · ¾ cup sugar · Lemon juice · Kirsch to taste*

Halve and peel the peaches. Remove the pits, saving two or three of them. Slice the peaches into a non-corroding saucepan. Crack the reserved pits with a hammer or nutcracker and add their kernels to the peaches. Add the water and cook, covered, over low heat, stirring often, until the peaches are heated through—10 to 15 minutes, depending on the variety. Purée the cooked peaches in a blender or food processor and measure. You should have 3 cups of purée. Stir in the sugar until it dissolves, then chill. Flavor with a little lemon juice and a few drops of kirsch to taste. Freeze according to the instructions with your ice cream maker.

Serve alone or in combination with Strawberry, Boysenberry, Blackberry, Raspberry, or Plum Sherbets, or with Bitter Almond or Vanilla Ice Cream, and cookies.

To make Nectarine Sherbet: Follow the above instructions, using 1¾ pounds ripe nectarines, but do not peel them.

170

PEACH TART

For 8 servings: *One 9-inch puff pastry shell (page 25), frozen, or one pre-baked 9-inch short crust shell (page 11) · 1⅛ pounds firm ripe freestone peaches · 1 tablespoon sugar · 2 tablespoons apricot jam or cooked-down fruit poaching liquid · ¼ teaspoon kirsch*

Cut the peaches in half, twist the halves in opposite directions to take them apart, and remove the stones. Peel them and cut in about ⅓-inch slices. Arrange circles of peaches in the short crust tart shell, overlapping them just slightly. Sprinkle with the sugar and bake in a preheated 375°F oven for about 35 minutes, or until the bottom is brown.

If you are using a puff pastry shell, set it on a baking pan or something from which you can slide it to a baking stone before you fill it with the sliced peaches. Bake it in a preheated 400°F oven. Check the tart after 10 minutes and again after another 5 minutes, and prick it if it is rising in the center. If the edges brown too fast, lay a piece of foil loosely over the tart while it finishes baking. Five or 10 minutes after removing the tart from the oven, warm the jam or poaching liquid, add the kirsch, and brush it evenly on the peaches.

Serve warm with Vanilla Ice Cream or crème Chantilly.

ANOTHER PEACH TART

For a 9-inch tart, serving 8: *One 9-inch pre-baked puff pastry (page 25) or short crust (page 11) tart shell · 2 cups water · ½ cup sugar · 1-inch piece of vanilla bean · 1¾ pounds firm ripe freestone peaches · 1 cup frangipane cream (page 7) · A few drops of kirsch · 1 or 2 tablespoons finely chopped toasted almonds or pistachios*

Put the water, sugar, and the scraped vanilla bean into a non-corroding saucepan and bring to a simmer. Meanwhile wash, quarter, and pit the peaches, and add them to the simmering liquid, skin side down. Cover with a round of parchment or a lid, and cook gently at a slight simmer for 10 to 15 minutes, or until the peaches are just cooked through. They should not get mushy. Using a slotted spoon, remove the peaches from the pan to a plate and let them cool. Cover and chill completely. Cook down the remaining syrup until it bubbles thickly and has reached the jellying stage, 220°F. Set aside.

When the peaches are chilled, slip their skins off, cut them into slices about ⅜-inch thick and drain them thoroughly on paper towels. Spread the frangipane cream in the tart shell and arrange the well-drained peach slices on top in circles, overlapping them just slightly. Heat the reduced poaching liquid until thin enough to brush, add a few drops of kirsch, and brush the peaches with it to glaze them. Sprinkle finely chopped almonds or pistachios around the edges and in the center.

This tart is really beautiful because the blush from the skin of the peaches cooks into the flesh when they are poached, giving the slices rosy edges.

PLUM SHERBET BOMBE
WITH GRAND MARNIER MOUSSE

For 10 to 12 servings: *1 quart Santa Rosa Plum Sherbet (page 174) · 1 recipe frozen mousse (page 9) · Grated peel of ⅓ to ½ orange · Grand Marnier to taste · Pinch of white pepper*

Please read about making and serving bombes on page 9. Make the sherbet and have it slightly softened. Chill a 1½-quart to 1¾-quart bombe mold in the freezer; then quickly line the bottom and sides with an even layer of the sherbet, using about two-thirds of it. Freeze this solid. Make the mousse and grate the orange peel into it in shreds as long and fine as possible. Flavor this to taste with Grand Marnier and add a pinch of white pepper. Taste a little of it with a bit of the sherbet to be sure the flavors are in balance, with neither dominating. Fill the bombe to within about an inch of the top with the mousse and freeze. Spread the remaining sherbet evenly over the top and freeze again, covered tightly with plastic and foil until you are ready to serve it.

Serve garnished with sprigs of mint; if you serve individual slices, garnish each with a mint sprig. Accompany with Lace Cookies, Langues de Chat, or crisp Ladyfingers.

172

SANTA ROSA PLUM ICE CREAM

Makes about 1 quart: *¾ pound soft ripe Santa Rosa plums · 1 cup whipping cream · ⅝ cup sugar · 2 egg yolks · Vanilla extract to taste · Optional: kirsch to taste*

Prepare the plum purée as in the sherbet recipe (page 174) and measure out 1¼ cups. Chill. Warm ½ cup of the cream with the sugar in a heavy non-corroding saucepan until the sugar dissolves. Whisk the egg yolks just enough to mix them and pour in a little of the warmed cream mixture, stirring constantly. Return to the pan and cook over low heat, stirring constantly, until the mixture coats the spoon. Strain through a medium-fine strainer into a container. Add the remaining cream and the plum purée and chill thoroughly. Add a few drops each of vanilla and kirsch to taste and freeze according to the directions with your ice cream maker.

PLUM CARAMEL SAUCE

Makes about ⅞ cup sauce: *¾ pound tart flavorful plums (Santa Rosas are very good) · ½ cup plus 2 tablespoons water · ½ cup sugar · Kirsch to taste*

Wash the plums, cut them in half, and pit them. Slice into a non-corroding saucepan, add ¼ cup of the water and cook slowly, stirring occasionally, until they are very tender—15 to 20 minutes. Purée very fine in a blender and set aside.

Put the sugar in a heavy saucepan with the 2 tablespoons water. As soon as the sugar is moistened, cook over high heat, watching carefully and swirling the pan occasionally until the sugar is light golden brown. Remove from the heat and carefully pour another ¼ cup water into the caramel, being very careful that it doesn't spatter you. Cook over medium heat, stirring constantly, until the caramel has dissolved. Add to it the reserved plum purée and cook briefly to blend them. Strain through a very fine strainer, add a few drops of kirsch to taste, and cool or chill.

Serve the sauce either chilled or at room temperature, with crêpes filled with Fresh Peach Ice Cream, or with Baked Stuffed Nectarines, or with Noyau, Bitter Almond, or Vanilla Ice Cream.

SANTA ROSA PLUM SHERBET

Makes about 1 quart: *1⅓ pounds soft ripe Santa Rosa plums · ⅞ cup water · ⅞ cup sugar · Kirsch to taste*

Wash the plums, cut them in half, and pit them. Crack 4 or 5 of the pits and reserve their kernels. Cut the fruit in ½-inch slices into a heavy non-corroding saucepan and add ¼ cup of the water and the reserved kernels. Cook over low to medium heat, stirring often to keep the plums from sticking, until they are tender, about 15 minutes. Purée them through a food mill or in a blender or food processor. The blender will make the smoothest purée, the processor a little chunkier, and the food mill the coarsest. I use the food mill, but you might prefer a smoother sherbet. Measure 2⅓ cups and chill. Boil the sugar with ⅝ cup water for 5 minutes and add to the purée. Chill thoroughly. Freeze according to the instructions with your ice cream maker.

Serve accompanied by crisp cookies, or as part of an assortment of various plum sherbets.

WILD PLUM SHERBET

Makes a scant quart: *About 2½ pounds wild plums · 1 cup water · 1 cup sugar · Kirsch to taste*

Wash the plums and put them in a non-corroding saucepan with ¼ cup of the water. Cook, covered, over medium heat, stirring occasionally, until they are soft. Put them through a food mill and measure 3 cups purée. Boil the remaining ¾ cup water with the sugar for a few minutes. Add to the purée and taste. It may be necessary to add more sugar if you have very tart plums. Before you add extra sugar, boil with a little of the sherbet mixture. Add to the purée and chill thoroughly. Flavor with a few drops of kirsch to taste and freeze according to the directions with your ice cream maker.

Serve as a part of an assortment of sherbets made from different plum varieties. This makes a nice bombe with Vanilla or Bitter Almond Ice Cream and Strawberry or Raspberry Ice Cream.

PLUM TART

For 8 servings: One 9-inch puff pastry tart shell (page 25), chilled or frozen · 1 pound plums (Santa Rosa or other flavorful plums, ripe but firm) · 1½ to 2 tablespoons sugar · 1 to 2 tablespoons raspberry or red currant jam · Kirsch

Heat your oven to 400°F. If you want to bake the tart on a baking stone or brick, preheat it according to the manufacturer's instructions.

Wash and dry the plums, cut them in half and stone them. The fruit will usually come off the pit more easily if you twist the halves in opposite directions as you take them apart. Slice each half into pieces about ⅜-inch thick and set them aside.

Set the frozen tart shell on a lightly floured flat pan if you are baking it on a stone, or on an unfloured baking sheet, preferably a dark one. Arrange the plums in circles in the shell, letting the slices overlap by about ⅛ inch. If you overlap them too much, you will have too many plums in the tart and it will be so juicy that the pastry will get soft. Work quickly so the pastry doesn't soften too much. Sprinkle the tart with the sugar and set the pan in the center of the preheated oven. If you are baking it on a stone, be sure that the pastry is still rigid so you can easily shake it off the pan onto the stone. If it has softened, set it back in the freezer for a few minutes to harden again before slipping it onto the stone.

Bake 35 to 40 minutes, or until the pastry is golden brown on the bottom. If the shell puffs in the center in the first few minutes, prick it with a knife. After the first 15 to 20 minutes the tart should be set. Cover it loosely with a piece of foil if the sides brown before the bottom is done. Remove the tart to a cooling rack. After about 10 minutes, warm the jam, add a few drops of kirsch, and brush the plums with it.

Serve while warm if possible, but the tart will keep very well for at least 2 hours. Serve it with Angelica or Vanilla Ice Cream or with a glass of Sauternes. This is one of the most beautiful tarts we make—rich red plums with their darker skins resting in the golden shell.

8

FIGS,
MELONS,
AND OTHER
FALL FRUITS

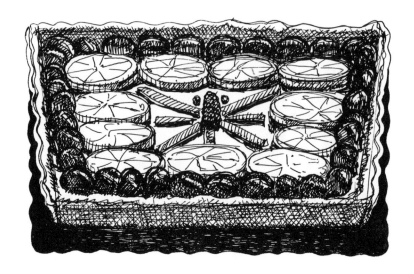

FIGS ARE one of the greatest pleasures of the fall. They are plentiful here, but may be hard to find in some parts of the country because they are next to impossible to ship ripe. A real treat is a mixed platter of halved green and black figs sprinkled with dark red raspberries and bright little dots of fraises des bois. If you have figs that are slightly underripe, try poaching them in a flavored syrup. We often serve whole figs dipped in caramel—much more easily done at home than at the restaurant—with anise or Chartreuse creams. The herbal flavors complement perfectly the sweet muskiness of the figs. Or try serving halved Adriatic figs, with their bright apple-green skins and dark strawberry-red centers, with honey mousse and strawberry purée. Or serve fig tarts warm with lavender honey ice cream. When the figs are too soft for anything else, they make luscious ice cream; they may be too mushy to look nice, but their flavor is at its peak.

178

The first good melons begin to arrive in early fall—the ones that are available in summer are from Central America and are picked green and never ripen properly. Although melons are not as versatile as some other fruits, it is difficult to improve on a slice of perfectly ripe, chilled melon, or half a small Charentais melon, seeded and filled with a little port or Beaumes-de-Venise wine, or heaped with strawberries or fraises des bois. Melons make wonderful sherbets and ice creams to go with the last of the summer berries, especially the Cranshaws with their spicy-floral scent—nothing is more refreshing on a hot Indian summer day. When there are many different melons to be had, it is fun to serve a plate of sherbets made from four or five different varieties, with their subtle differences in flavor, aroma, color, and even texture.

During the wine grape harvest in September and October, we serve sherbet plates with grape garnishes, and once or twice in the short season it is possible to make sherbets and ice creams from the grapes themselves. The colors are soft beige-greens and pale lavenders, depending on the grapes, and together they present a beautiful combination of muted fall pastels. In California, we use Cabernet, Zinfandel, Chardonnay, and other premium wine varietals along with the traditional American Concords. Any distinctively flavored variety available to you is worth trying—there are many we never see in California, like the Catawbas and Scuppernongs.

Rhubarb, a traditional American plant, comes from hothouses in the fall, just in time to have something red to use for tarts when it seems everything is apples, oranges, or lemons. Soft-ripe persimmons are another treat at this time of year. Served chilled and cut so they fall open like flowers, and sprinkled with a little kirsch, they make a beautiful simple dessert for an autumn meal. Warm glossy brown persimmon pudding needs nothing more than a drift of crème Chantilly to satisfy utterly. The tiny native American persimmons are not available in the Bay Area, but they are said to have an even better flavor than the Oriental varieties.

The climax of autumn is Thanksgiving, made special with its cranberries, pumpkins, and pomegranates. It is a chance to make really substantial yet festive desserts that link the farms and gardens to the kitchen. Over the years, as we have come to understand this link, the fall desserts at the restaurant have become less European and more American. A few years ago we would never have served pumpkin pie; now it is one of our best-loved desserts.

FIGS AND RASPBERRIES WITH ANISE CREAM

For 8 to 10 servings: *2 pounds figs (or enough to arrange on your platter) · 1 or 2 half-pint baskets raspberries · About 1 cup whipping cream · Sugar to taste · A few drops Pernod, to taste*

If the figs are dusty, wipe them with a clean towel and cut off the tough tips of the stem ends. Slice them in half through the stem end and arrange them on the platter. Overlap each fig and each row slightly so the design looks like a large flower. Leave an opening in the center and fill that with a pile of raspberries, sprinkling a few more over the figs. Whip the cream until it just barely holds a shape and sprinkle in sugar and a few drops of Pernod to taste. Be careful: a little Pernod goes a long way.

Serve immediately with a small bowl of the cream on the side and some crisp cookies.

FRESH FIGS WITH BEAUMES-DE-VENISE
ICE CREAM AND PEACH CARAMEL SAUCE

For 6 servings: *¾ pound very ripe peaches · 1-inch piece of vanilla bean · 6 to 7 tablespoons water · 4 tablespoons sugar · Kirsch to taste · 9 large, very ripe figs · 1 recipe Beaumes-de-Venise Ice Cream (page 252)*

For the sauce: Slice the peaches in half, pit, and peel. Slice thin into a heavy non-corroding saucepan, add the vanilla bean and 1 tablespoon of the water, and cook over low heat, stirring often, until the peach slices have cooked through. Remove the vanilla bean, purée the peaches, and set aside. Put the sugar in a small heavy saucepan with 1 tablespoon water. Let stand until moistened and cook quickly until the sugar is pale gold. Carefully add 4 tablespoons water and cook over medium heat to dissolve

180

the caramel. Pour into the purée, then strain the sauce through a very fine strainer. Chill a drop in the freezer to check its consistency; if it is too thick, add another tablespoon of water. If too thin, cook a little longer. The sauce should be the consistency of a light syrup. Taste and add a few drops of kirsch to heighten the peach flavor. Cool to room temperature.

To serve the figs: Cut the tough ends from the stems and slice the figs in half through the stem end. Arrange three halves on one side of each plate. On the other side put two ovals of the ice cream, shaped with a soup spoon, and pour a little of the sauce over and around the ice cream. Serve with Lace Cookies.

You may substitute Lavender Honey Ice Cream, Frozen Caramel Mousse, or Honey Mousse for the Beaumes-de-Venise Ice Cream in this recipe.

FIGS IN CARAMEL

For 6 to 8 servings: *1¼ pounds figs (a mixture of green and black figs makes a nice arrangement; use more or less according to the number of people to be served)* · *1½ cups sugar* · *½ cup water* · *¼ teaspoon lemon juice* · *⅔ cup whipping cream* · *Sugar and Pernod or Chartreuse to taste*

Have the figs at room temperature—if they are cold they will sweat as they warm and dissolve the caramel too quickly. Cut off the tough stem ends. Put the sugar, water, and lemon juice in a heavy, light-colored saucepan and let stand until all the sugar is moistened. Cook over medium to high heat, occasionally swirling the pan gently so the sugar colors evenly. Butter a fork and lightly butter a serving plate on which to arrange the figs.

When the caramel is light golden brown, remove it from the heat and quickly dip the figs in one by one, rolling them with the buttered fork to coat them with the caramel. Dip the figs as fast as you can because as the caramel in the pan cools it will thicken and make a very unpleasant coating for the fruit. Remove the figs quickly to the buttered plate. Arrange them as you set them on the plate—you won't be able to move them easily once the caramel hardens. If you work fast and reheat the caramel once or twice to thin it, you will get a fine, crisp coating that will usually last at least a couple of hours if the air is dry. On damp days, coat the figs just before serving them.

Whip the cream until it just begins to hold a shape and flavor with sugar and Pernod or Chartreuse to taste—Pernod is very strong, so you will need only a few drops of it. Serve the figs with some of the cream on the side.

FIG ICE CREAM

Makes 1 quart: *1 pound very ripe figs · 3 tablespoons water · 1½ cups whipping cream · ½ cup plus 1 tablespoon sugar · 3 egg yolks · Vanilla to taste · Optional: Cognac or brandy to taste*

Wash the figs, cut off the stem ends, and cut in quarters into a non-corroding saucepan. Add the water and cook slowly until very tender, about 20 minutes, stirring often. The cooking time will depend on the variety of fig you are using and how thick the skin is. Coarsely chop the figs in a food processor, or put them through a food mill, or crush well with a potato masher. Warm 1 cup of the cream with the sugar in a non-corroding saucepan, stirring occasionally, until the sugar has dissolved. Whisk the egg yolks just enough to mix them and whisk in some of the hot cream mixture to warm them. Return to the pan and cook over low heat, stirring constantly, until the custard coats the spoon. Strain through a medium-fine strainer into a container. Add the remaining cream and 1½ cups of the fig purée. Flavor to taste with a few drops each of vanilla and Cognac or brandy. Chill thoroughly. Freeze according to the instructions with your ice cream maker.

Serve with Langues de Chat, Lace Cookies, or Walnut Drops. I have used both black and white figs for this recipe; each seems to work equally well.

FIGS POACHED IN RED WINE
AND CINNAMON BASIL

For 6 to 8 servings: *1 cup sugar · 1 cup water · 2 cups Zinfandel or other full-bodied fruity red wine · 4 sprigs cinnamon basil (with a flower head and 4 to 6 leaves on each sprig) · 1½ pounds small Kadota or Black Mission figs*

Heat the sugar, water, wine, and basil in a non-corroding saucepan and simmer 5 minutes. Rinse the figs if they seem dusty, and cut off the tough tips of the stems. Add to the poaching liquid and simmer about 10 minutes. Chill in the poaching liquid and serve cold with a little cream to pour on, or with crème fraîche.

STEAMED FIG PUDDING

For 6 to 8 servings: *1 cup chopped dried figs (about 5 ounces) · 2 tablespoons Cognac · ¾ cup milk · ¼ cup unblanched whole almonds · 1 cup finely ground suet (3½ ounces) · ½ cup sugar · 1 egg · 1 cup fresh bread crumbs · 2 teaspoons finely chopped candied orange peel, or 1 teaspoon grated orange rind · 1 cup flour · 1 teaspoon baking powder · ¼ teaspoon salt · ½ teaspoon nutmeg · ½ teaspoon cinnamon*

Use moist dried figs for this recipe. They should be pliable when squeezed.

Chop the figs in ⅓-inch to ½-inch pieces and put them in a non-corroding saucepan with the Cognac. Cover and heat over low heat until the Cognac is absorbed. Add the milk and continue cooking, stirring often, until the mixture is thick but still moist and the figs are tender. Add a little more milk, if necessary. Set aside to cool. Toast the almonds in a preheated 350°F oven for 6 to 8 minutes, or until they smell nutty. Cool and chop them coarse. Grind the cold suet in a food processor, or grate it, or put it through the fine blade of a meat grinder. Cream it with the sugar and beat in the egg well. Beat in the bread crumbs and the orange peel. Stir in the almonds. Mix the flour, baking powder, salt, nutmeg, and cinnamon. Stir into the suet mixture alternately with the cooled figs. The mixture will be quite heavy; be sure to mix it thoroughly. Butter well a 5-cup pudding mold and the inside of its lid and fill it with the pudding. Smooth the top, cover the mold, and set on a rack in a deep pot. Fill halfway up the sides of the mold with boiling water, cover, and steam for 2 hours, keeping the water at a simmer. Cool about 20 minutes and unmold.

Serve the pudding warm, accompanied by Hard Sauce. You might flavor the Hard Sauce with a little Pernod rather than brandy if you want to be untraditional—or make brandy butter using the same proportions as for Hard Sauce, but substituting brown sugar for powdered sugar.

FIG TART

For 8 servings: *One 9-inch puff pastry tart shell (page 25)* · *1½ to 2 pounds very ripe Black Mission figs* · *1 egg yolk* · *2 teaspoons milk or cream* · *1 tablespoon unsalted butter, melted* · *1 teaspoon sugar* · *About 2 tablespoons honey to glaze the tart*

Have the tart shell frozen so that it will be easier to work with. Cut the stem ends off the figs—just the tough parts—and slice the figs in half lengthwise. Remove the tart shell from the freezer and brush the edge with a glaze made from the egg yolk lightly beaten with the milk or cream. Put it on a baking sheet—a pizza pan works well—and arrange the fig halves in it, slightly overlapping, cut side up and pointed ends to the center. Brush the tops of the figs with the melted butter and sprinkle them lightly with sugar.

Bake in a preheated 400°F oven for about 35 minutes, or until the bottom is thoroughly browned and the figs are cooked through. If the sides of the tart brown too quickly, lay a piece of foil loosely over it while it finishes baking. Remove from the oven and cool on a rack. Bring the honey to a boil and cool it until it thickens slightly. Brush the figs with it 5 or 10 minutes after removing the tart from the oven. You can also glaze the tart with fruit poaching syrup that has been cooked down until slightly thick, or with apricot jam flavored with a few drops of kirsch and Grand Marnier. It depends on the flavor you want.

This tart tastes good with honey and served with Beaumes-de-Venise Ice Cream with fraises des bois sprinkled on top. It would also be good with Anise Ice Cream or Lavender Honey Ice Cream and a few raspberries.

ANOTHER FIG TART

For 8 servings: *One 9-inch short crust tart shell (page 11) · 1½ to 2 pounds ripe figs · 1 teaspoon sugar · 2 tablespoons apricot jam · A few drops each of kirsch and Grand Marnier*

Bake the tart shell in a preheated 350°F oven until evenly golden brown and cooked through. Meanwhile, cut off the tough ends from the stems of the figs. Peel the figs—the peel should pull off easily if the figs are ripe; if they are thick-skinned green figs, you will have to cut the peel off. Slice the figs in half and overlap them in the cooled shell as in the preceding recipe. Sprinkle them lightly with the sugar and bake the tart in the 350°F oven until the figs are cooked through and juicing a little—about 30 minutes.

Cool the tart on a rack. In 5 or 10 minutes, warm the jam and add the liqueurs to it. Brush the figs with the glaze, and serve the tart warm with a little crème Chantilly.

CHARENTAIS MELON ICE CREAM

Makes a scant quart: *2 to 2½ pounds ripe Charentais melons · ¾ cup sugar · 1¼ cups whipping cream · A few drops of kirsch or a little Beaumes-de-Venise wine*

Cut the melons open and scoop out all the seeds. Scoop out the flesh with a stainless steel spoon. Be sure to taste the melon when you get close to the rind to make sure you use only the sweet ripe part. Purée the melon in a blender or food processor. You should have 1¾ cups of purée. Warm the sugar in ¾ cup of the cream until it is dissolved and mix it with the melon purée, the remaining cream, and a few drops of kirsch or the wine, if you like. Chill, then taste again and adjust the flavoring if necessary. Freeze according to the instructions with your ice cream maker.

Flavorful ripe cantaloupes or similar melons work well for this ice cream, too.

Serve garnished with strawberries or fraises des bois.

CHARENTAIS MELON
WITH BEAUMES-DE-VENISE SABAYON

For about 1½ cups sabayon: *3 egg yolks · 2 tablespoons sugar · ⅓ cup Beaumes-de-Venise wine · ⅔ cup whipping cream · Chilled melons (allow 1 melon for 2 to 4 persons) · Optional: a few strawberries or fraises des bois*

Heat water to simmering in the bottom of a double boiler or in a pan on which you can set a copper bowl or a stainless steel mixing bowl. Whisk together the egg yolks and sugar in the bowl or the top of the double boiler, and whisk in the wine. Set this over the simmering water and whisk it constantly until it holds a shape for 3 seconds when you drop some from the whisk. Remove from the heat and chill, either over an ice bath or in the refrigerator, whisking occasionally. When cold, whip the cream until it just begins to hold a shape and fold it into the sabayon. Chill.

Cut the melons in half and seed them. Slice them, cut off their skins, and arrange them nicely on a serving platter. Wash, hull, and dry the strawberries and scatter them over the melon slices. Slice the strawberries if they are large.

Serve very cold with the sabayon to spoon over.

CRANSHAW MELON SHERBET

Makes about 1 quart: *3 pounds ripe sweet Cranshaw melon (or any ripe flavorful melon) · ⅞ cup sugar · A few drops of kirsch or Beaumes-de-Venise wine*

Cut the melon open and scoop out the seeds with a stainless steel spoon. Scoop out the flesh, being careful not to cut too close to the rind—you want only the best, sweetest part. Purée in a blender or food processor, or through a food mill, and measure out 4 cups. Put about 1 cup of the purée in a heavy non-corroding saucepan with the sugar and heat, stirring constantly, until the sugar is dissolved. Pour this into the remaining melon purée, flavor with the kirsch or wine, and chill. Freeze according to the instructions with your ice cream maker.

FALL FRUIT COMPOTE

For 4 to 6 servings: *1 cup water · ½ cup sugar · ½-inch piece of vanilla bean · 1 quince (about 10 ounces) · 2 cups water · ⅔ cup sugar · 1 strip lemon zest · 1 pound firm ripe Bosc pears · 10 ounces ripe figs, black or green · ¼ to ⅓ half-pint basket raspberries · Lemon juice to taste*

Poach the quince first: Make a syrup of the 1 cup water, ½ cup sugar, and vanilla bean in a non-corroding saucepan. Quarter, core, and peel the quince, cut it into ½-inch slices, and add it to the syrup. Bring to a simmer, cover, and let cook, barely simmering, for about 2½ hours, until the slices are a deep rose color. Don't stir: instead, push them gently under the liquid from time to time so the slices don't break up. When cooked, chill the quince slices in their poaching liquid.

Poach the pears: Make a syrup of the 2 cups water, ⅔ cup sugar, and the strip of lemon zest. Halve, peel, and core the pears. Put them into the simmering syrup and cook, barely simmering and covered, for 20 to 30 minutes, or until they are tender and translucent but not falling apart. Chill them in all but 1 cup of their syrup.

Poach the figs: Take 1 cup of the syrup the pears were poached in and heat it to a simmer. Rinse the figs, cut off any tough tips from their stem ends, add to the syrup, and again barely simmer for 10 to 12 minutes, or until they are heated through. Then chill the figs in their syrup.

When you are ready to serve the compote, slice the pears lengthwise into pieces about ⅓-inch thick and arrange a layer in the bottom of a pretty serving bowl. Make a layer of quince slices and sprinkle it with a few raspberries. Slice the figs in half lengthwise and arrange them over the other fruit. Repeat the layering until you have used all the fruit. Try to arrange it in open layers so you can see all the different fruits at once. Add enough of the quince syrup to the pear syrup to turn it pale pink and add lemon juice to taste. Pour some of the syrup over the fruit and serve cold.

This needs nothing but some simple plain cookies or Walnut Drops. The colors are beautiful, with white pear slices, deep rose-colored quinces, red raspberries, and dark or green fig halves. The tart raspberries make a nice counterpoint to the sweet poached fruits. If you have been drinking

Zinfandel or a spicy Rhone or Provencal wine with dinner, this dessert
will help integrate the flavors of the entire meal.

CRANBERRY ICE CREAM

Makes 1 quart: *One 12-ounce package cranberries · ¼ cup water · 2¾ cups
whipping cream · 1 cup sugar · A few drops of vanilla extract*

Pick over the cranberries, removing any soft or spoiled berries, and rinse
them. Put in a non-corroding saucepan with the water and cook, covered,
stirring occasionally, for about 10 minutes, or until the berries are soft.
Purée through a food mill and strain to remove the seeds. Measure 1¼
cups. Warm the cream with the sugar, stirring occasionally, until the
sugar has dissolved. Whisk the purée into the cream mixture and chill.
Add a few drops of vanilla to taste and freeze according to the instructions
with your ice cream maker.

   Serve as part of an assortment of Thanksgiving or Christmas desserts
or with crisp cookies.

CRANBERRY SHERBET

Makes 1 quart: *Two 12-ounce packages cranberries · 2½ cups water · 1 cup
sugar · 1 or 2 teaspoons kirsch, to taste*

Pick over the cranberries, removing any soft or spoiled berries, and rinse
them. Put in a non-corroding saucepan with ½ cup of the water and cook,
covered, stirring occasionally, for about 10 minutes, or until the berries
are soft. Purée through a food mill and strain to remove the seeds. Measure
2 cups. Boil the remaining 2 cups water with the sugar for a few minutes.
Cool slightly and stir in the purée. Chill. Flavor with kirsch and freeze
according to the instructions with your ice cream maker.

   Serve as a bombe, filling the center with frozen mousse flavored with
Grand Marnier, or layering with Tangerine and Champagne sherbets. Or
serve the sherbet alone between the courses of Thanksgiving dinner as a
refresher.

MUSCAT GRAPE SHERBET

Makes about 1 quart: *3½ pounds ripe Muscat grapes · ½ cup water · 3 tablespoons sugar · 1⅓ tablespoons corn syrup*

Wash the grapes and pull off the stems. Put the grapes with the water in a non-corroding saucepan, cover, and cook over medium heat, stirring occasionally, for about 15 minutes, or until they are tender and juicy. Purée them through a food mill, then put them through a very fine strainer to remove any bits of seed that might have gone through the mill. Measure 4 cups, add the sugar and corn syrup, and stir until dissolved. Chill. Freeze according to the instructions with your ice cream maker.

Serve with other grape sherbets or with crisp cookies. We usually serve this with two other sherbets, choosing from Zinfandel, Chardonnay, Riesling, or Concord grapes.

WINE GRAPE SHERBET

Makes 1 quart: *4 pounds Riesling, Zinfandel, or Chardonnay grapes · ¼ cup water · 2 tablespoons corn syrup · 1 tablespoon sugar*

Wash the grapes and pull them off their stems. Put them in a non-corroding saucepan with the water. Cook, covered, over medium heat, until the grapes are soft and have released their juices. Put them through a food mill, being careful not to break the seeds or push them through. Strain through a fine strainer and measure 4 cups. While the grape juice is hot, stir in the corn syrup and the sugar until the sugar dissolves. Chill thoroughly. Freeze according to the instructions with your ice cream maker.

Serve sherbets singly or as part of an assortment of wine grape sherbets and ice creams. Accompany with Bow Ties or Walnut Drops.

PERSIMMON PUDDING

For one 8-inch or 9-inch pudding: *About 1½ pounds persimmons · 1¼ cups flour · ⅛ teaspoon salt · ¾ teaspoon baking soda · ¾ teaspoon baking powder · 1 teaspoon cinnamon · ¾ cup sugar · 3 eggs · 1½ cups milk · ¼ cup whipping cream · 1 tablespoon honey · 1 cup walnuts or mixed walnuts and black walnuts · 6 tablespoons unsalted butter*

The persimmons should be completely soft when they are ripe, and the flesh should look translucent and a little like jelly. Scrape the pulp off the peel and put through a strainer, or purée in a blender or food processor. Mix the flour, salt, baking soda, baking powder, and cinnamon in a large mixing bowl. Combine the persimmon pulp, sugar, eggs, milk, cream, and honey. Gradually stir the liquid mixture into the flour mixture. It will be thin at first but will thicken quickly. Let the batter stand to thicken.

Lightly toast the walnuts 5 to 6 minutes in a preheated 350°F oven; then let them cool. Butter an 8-inch or 9-inch springform pan and line the bottom with baking parchment. Melt the butter, let it cool slightly while you chop the nuts coarse, then stir both butter and nuts into the batter. Pour into the prepared pan and bake in the 350°F oven for 2 to 3 hours, or until the pudding is set. Remove from the pan while warm. The top will be a dark glossy brown and needs no embellishment other than a pretty plate or tray.

Serve warm with crème Chantilly. This pudding is meant to taste like persimmons, so I have left out such things as liquor-soaked raisins. You may add them if you wish.

PUMPKIN PIE

For one 9-inch pie: *One 9-inch pre-baked pie shell (page 23)* · *1½ cups pumpkin purée* · *¼ cup light brown sugar* · *1½ teaspoons granulated sugar, to taste* · *1 teaspoon cinnamon* · *¾ teaspoon ground ginger* · *⅛ teaspoon ground cloves* · *⅛ teaspoon or a few grinds white pepper* · *2 teaspoons brandy* · *3 eggs* · *1 egg yolk* · *1 cup half-and-half*

To prepare the pumpkin filling: Split a small pumpkin in half, scoop out its seeds, and lay it cut sides down on a baking sheet with sides. Bake in a preheated 325°F oven for 1 hour, or until it is soft. Scoop the flesh from the skin and purée in a food processor, food mill, or ricer. Measure 1½ cups into a bowl. Whisk in the sugars, spices, and brandy. Whisk in the eggs, egg yolk, and half-and-half. Taste for sweetness because some varieties of pumpkin are sweeter than others—I usually use Sugar Pumpkins, which are both sweet and flavorful. Also, if you are serving the pie with Hard Sauce, you will want it to be less sweet.

Pour into the pre-baked shell and bake in the middle of a preheated 350°F oven for about 45 minutes, or until a knife inserted in the filling halfway between the edge and the center of the pie comes out clean. The custard will finish cooking in the center from its own heat after it comes out of the oven.

Serve warm with brandy or bourbon Hard Sauce, or cool with crème Chantilly. You may also decorate the pie with pecan halves laid on top after the first 20 minutes of baking. This is one of my very favorite pies of all.

RHUBARB CRISP

For 6 to 8 servings: *½ cup walnuts* · *⅞ cup flour* · *⅓ cup brown sugar* · *4 teaspoons granulated sugar* · *⅛ teaspoon cinnamon* · *⅓ cup softened salted butter* · *1½ to 2 pounds rhubarb* · *Optional: ½ pint ripe strawberries* · *¾ cup sugar* · *3 tablespoons flour*

Toast the walnuts in a preheated 375°F oven for 4 to 6 minutes, or until they smell nutty, then cool them. Chop in the food processor, or by hand, into coarse ¼-inch chunks—if they are larger they will stick out of the topping and burn.

Make the topping: Mix the flour, sugars, and cinnamon, and work in the butter until the mixture begins to hold together and look crumbly. Add the walnuts. Wash the rhubarb and cut off the leaves and any brown tips. Cut into ½-inch-thick slices and measure out 6 to 7 cups. You may wish to add about half a pint basket of ripe strawberries, washed, hulled, and sliced, to the rhubarb. Toss the fruit with the ¾ cup sugar and 3 tablespoons flour and let stand until slightly moistened. Pile into a 9-inch pie plate or a gratin dish and smooth the top. Sprinkle with an even layer of the topping. Bake in preheated 375°F oven for 45 minutes, or until the juices bubble thick around the edges, and the rhubarb is tender and the top is golden brown. If the top browns too quickly, lay a sheet of foil over it while it finishes baking. You may make the crisp a few hours ahead and put it in the oven to bake just as you sit down to dinner.

Serve warm with thick cream to pour over each serving, or with crème Chantilly or Vanilla Ice Cream.

RHUBARB AND STRAWBERRY PIE

For 8 servings: *Pastry for a 2-crust 9-inch pie (page 23) · 1¼ pounds rhubarb · 1 pint basket strawberries · 2½ tablespoons flour · ⅔ to 1 cup sugar · 1 egg yolk · 2 teaspoons milk or whipping cream*

Roll out the pastry, line the pan with it, and chill. Roll out the top and chill it on a baking sheet while you make the filling. Wash the rhubarb, cut off the ends, cut in slices about ⅓-inch thick, and measure out about 3¾ cups. Wash, dry, and hull the strawberries and chop them medium fine. Add them to the rhubarb and toss with the flour and sugar. Use the smaller amount of sugar if you are serving the pie with ice cream or if you like the flavor tart.

Fill the chilled bottom shell with the rhubarb-strawberry mixture, brush the edge of the shell with cold water, and lay the chilled top over it. When the top crust is pliable, press it lightly around the edge to seal; then trim it about ½ inch beyond the edge of the bottom crust. Fold it under the

192

edge of the bottom crust and make a fluted edge. Beat the egg yolk and milk or cream with a fork and brush it on top of the pie. Prick the top with a fork in several places, or cut a decorative design in the top, using the tip of a paring knife and cutting halfway through the crust, or about ¹⁄₁₆-inch deep. Pierce the pastry in a few places to allow steam to escape.

Bake in a preheated 400°F oven about 1 hour, or until the crust is golden and the rhubarb is tender. Allow to cool for an hour. Serve warm with Vanilla Ice Cream.

RHUBARB SHERBET

Makes a scant quart: *1½ pounds rhubarb · ¾ cup water · 2 cups sugar · Kirsch to taste*

Chop the rhubarb fine with ½ cup of the water in a food processor, or by hand with a stainless steel knife. Cook the chopped rhubarb with ½ cup water and sugar in a non-corroding saucepan, stirring often, until tender—15 to 30 minutes. When tender, add the remaining ¼ cup water and kirsch to taste, and chill thoroughly. Freeze according to the instructions with your ice cream maker.

Serve as part of a plate of assorted sherbets, such as Pineapple and Strawberry sherbets, accompanied by crisp cookies. This is also good between courses of a complicated dinner.

RHUBARB AND STRAWBERRY SHERBET

Makes about 1 quart: *1½ pounds rhubarb · ¼ cup water · 2 cups sugar · 1 pint basket strawberries · Kirsch to taste*

Chop the rhubarb as fine as possible, either in a food processor (with the water) or by hand with a stainless steel knife. Put the chopped rhubarb and water in a non-corroding saucepan and cook it over low to medium heat, stirring often, for 15 to 30 minutes, or until very tender. Purée it in a food processor or a blender, or put through a fine strainer. You should have 2 cups of purée. Add the sugar while the purée is still hot. Stir until

193

the sugar has dissolved and then refrigerate it. Wash, dry, and hull the strawberries. Purée them and measure 1 cup. Stir this into the rhubarb mixture. Chill thoroughly; then add a little kirsch to taste. Freeze according to the directions with your ice cream maker.

Serve with a little sweetened strawberry purée drizzled over, or in combination with Vanilla Ice Cream garnished with strawberries.

RHUBARB TART

For one 9-inch tart: *One 9-inch short crust tart shell (page 11) · About 2 pounds rhubarb · 1 cup sugar · Kirsch or Grand Marnier · Crème Chantilly*

Bake the tart shell and cool it. Make the rhubarb filling: Wash rhubarb, cut off any leaves, and trim away any dry or brown spots. Stack a handful of stalks together and slice the rhubarb into ⅓-inch to ½-inch slices with a stainless steel knife. Put them into a non-corroding saucepan with the sugar and cook, covered, over medium heat for 10 to 15 minutes, or until tender. Remove the lid, turn the heat up high and cook, stirring constantly, until you have a thick purée that will hold a shape when cool. Test the consistency by dropping a bit of the purée onto a plate that has been chilled in the freezer. Cool and add a little kirsch or Grand Marnier to taste.

When you are ready to serve the tart, spread the filling in the shell. Pipe rosettes of crème Chantilly in rings over the top of the filling. Leave a small circle of the filling uncovered in the center. This makes a very pretty pink and white tart.

This is a variation of a Patricia Lenz recipe which appeared in *Cuisine* magazine (February 1983) and quickly became a favorite at the restaurant.

Two kinds of rhubarb are generally available in the stores. The one that appears earlier in the fall and winter is usually hothouse rhubarb; it has soft, coral pink, satiny-looking stalks. The field-grown rhubarb arrives in the spring; it has dark red stalks that are usually stringier. If you use field-grown rhubarb you might want to purée half of it in your food processor or blender after you have cooked it until tender but before the final cooking. I usually purée only half of it because I like the filling to have some texture.

194

9

NUTS AND
DRIED FRUITS

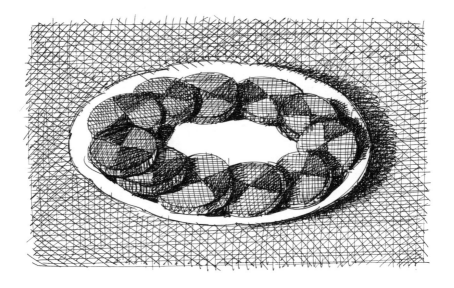

FIGS HAVE been dried in the same way for thousands of years—they fall from the tree and dry naturally. The Romans ate them with bread, instead of butter. They also ate Agen prunes, the most widely grown variety in both France and California to this day. Provençal tradition requires that figs be on the table at the beginning of the meal and that they be consumed first. At the restaurant we make rich and colorful compotes of dried fruits in the winter, sometimes poaching them in wine and spices as was done in the Middle Ages, and sometimes with raspberry purée added to the poaching liquid to give them a lighter, fresher fruitiness. We use not only prunes and figs, but also apricots, pears, raisins, and currants. Dried fruits are very versatile; they can be made into ice creams or fillings for a tart or a dartois. I still remember a prune tart that I was served in a small town in France in the Auvergne—nothing but a delicious prune purée in a yeast-raised pastry shell.

The nut harvest comes in the fall as the weather turns damp and cold and people are ready to eat rich nut tarts and butterscotch pecan pies. But nuts lend themselves to delicacy as well. Lace Cookies made with almonds are an old standby as the perfect accompaniment to almost any ice cream, mousse, or sherbet. And walnut or hazelnut cookies seem the perfect foil to desserts made of autumn pears and apples.

Sometimes it is important to make just the right dessert to accompany a fine old Sauternes—a powerful and complex wine that clashes with chocolate or citrus fruit, for example. Almond blancmanges suit the moment perfectly, but when the wine is younger and less demanding, blancmanges can be made with hazelnuts or walnuts. Our blancmange has been reduced to its essence: almond milk, made with a few bitter almonds, and sugar. It is an aromatic dessert with a taste that stays in the mouth admirably after the last bite is gone.

The bitter almond provides the characteristic flavor of marzipan and almond paste. Diners at Chez Panisse seem to have an insatiable appetite for new, unusual delights, and they have suddenly taken up the bitter almond, which we use in ice creams and macaroons as well as blancmanges. Perhaps the fascination lies in their purported danger: the bitter flavor is from small amounts of prussic acid.

Wild nuts usually have a more distinctive flavor than cultivated ones, and one variety or another grows in every part of the country. Native black walnuts have an unusual flavor that is not appreciated by everyone, a little like that of a good cheese; but they make inimitable ice creams and cakes. Black walnut trees grow wild along the Russian River where I grew up, doubtless springing from nuts that are carried by the river every fall. My father still finds sources of them for the restaurant. Look for hazelnuts and other old-fashioned nuts such as beechnuts, butternuts, and hickories—they grow wild in many parts of the country. Wild Missouri pecans and hickory nuts are a rare treat when they are available, still the best-tasting nuts of the pecan family that I have eaten.

197

BLANCMANGE

Makes 1 quart, for 4 to 8 servings: *2 cups (8 ounces) unblanched almonds and a few bitter almonds, if you have them · 1 cup half-and-half · 1 cup water · 1 tablespoon gelatin · 1⅜ cups whipping cream · ¼ cup sugar · A pinch of salt · Optional: a few drops of almond extract*

Toast the almonds (and the bitter almonds) in a preheated 375°F oven for about 6 minutes, or until they smell nutty. Grind them very fine in a blender or food processor and gradually add the half-and-half along with ½ cup of the water. You should have a rather thick gruel.

Dampen the center of a very sturdy kitchen towel with cold water and wring it out well. Set a strainer over a mixing bowl and center the wet part of the towel in the strainer. Pour in about 1 cup of the almond mixture, twist the towel closed over the top, and squeeze out as much almond milk as you can into the bowl. Empty the dry almond mixture from the towel and repeat the process until you have squeezed all of the mixture. This should give you about 1⅛ cups of almond milk. Be sure to use a very stout towel when squeezing the almond milk—it is very demoralizing to have to start squeezing all over again when the nuts break through a weak towel into all the milk you have laboriously produced. The squeezing can be left to a strong assistant who wants to lend a hand.

Sprinkle the gelatin over the remaining ½ cup water in a small saucepan and let stand 5 minutes. Whip the cream until it holds a slight shape when some is dropped from the beater. Warm the gelatin mixture over low heat, stirring, until completely dissolved. Add the sugar and a pinch of salt and stir until that has dissolved. Stir the gelatin-sugar mixture into the almond milk and set it over an ice water bath. Stir constantly with a rubber spatula, scraping the bottom and sides to keep the mixture from jelling there first, until the mixture coats your spatula thickly. Remove from the ice water and immediately and quickly fold the almond mixture into the whipped cream. Taste the blancmange and add a few drops of almond extract if necessary to bring out the almond flavor.

Oil a 1-quart mold very lightly with sweet almond oil or other flavorless oil by rubbing it on with a paper towel. Pour the mixture into the mold and chill for several hours, or until completely set.

To serve: Loosen one edge gently with the tip of a silver knife, set a plate on top of the mold, and invert. If the dessert won't come loose, lift one corner of the mold away from the plate and loosen one edge of the blancmange with the knife; it will usually slide out then. This is perfect with a glass of Sauternes.

AUNT VICTORIA'S BISCOTTI

For 4½ dozen cookies, 2½ inches long: *½ cup (2 ounces) whole unblanched almonds · ½ cup unsalted butter · ¾ cup sugar · 2 eggs · 1 tablespoon plus 1 teaspoon grappa · 1 teaspoon anise extract · 1 teaspoon aniseed · 2 cups plus 2 tablespoons flour · 1½ teaspoons baking powder · ¼ teaspoon salt*

Toast the almonds in a preheated 350°F oven for a few minutes until they smell nutty. Cool them and chop by hand into ¼-inch chunks. Cream the butter until fluffy and add the sugar. Cream again until fluffy and beat in the eggs until the mixture is smooth. Beat in the grappa, anise extract, and aniseed. Mix the flour, baking powder, and salt and beat them in just until mixed. Stir in the chopped almonds.

On a lightly floured board, make sausagelike rolls of the dough an inch or so in diameter and the length of your baking sheet. Set them on the baking sheet about 2 inches apart and bake in the top third of a preheated 325°F oven for about 25 minutes, or until they are set and lightly browned on top. Cool the rolls on a rack for 5 minutes or so; then slice them diagonally about ½-inch thick.

Lay the slices back on the baking sheets and return to the oven for 5 minutes to dry them. Turn the slices and dry for another 5 minutes. Cool on a rack and store in a tightly covered container, where they will keep for months.

Biscotti—the word means "cooked again," and is the same word as "biscuit"—are wonderful served with a cup of coffee and a glass of grappa. They are even better dipped in the fruity red wine you may have had for dinner. My 85-year-old Italian aunt Victoria still makes these for all the relatives; everyone brings back a couple of coffee cans full from visits to Seattle.

The almonds are my addition to her recipe. You can make these cookies larger or smaller simply by changing the size of the roll and altering the baking times accordingly.

LACE COOKIES

For twenty 3-inch cookies: *¼ cup (1 ounce) whole unblanched almonds · ¼ cup unsalted butter · ¼ cup sugar · 1 tablespoon whipping cream · 1½ teaspoons flour · A few drops of vanilla extract · A pinch of salt · Baking parchment to line the baking sheet*

Chop the almonds very fine, preferably by hand. Shake them in a strainer to remove any dust before measuring. Put the nuts in a small, heavy non-corroding saucepan with the butter, sugar, cream, flour, and flavorings. Stir over low heat until the sugar has dissolved and the mixture is smooth. Set aside and cut baking parchment to fit your baking sheet. You might be able to make these cookies on a buttered and floured pan, but it would be difficult—it is best to use the parchment on a baking sheet. Also, these cookies need a flat surface to spread out on, so it is very important that you use a baking sheet that will not flex in the oven. Drop the batter by level teaspoonfuls onto the parchment, allowing 4 inches between cookies. When you bake successive batches be very sure to use new parchment for each one, or you will have odd-shaped cookies wherever the parchment is not perfectly flat.

Bake in a preheated 375°F oven for 4 to 6 minutes, or until the cookies are caramel colored. Take the sheet from the oven and slide the parchment off it. The cookies need to cool briefly so you can handle them. As soon as they are stiff enough to pick up, roll them quickly around the handle of a wooden spoon with the top side of the cookie facing out. Set on a rack to cool. If they stiffen too much to roll while you work on them, set them back on the warm baking sheet and put it back in the oven long enough to soften them. Continue until all have been rolled. The cookies can also be left flat and drizzled with melted chocolate just before serving. Sometimes Mary Jo pinches them into tortellini-like shapes. You can make any shape you like, as long as you work quickly.

200

Store these cookies in a tightly covered container and serve within 2 to 3 hours; they will lose their crispness if they are exposed to moisture in the air. Serve with almost any ice cream, mousse, floating island, or the like. These are one of my favorite cookies, delicate, crisp, and nutty, and very easy to make. I am indebted to my friend Diane Dexter for this recipe, which became a staple at the restaurant as soon as she introduced it.

SARAH'S MACAROONS

Makes 3 dozen cookies: *½ cup (2 ounces) whole unblanched almonds · 1 cup vanilla powdered sugar (page 4) · 2 egg whites · ¼ teaspoon cream of tartar*

Toast the almonds in a preheated 350°F oven for 5 to 7 minutes, or until they smell nutty. Cool. Grate fine with a nut grater. Sift the powdered sugar into a bowl and lightly toss with the cooled almonds. Butter and flour a baking sheet or cover it with baking parchment. Beat the egg whites with the cream of tartar until they hold stiff peaks, and fold quickly into the nut mixture. Pipe 1-inch mounds from a pastry bag with a ½-inch tip, keeping them 1½ inches apart. Bake the cookies in a preheated 400°F oven for 5 to 7 minutes, or until they are lightly browned. Let them firm slightly and remove from the baking sheet to a rack to cool. If they have cooled too much and stick to the parchment, just turn the parchment over, cookies and all, and moisten it a bit under each cookie—they will pull right off. Store in a tightly covered container, where they will keep for a couple of days. You may substitute other nuts for the almonds. You may also fill these macaroons with the following filling.

Almond Filling: *3½ ounces almond paste · 1 teaspoon rum · 3 tablespoons unsalted butter · A scraping of a vanilla bean*

Beat the almond paste with the rum to soften it slightly. Beat in the softened butter and a little vanilla bean. Spread a thin layer on the back of a macaroon and sandwich another macaroon to it. You may also pipe it onto the cookies. Serve within an hour or two of filling.

To make Chocolate Macaroons: Follow the basic recipe above, but add 3 tablespoons unsweetened cocoa powder to the nut and sugar mixture. To make a chocolate filling: Pour 3½ tablespoons hot cream over 2 ounces chopped semisweet chocolate and stir until melted. Cool and use to fill the macaroons.

OSSI DEI MORTI

For 12 dozen: *2 cups (8 ounces) unblanched almonds · 3 cups sugar · 2 teaspoons lemon juice · 1½ teaspoons baking powder · ⅛ teaspoon salt · 3 eggs · A few drops of almond extract · 2 cups flour · Vanilla powdered sugar (page 4)*

Toast the almonds lightly in a preheated 350°F oven and cool them; then chop them fine by hand. Mix together sugar, lemon juice, baking powder, and salt. Add the eggs and almond extract and beat with a mixer until spongy, about 3 minutes. Mix in the flour and almonds.

Roll the dough into ropes the thickness of a fat pencil and cut them into 2-inch lengths. This will make cookies about 2½ inches long by 1¼ inches wide when they are baked; they can be made in larger shapes, too, if you prefer. Space the cookies 3 inches apart on a buttered baking sheet and bake in a preheated 300°F oven for 15 to 20 minutes, or until very lightly browned. Cool on a rack, then shake sugar over them and store in an airtight container.

This recipe came to me through pastry assistant Lisa Goines, who got it from Alma Glooschenko, the mother of her friend, Sandra Jaeger; Mrs. Glooschenko got it in turn from her mother, Grandma Peretti.

ALMOND SEMIFREDDO

This semifreddo is a sponge cake layered with mousse and praline; it freezes very well. I have given ingredients for two cakes here—freeze the

202

extra one or use it for tea. Or make a second semifreddo with one of the other filling recipes that follow.

Makes 2 cakes, 10 to 12 servings each: *3 eggs · ½ cup sugar · ⅔ cup cake flour · ⅛ teaspoon salt · 2 tablespoons unsalted butter · ½ teaspoon vanilla extract*

Make the cake first: Butter a 9-inch square cake pan and line the bottom with parchment or waxed paper. Put the eggs and sugar in a stainless steel mixing bowl. Sift the cake flour onto a piece of waxed paper, measure it, and then mix in the salt. Meanwhile, melt the butter.

Beat the eggs and sugar together over hot water until they are warm to the touch. Remove from the heat and beat until they are thick and almost white. The bubbles in the mixture should be very fine and it should hold a shape for 2 or 3 seconds when the beater is lifted from it. Put the flour into a sieve and begin to shake a thin layer of flour over the egg mixture. Fold it in, giving the spatula a shake as you bring it up through the flour to break up any lumps that might form. Do not fold in the flour completely. Shake in some more flour and continue in this way until all the flour is almost, but not completely, folded in.

Check the butter to be sure it feels slightly warm to the touch and put the vanilla in it. Dribble some of it very lightly over the top of the batter; don't let it sink through. Fold it in carefully with a few strokes and finish adding the rest of the butter in the same way. Be very careful not to overwork the batter or it will deflate. The batter should take about three additions of butter altogether.

Pour into the prepared pan and bake in a preheated 350°F oven for about 25 minutes, or until the top springs back when it is pressed lightly and the cake is beginning to pull away from the sides of the pan. Cool in the pan 5 minutes; then turn out on a rack to finish cooling.

Praline: *¼ cup sugar · 1 tablespoon water · ¼ cup (1 ounce) whole unblanched almonds*

Make the praline next: Butter a 9-inch square pan. Heat the sugar and water in a small, heavy, light-colored saucepan. It is hard to keep track of the color of the cooking sugar in a dark pan. When the sugar has melted, put in the almonds and continue cooking, stirring occasionally, until the sugar has turned a light caramel color. If sugar begins to crystallize on the almonds, stir them around gently until the sugar melts off. When all the sugar is melted and caramelized, pour it into the buttered pan, making sure the nuts are in a single layer. Cool, turn out, and chop fine by hand.

Soaking liquid: *3 tablespoons kirsch · 3 tablespoons water*

To soak the cake: Line a 9-inch by 5-inch loaf pan with plastic wrap and cut a piece of the cake to fit the bottom. Sprinkle the cake with the mixed kirsch and water.

Filling: *¼ cup sugar · 4 tablespoons water · 3 egg yolks · 1 cup whipping cream · 1½ tablespoons kirsch · 1 ounce semisweet chocolate · praline*

Make the filling: Put the sugar and water in a small saucepan and cook to 230°F, or until it spins a 1-inch thread when a spoon is dipped in and pulled out. While that cooks, beat the egg yolks until they hold a shape. When the syrup is ready, pour it into the egg yolks in a thin stream, being careful to beat constantly and to beat where the syrup is hitting the yolks so they don't curdle. Beat over ice until cool and thick enough to hold a shape.

Whip the cream with the kirsch until it is as thick as the egg mixture. Fold them together—the resulting mixture must be thick enough to hold the praline and chocolate in suspension. Chop the chocolate fine by hand. Fold in the chocolate and the praline and pour into the pan on top of the cake. Cover with plastic wrap and freeze for several hours.

To serve, unmold and cut in slices about ¾-inch thick. Melt a little chocolate and put through a very fine pastry tube in slanting lines across the slice, or use the tines of a fork to dribble chocolate across the slice.

To make a Hazelnut Semifreddo: Substitute ¼ cup hazelnuts for the almonds. Toast them in a 375°F oven for 5 minutes, then cool them and rub off as much of their skins as possible. Proceed, substituting Cognac for the kirsch in the above recipe.

To make a Walnut Blood Orange Semifreddo: Make the cake as usual, or add a grating of blood orange peel to the batter. Add walnuts instead of almonds to the praline when the sugar begins to color. Add the finely grated peel of 1 blood orange to the egg yolks for the filling. Make the syrup with 3 tablespoons of blood orange juice and ¼ cup sugar. The mixture will turn beige when you put them together, but don't worry

204

about it. Whip 1½ tablespoons Cognac with the cream. Soak the cake with a mixture of 3 tablespoons blood orange juice and 3 tablespoons Cognac.

LINDSEY'S ALMOND TART

For one 9-inch tart: *One 9-inch short crust tart shell (page 11) · A small piece of tart pastry for patching · ¾ cup whipping cream · ¾ cup sugar · 1 teaspoon Grand Marnier · 2 or 3 drops of almond extract · 1 cup (about 3 ounces) sliced unblanched almonds*

Bake the shell in a removable-rim tart pan in a preheated 375°F oven until golden brown all over. It should be fully baked because the pastry will not continue to bake once it is filled. Mix cream, sugar, and flavorings in a saucepan large enough for the mixture to triple in volume, stirring well. Heat until it comes to a rolling boil and bubbles thickly, stirring occasionally. Remove from the heat, mix in the almonds, and let the mixture stand about 15 minutes.

Meanwhile, patch the tart shell if necessary. Smooth a small piece of very soft dough gently over any crack that looks as if it goes all the way through the shell. Be careful not to break through the crisp top of the baked crust if you can avoid it; if the filling leaks through, it will caramelize on the bottom of the shell. Fill the shell with the still warm filling, which will be quite liquid. Make sure the almonds float evenly in the filling. If they are gathered on the top of the liquid mixture, the finished tart will have a cornflake-like texture instead of the glossy surface you want.

Set the tart into a preheated 400°F oven, the bottom of which has been lined with aluminum foil, dull side up—the tart may bubble over. Bake 30 to 35 minutes, or until the top is a nice shade of creamy-and-russet caramel; remember that it will continue to brown a little more after you take it out of the oven. Cool the tart on a rack, loosening the sides of the pan slightly every minute or two for 5 to 10 minutes or until set. Then remove the tart from the ring and return it to the rack to cool. If you remove the ring of the pan too soon the sides will fall off the tart.

If you want to remove the tart from the bottom of its pan, carefully slide a thin sharp knife between pastry and pan while the tart is still warm—

15 to 20 minutes after it comes out of the oven. Then lift the tart off the bottom of the pan with a wide spatula and return it to the rack to finish cooling.

This tart is best eaten with the fingers; it is too hard to cut easily with a fork. It is good accompanied by a glass of Sauternes (but not too sweet, or too rare!) or Champagne—or a glass of milk, or coffee. It is a good picnic dessert because it is virtually indestructible.

This recipe was adapted from Mapie's *La Cuisine de France*, and modified for a different texture. It immediately became identified, for better or worse, as the house specialty of Chez Panisse.

ALMOND TORTE

For 12 servings: *1¼ cups sugar · ⅞ cup (about 8 ounces) soft almond paste · 1¼ cups softened unsalted butter · 1 teaspoon vanilla extract · 6 eggs · 1 cup flour · 1½ teaspoons baking powder · ¼ teaspoon salt*

Beat the sugar with the almond paste until the almond paste is in fine pieces. Or, better, pulverize it in a food processor. Beat in the butter and the vanilla, then cream the mixture until it is light and fluffy. Beat in the whole eggs, one at a time—the eggs should be at room temperature—beating well after each addition so the eggs are thoroughly mixed in. Mix the flour, baking powder, and salt, and beat in just until thoroughly blended.

Butter and flour a 9-inch springform pan and turn the batter into it, smoothing the top evenly. Bake in a preheated 325°F oven for 1 to 1¼ hours, or until a toothpick inserted in the center comes out clean and the center feels springy when you push it gently.

This cake is for marzipan lovers and is nice just powdered lightly with vanilla powdered sugar and served with a cup of coffee or tea or a glass of sherry, or better, an Italian Aleatico or Passito. It is also good with sliced peaches or nectarines and crème anglaise.

206

VALENTINE VACHERINS

For 2 hearts, to serve as many: *3 tablespoons (scant ounce) whole unblanched almonds · 2 egg whites · ¼ teaspoon cream of tartar · A pinch of salt · ½ cup sugar · White Chocolate Ice Cream (page 235) · Strawberry Ice Cream (page 142) · Raspberry purée*

Toast the almonds in a preheated 350°F oven for 6 to 8 minutes, or until they smell nutty. Cool them and chop them fine. Butter and flour a baking sheet and draw on it the outlines of two hearts about 5 inches wide at their tops, using the tip of a chopstick or a toothpick or something similar. Or use a piece of baking parchment and draw the hearts with a pencil—lay the parchment pencil side down on the sheet or the pencil marks will transfer to the meringue.

Warm the egg whites over hot water or swirl them above a gas flame until they are barely warm, and beat them with the cream of tartar and salt until they hold stiff peaks. Beat in two-thirds of the sugar until they hold stiff peaks again. Fold in the remaining sugar and nuts quickly. Put the meringue in a pastry bag with a ½-inch round opening and pipe an even layer covering the hearts. Pipe another layer on top around the edge to make a container. Or shape with a spoon, building up the edge to make the sides higher than the center.

Bake in a preheated 200°F oven for 1½ to 2 hours, or until the hearts are thoroughly dry and crisp and the palest cream color. Store in an airtight container until you are ready to use them.

To serve, fill each heart with a scoop each of White Chocolate Ice Cream and Strawberry Ice Cream and drizzle tart raspberry purée over them.

BITTER ALMOND ICE CREAM

Makes about 1 quart: *¼ cup (1 ounce) shelled bitter almonds · 1¼ cups half-and-half · 2½ cups whipping cream · ⅞ cup sugar · 7 egg yolks*

Bitter almonds—*Prunus dulcis "amara"*—are the fruits of a wild almond tree on whose rootstocks the cultivated varieties are often grafted.

Toast the almonds in a preheated 350°F oven for 5 to 6 minutes, or until they smell nutty. Grind them in a blender or food processor, then put them in a non-corroding saucepan with the half-and-half, cream, and sugar. Heat to 180°F to 200°F and keep the temperature there for 15 to 30 minutes, or until the flavor is strong enough to suit you.

Break up the egg yolks with a whisk and pour in some of the hot mixture, stirring constantly. Return to the pan and cook over low heat, still stirring constantly, until the custard coats the spoon. Strain through a very fine strainer into a container; then chill completely. Freeze according to the instructions with your ice cream maker.

Serve with Baked Stuffed Nectarines or Peach or Nectarine Pie.

HAZELNUT OEUFS À LA NEIGE

For 6 to 8 servings: For the custard: *7 tablespoons (2 to 3 ounces) hazelnuts · 3 cups milk · ¼ cup sugar · 4 egg yolks*

Make the custard: Toast the nuts in a preheated 350°F oven for about 5 minutes, or until they smell nutty and their skins begin to look brittle and cracked. Cool them, and rub off as many of their skins as you can in a coarse strainer. Reserve 2 tablespoons whole hazelnuts for the garnish. Grate the remaining nuts in a nut grater or grind them fine in a blender or food processor. Put them into a non-corroding saucepan with the milk and heat to just under boiling. Let stand for 15 to 20 minutes, reheating as necessary to keep the mixture hot. Strain through a very fine strainer and measure, adding more milk if necessary to make 2 cups. Return to the cleaned saucepan, add the sugar, and reheat. Whisk the egg yolks to break them up and stir in some of the hot mixture. Return to the saucepan and cook over low heat, stirring constantly, until the custard coats the spoon. Strain into a container, cover tightly and chill. Whisk once when it has cooled.

For the meringues: *3 egg whites · ¼ teaspoon cream of tartar · 6 tablespoons sugar · A few drops of vanilla extract*

Make the meringues: Heat about 1 inch of water in a shallow non-corroding sauté pan to 170°F and keep the water at that temperature. Warm

208

the egg whites over hot water or swirl them over a gas flame until they are barely warm. Beat them with the cream of tartar until they hold straight peaks when you withdraw the beater. Gradually beat in the sugar and beat until they hold stiff peaks again. Beat in a few drops of vanilla until they are stiff once again. Form egg-shapes by scooping a rounded tablespoonful of the meringue and pushing it into the hot water. You can also use an oval or round ice cream scoop. Leave plenty of room for them to expand while they cook and let them cook for 3 to 4 minutes. Turn them gently and cook 3 to 4 more minutes. Be sure that the temperature of the water does not go above 170°F—this is the temperature at which egg proteins coagulate; higher temperatures will toughen them. Remove from the pan with a slotted spoon and drain on a pan lined with a cloth or paper towel. Repeat until all the meringues are cooked. You might prefer to make slightly smaller meringues and serve two to each person. Cool them but don't refrigerate. They will keep for several hours until you are ready to serve them.

At serving time put the custard into a bowl and arrange the meringues over it. Drizzle with caramel syrup, or make the following caramel garnish:

4 tablespoons sugar · 1½ tablespoons water

Make the caramel and cool it until you can drizzle thin threads of it over the meringues. (See page 34 for caramel instructions.) Chop the reserved hazelnuts fine and sprinkle them over. Serve immediately. Serve a meringue and some custard to each person, and accompany with crisp cookies. Our French exchange daughter, Dominique, thought this was better than her grandmother's oeufs à la neige.

HAZELNUT LOGS

Makes 40 cookies: *½ cup (2½ ounces) hazelnuts · 4 tablespoons salted butter · 4 tablespoons unsalted butter · 2 tablespoons sugar · 1 teaspoon vanilla extract · 1 cup flour · Powdered sugar to sprinkle over the cookies*

Toast the nuts in a preheated 350°F oven for 5 to 7 minutes, or until they smell nutty and their skins are beginning to loosen. Cool them, and rub off as much of their skins as you can, being especially careful to remove any furry-looking skin. Don't worry about other pieces of skin that stick. Chop the nuts very fine by hand. Cream the slightly softened butter until it is light and fluffy, then add the sugar and vanilla. Cream again until light and fluffy. Stir in the flour and the nuts and mix until the dough holds together. Flour your hands lightly, take small handfuls of dough, and roll lightly into long ⅝-inch-thick rolls. Pinch off in 2-inch-long pieces, smooth their ends, and lay them on a baking sheet 1 inch apart. Bake them in the 350°F oven 15 to 20 minutes, or until they have browned very lightly on their tops. Cool on a rack and sift powdered sugar over them. Handle them carefully as they are quite fragile. Keep them in a tightly closed container until serving time.

HAZELNUT SOUFFLÉS

For 6 servings: *⅔ cup (3⅓ ounces) hazelnuts · ⅔ cup milk · 1 tablespoon plus 2 teaspoons flour · 5½ tablespoons sugar · 5 egg yolks · 1 tablespoon unsalted butter · 1½ teaspoons Cognac · 6 egg whites · 1¼ teaspoon cream of tartar*

Toast the hazelnuts in a preheated 350°F oven for about 5 minutes, or until they smell nutty. Cool them and rub off as many of the skins as you can easily; it doesn't matter if some are left. Grind or grate fine ⅓ cup of them. Put in a non-corroding saucepan with the milk and bring to a bare simmer. Turn off the heat and let the nuts steep for 15 minutes. Strain through a very fine strainer and whisk the milk gradually into the mixed flour and 2½ tablespoons of the sugar. Return to the cleaned saucepan and cook over medium heat, stirring constantly, until the mixture has thickened and boiled for a minute or two. Beat the egg yolks until they are light colored and slightly thickened, then beat in some of the hot milk mixture to warm them. Return to the pan and cook over low heat, stirring constantly, until the eggs have cooked and the mixture has thickened again—the temperature should reach 170°F. Beat in the butter and cool or chill the mixture, tightly covered.

When you are ready to bake the soufflés, butter and sugar 6 individual

5-ounce soufflé dishes. Chop fine by hand the remaining ⅓ cup hazelnuts. Whisk the soufflé mixture slightly to smooth it out and beat in the Cognac. Warm the egg whites over hot water or swirl them above a gas flame until barely warm, then beat them with the cream of tartar until they hold soft peaks. Beat in the remaining 3 tablespoons sugar until they hold soft peaks again. Fold about a quarter of the beaten whites into the soufflé mixture to lighten it, and then fold in the remaining whites with the chopped nuts. Fill the soufflé dishes to within ½ inch of the tops and bake in a preheated 400°F oven for 7 to 9 minutes, or until they are puffed and browned but still a little shaky when you jiggle them.

Powder the tops very lightly with vanilla powdered sugar and serve immediately with very cold crème anglaise.

CRAIG'S MACADAMIA CAKE

For 12 servings: For the cake: *1¼ cups (5 ounces) macadamia nuts · ¼ cup cake flour · 6 egg yolks · ¾ cup sugar · A few drops of vanilla extract · 1 teaspoon kirsch · 7 egg whites · ⅛ teaspoon salt · ½ teaspoon cream of tartar*

Butter and flour a 9-inch springform pan. Toast the nuts in a preheated 325°F oven for 5 to 7 minutes, or until they smell nutty. Cool. Grate the nuts fine with a hand nut grater and stir in the flour, or grind them fine with the flour in a food processor.

Beat the egg yolks with half the sugar, the vanilla, and the kirsch to a 3-second ribbon. Warm the egg whites over hot water or swirl them over a gas flame until barely warm, then beat them with the salt and the cream of tartar to soft peaks. Gradually beat in the remaining sugar until the whites hold soft peaks again. Spread the yolk mixture over the whites and sprinkle with a quarter of the nuts. Fold until partially mixed, sprinkle with another quarter of the nuts, and fold. Repeat until all the nuts have been folded in. Be careful not to overwork the batter and deflate the eggs. Pour into the prepared pan and bake in a preheated 325°F oven for 30 to 40 minutes, or until the sides of the cake just begin to pull away from the sides of the pan. Cool.

211

For the filling: *2 cups (8 ounces) macadamia nuts · ½ cup sugar · 3 table-spoons water · 2 tablespoons corn syrup · 1 tablespoon unsalted butter · 1 tablespoon whipping cream*

Toast the nuts in a preheated 325°F oven for 5 to 7 minutes, or until they smell nutty. Cool and chop coarse. Shake the nuts in a coarse strainer to remove any dusty particles.

Put the sugar in a small non-corroding saucepan, add the water, and cook over medium heat until light gold. Remove from the heat and carefully add the corn syrup, butter, and cream. Stir over low heat until the caramel has dissolved, then stir the caramel into the nuts to bind them. Slice the cake into two layers and spread the warm filling between them.

For the icing: *2 cups flaked unsweetened coconut · 1 cup whipping cream · 2 tablespoons sugar, to taste · 1 teaspoon vanilla extract*

Toast the coconut in a preheated 325°F oven for 5 to 8 minutes, stirring often until pale golden brown. Cool. Whip the cream with the sugar and vanilla until it holds soft peaks and is just stiff enough to spread on the cake. Ice the cake with the cream and press the coconut all over the surface of the cake.

This cake is delicious served with kumquats poached in honey. The recipe was developed by Craig Sutter, a pastry assistant for several years at Chez Panisse.

WILD MISSOURI PECAN ICE CREAM

Makes a generous quart: *2 to 2½ cups (8 to 10 ounces) pecans · 1¼ cups milk · 2½ cups whipping cream · ¾ cup plus 1 tablespoon sugar · 6 egg yolks · Vanilla extract and brandy or Cognac to taste*

Toast the pecans in a preheated 350°F oven for 5 minutes, or until they smell nutty. Use the larger amount if you want to have chopped nuts in the finished ice cream, setting aside ½ cup of the nuts and grinding the rest fine in a food processor or blender. Combine the ground nuts with the milk in a non-corroding saucepan and heat to just under boiling. Turn off the heat and let the mixture steep for about 20 minutes. Strain the liquid through a very fine mesh strainer or squeeze through a dampened dishtowel. Add the cream and sugar and heat again.

Whisk the egg yolks just to break them up and whisk in some of the hot mixture. Return to the pan and cook over low heat, stirring constantly, until the custard coats the spoon. Strain into a container, flavor with a few drops each of vanilla and brandy or Cognac to bring out the nut flavor, and chill. Taste again, correct the flavoring if necessary, and freeze according to the instructions with your ice cream maker. If you want to add the reserved nuts, chop them into ¼-inch chunks and fold them in when the ice cream comes from the machine. Freeze.

Serve in crêpes, cookie cups, or bombes, or with crisp cookies.

To make Walnut Ice Cream: Substitute 1½ to 2 cups (8 to 10 ounces) walnuts for pecans, and use 1 cup milk, 2 cups whipping cream, and ¾ cup sugar. Proceed as in above recipe.

To make Hazelnut Ice Cream: Use 1¾ to 2¼ cups (8 to 10 ounces) hazelnuts, 1⅓ cups milk, 2½ cups whipping cream, and ¾ cup sugar.

BUTTERSCOTCH-PECAN PIE

For a 9-inch pie: *One 9-inch pie shell (page 23), baked · 1 cup milk · 5 tablespoons unsalted butter · ¾ cup light brown sugar · 3 tablespoons flour · A pinch of salt · 6 egg yolks · ¾ teaspoon vanilla extract, to taste · ¾ cup (3 ounces) pecans · 1 cup whipping cream · Sugar and vanilla extract to taste*

Warm the milk just until it begins to steam, about 130°F. Be careful: if it gets too hot it will curdle in the sugar mixture. Brown the butter in a heavy-bottomed non-corroding saucepan, stirring constantly, until it is a very light golden brown. Remove from the heat and continue stirring as long as it darkens from the heat of the pan. Strain through a fine strainer to remove any brown pieces in the butter. Return to the pan and add the sugar, flour, and salt. Heat briefly to warm the mixture again, then whisk in the warmed milk. Whisk the egg yolks lightly and stir in a little of the sugar mixture. Return to the pan and cook over low heat, stirring constantly, until the mixture is thick enough to hold a shape. The temperature will be about 180°F. The mixture will look very lumpy as it begins to thicken but will smooth out when it is finished. Remove from the heat, add the vanilla, and whisk 10 to 15 times to smooth out the mixture. Do not overbeat or the pie filling will be too thin. Chill, covered tightly.

Toast the pecans in a preheated 350°F oven for about 5 minutes, or until you begin to smell the nuts. Cool them completely. When you are ready to assemble the pie, whisk the cooled filling slightly to smooth it out. Chop ⅝ cup of the pecans coarse and stir them in. Spread the filling in the cooled baked pie shell. Whip the cream until it just holds a firm shape but is not grainy, and flavor it to taste with sugar and vanilla. Spread it decoratively over the filling and garnish it with the remaining nuts, either chopped or arranged in halves on top of the pie. Chill the pie if you are not serving it immediately, but serve it before the crust can get soggy.

Serve a cup of coffee after the pie—it is very rich!

PECAN TORTE

For 1 torte, serving 10 to 12: *1½ cups (6 ounces) fresh pecans · 2 tablespoons flour · 6 eggs · ½ cup plus 2 tablespoons sugar · ½ teaspoon cream of tartar · ⅛ teaspoon salt · ½ teaspoon vanilla extract*

Toast the pecans in a preheated 350°F oven for 5 to 6 minutes until they smell nutty. Cool, then grate in a nut grater and toss them lightly with the flour. Butter and flour a 9-inch springform pan. Separate the eggs and beat the yolks with half the sugar until they hold a 1-second ribbon. Warm the egg whites over hot water or swirl them above a gas flame until barely warm, then beat them with the cream of tartar and salt until they just hold stiff peaks. Beat in the remaining sugar until they hold stiff peaks again. Drizzle the vanilla over the egg whites and spread the egg yolk mixture over that. Sprinkle one-fourth of the nut mixture over the yolks and partly fold together. Sprinkle over another fourth of the nuts and partly fold them in. Continue until the last of the nuts have been added and fold them in completely. Spread evenly in the prepared pan and bake in a preheated 300°F oven about 55 minutes, or until a toothpick inserted in the center comes out clean. Cool in the pan. Frost thickly with bourbon-flavored crème Chantilly, or powder lightly with vanilla powdered sugar and serve with the cream to spoon over.

You can make a Walnut Torte or a Hazelnut Torte by substituting the appropriate nuts. You will need 2 cups of grated nuts for either torte.

PISTACHIO ICE CREAM

Makes a generous quart: *1½ to 2 cups (6 to 8 ounces) shelled unsalted pistachio nuts · 1½ cups milk · 3 cups whipping cream · 8 egg yolks · ⅞ cup sugar · Vanilla extract to taste · Kirsch to taste*

Toast 1⅓ cups of the pistachios in a preheated 350°F oven for 5 to 10 minutes, or until they smell nutty. Don't let them brown. Grind them fine in a blender or food processor and put them in a non-corroding saucepan with the milk and cream. Heat to just under boiling and steep for about 20 minutes. Put through a very fine strainer into a bowl. Whisk the egg yolks to break them up and add the sugar and the warm pistachio milk, stirring constantly. Return to the cleaned pan and cook over low heat until the custard coats the spoon. Add a few drops each of vanilla and kirsch to taste—just enough to heighten the pistachio flavor. Strain into a container and chill. If you want to add chopped pistachios to the ice cream, dry out another ⅜ cup of pistachios in a 200 °F oven until they are crisp but have not lost their green color—mine take about 1 hour. Cool them and chop fine by hand. Freeze the ice cream according to the instructions with your ice cream maker, then fold in the chopped pistachios if you are using them.

Serve with Chocolate Truffle Ice Cream as we did one Christmas season, or with crisp cookies.

215

NOUGAT ICE CREAM

Makes about 1 quart: *1½ cups whipping cream · ¾ cup half-and-half · 3 egg yolks · ⅜ cup honey · About ½ tablespoon orange flower water, to taste · ⅜ cup (1½ ounces) shelled, unsalted pistachios · ¼ cup (1 ounce) whole unblanched almonds*

After trying many honeys, I have settled on a light delicate thistle honey for this ice cream; any mild honey that you like should be very nice.

Heat ½ cup of the cream with the half-and-half. Whisk the egg yolks just enough to mix them and gradually add the hot creams, stirring constantly. Return to the pan and cook over low to medium heat, stirring constantly, until the mixture coats the spoon. Strain into a bowl and stir in the honey. Add the remaining cream, and the orange flower water to taste; then chill.

Toast the pistachios on a baking sheet in a preheated 350°F oven for about 5 minutes, or until they are dried and crisp but still have their green color. Rub off as many of the skins as you can by putting the nuts in a dishtowel or coarse strainer and rubbing them against one another. If they are not completely dry and crisp, dry them in a 200°F oven until they are. Blanch the almonds—their flavor will be much more intense and characteristic if you blanch them yourself: Put them in 1 cup of boiling water for 2 to 3 minutes. Remove them from the hot water one by one, squeeze off their skins, and halve them by inserting the tip of a paring knife into the natural separation between the halves. Put them on a baking sheet in a preheated 300°F oven, then turn off the oven and let them stay in for 20 minutes or so, until completely dry. Freeze the cream mixture according to the instructions with your ice cream maker and fold in the nuts. Pack into a container and freeze.

Serve with crisp Ladyfingers or Langues de Chat.

This is an adaptation of Alice B. Toklas' recipe for Nougat Ice Cream from *The Alice B. Toklas Cook Book* (Garden City, N.Y., 1960).

216

PISTACHIO TORTE

For a 9-inch torte serving 12: Cake: *1½ cups (6 ounces) shelled, unsalted pistachio nuts · ¼ cup cake flour · 7 egg whites · 6 egg yolks · ¾ cup sugar · A pinch of salt · ½ teaspoon cream of tartar · ¼ teaspoon grated orange rind · ½ teaspoon kirsch · Optional: 1 teaspoon orange flower water*

Toast the pistachios in a preheated 300°F oven for 12 to 15 minutes, or until they are dried out and their skins are beginning to loosen. Be sure that the nuts don't brown, however, or the cake will not be a pretty green color. Grind the nuts in a nut grater, blender, or food processor. If you are using the grater, stir in the flour after grating the nuts. Otherwise, grind the nuts with the flour—it will help to keep them from turning to nut butter. Warm the egg whites over hot water or swirl them above a gas flame until barely warm. Beat the egg yolks with half the sugar until they are thick and light and hold a 1-second ribbon. Beat the egg whites with the salt and cream of tartar to stiff peaks. Gradually beat in the remaining sugar until they hold stiff peaks again. Spread the egg yolks over the beaten whites, sprinkle the grated orange rind over them, and drizzle with kirsch and orange flower water, if you like.

Sprinkle one-quarter of the pistachio mixture over this mixture. Fold in partly, then sprinkle another quarter of the nuts over and fold again. Continue until all the nuts are used. The last time, fold until evenly mixed and spread in a buttered and floured 9-inch springform pan. Mound the batter in the center and bake on the center rack in a preheated 325°F oven for about 40 minutes, or until the cake is set and a toothpick inserted in the center comes out clean. Cool on a rack.

Dust with vanilla powdered sugar and serve with kirsch cream or Johannisberg Riesling sabayon. Or cover with chopped pistachios, or ice with crème Chantilly flavored with kirsch, as follows:

Pistachio topping: *¾ cup (3 ounces) pistachio nuts · 5 to 6 tablespoons apricot jam · ½ teaspoon kirsch*

Dry out the nuts as in the cake recipe. Cool and rub in a coarse strainer to remove any loose skins. Chop fine by hand into about ⅛-inch chunks. Heat the apricot jam to boiling and stir in the kirsch. Slice off any uneven section from the top of the cake and turn it over. Brush all over with the apricot jam. Pat a layer of the chopped pistachios into the jam, covering the cake completely. Decorate the top with a few bits of candied violets or with fresh violets. Serve with kirsch cream (below) or Riesling sabayon.

Kirsch crème Chantilly: *1¼ cups whipping cream · 2 tablespoons sugar · Kirsch to taste*

Whip the cream with the sugar and kirsch to taste until it is spreadable but still soft. Ice the cake with it, decorate with some of the cream put through a pastry tube, and sprinkle with some chopped candied violets. If you have fresh violets you may scatter them on top, sugared or not. Unless the violets are sugared, leave an inch or two of their stems and put them on the cake just before serving.

WALNUT DROPS

For 5 to 6 dozen cookies: *1 cup (4 ounces) walnuts · 4 tablespoons very soft unsalted butter · 4 tablespoons very soft salted butter · ¼ cup sugar · 1½ teaspoons vanilla extract · 1 cup flour · Granulated sugar and vanilla powdered sugar (page 4) to sprinkle the cookies*

Toast the walnuts lightly in a preheated 350°F oven until they just begin to brown slightly, 5 to 7 minutes. Cool completely; then grind them in a food processor or blender, or better, grate them in a nut grater. Be careful that they don't turn to butter if you are grinding them with a machine. Cream the butters in a mixer or with an electric hand mixer until very light and fluffy. Beat in the sugar and vanilla, creaming again until very light. Mix in the nuts and flour just until thoroughly mixed.

Put half the mixture at a time in a pastry bag with a ½-inch (number 7) tip, and pipe out flat mounds about 1 inch in diameter on an unbuttered baking sheet, keeping the tip almost against the sheet. You may also drop the dough by teaspoons on the sheet, flattening each drop slightly. Bake in a preheated 300°F oven for 20 to 30 minutes, or until pale brown. Remove to a cooling rack and sprinkle very lightly with granulated sugar. When cool, sprinkle very lightly with vanilla powdered sugar, if you like.

BLACK WALNUT ICE CREAM

Makes 1 quart: *1 to 1½ cups (4 to 6 ounces) black walnuts · 1½ cups milk · 2 cups whipping cream · ¾ cup sugar · 3 egg yolks · Vanilla extract and Cognac or brandy to taste*

Toast the nuts in a preheated 350°F oven for 5 minutes, or until you can smell them. Grind 4 ounces (about 1 cup) of the nuts very fine in a blender or food processor. Put them with the milk in a non-corroding saucepan and heat them to just under boiling. Let the mixture steep about 15 minutes. Strain through a very fine strainer, return to the cleaned pan, and heat with the cream and sugar. Whisk the egg yolks to break them up and pour in a little of the hot cream mixture, whisking constantly. Return to the pan and cook over low heat until the mixture coats the spoon. Strain into a container and chill. Accent the flavor with a few drops of vanilla and Cognac or brandy. Freeze according to the instructions with your ice cream maker. Add the remaining nuts if you like, chopped medium fine, when you remove the frozen ice cream from the machine.

MIXED WALNUT TART

For 8 servings: *Pastry for a 1-crust pie (page 23), baked in a 9-inch tart pan, or one 9-inch puff pastry tart shell (page 25), baked · 4 tablespoons soft unsalted butter · ⅔ cup light brown sugar · 1 tablespoon egg white · ¼ teaspoon vanilla extract · ½ teaspoon brandy or Cognac · 1⅛ cups (4½ ounces) shelled walnuts · ⅓ cup (1¼ ounces) shelled black walnuts*

Cream the butter until fluffy and beat in the sugar until it is fluffy again. Beat in the egg white, vanilla, and brandy or Cognac until the mixture is smooth. Leave the walnuts in halves, or break them or chop coarse if you would like a smoother looking tart. Add the nuts to the creamed mixture and spread it gently and evenly in the pastry with your fingers. Bake in a preheated 400°F oven for about 15 minutes, or until the filling bubbles and browns slightly.

Serve with crème Chantilly or crème fraîche.

The original of this recipe came from Union Hotel chef Judy Rodgers' friend Beth Setrakian, whose pecan tarts I ate and loved. This is my adaptation of her recipe. It makes perfectly delicious pecan tarts, too.

ITALIAN NUT TORTE

For 12 to 16 servings: *1¼ cups (5 ounces) whole unblanched almonds · 1¾ cups (7 ounces) shelled walnuts · 2 teaspoons finely ground espresso or other dark roast coffee · 8 eggs · 1½ tablespoons unsalted butter · ½ cup sugar · ¼ teaspoon salt · ½ teaspoon cream of tartar*

Butter and flour the bottoms of two 9-inch layer cake pans. Toast the nuts in a preheated 350°F oven for about 5 minutes for the walnuts, a minute or two longer for the almonds, until they smell nutty. Cool them. Grate fine, preferably with a nut grater. You may use a food processor, but the texture of the cake will be a little coarser because you must stop the processing before the nuts become oily. Lightly mix the coffee into the nuts.

Separate the eggs and melt the butter. Warm the egg whites over hot water or swirl above a gas flame until barely warm. Beat the egg yolks with 3 tablespoons of the sugar until they hold a 3-second ribbon. Beat the warmed egg whites with the salt and cream of tartar until they hold soft peaks, then gradually beat in the remaining sugar. Beat until the whites hold peaks that stand straight when the beater is pulled out. Spread the egg yolk mixture over the whites and sprinkle with about a third of the nut mixture. Fold quickly until about half mixed, then sprinkle on another third of the nuts and repeat. Drizzle the melted butter over this, then sprinkle on the last third of the nuts. Fold together only until mixed, being careful not to deflate the eggs. Spread evenly in the prepared pans and bake in a preheated 300°F oven for about 45 minutes, or until the top springs back when lightly pressed and a toothpick inserted in the center comes out clean. The top will look lumpy. Cool the cake in the pans.

Filling: *⅓ cup water · ⅔ cup sugar · ⅓ cup light brown sugar · ½ teaspoon cream of tartar · 1 tablespoon unsalted butter · 3 tablespoons rum · ¼ teaspoon ground cloves · ⅓ cup (1⅓ ounces) toasted chopped walnuts*

Put the water and then the sugars in a small heavy saucepan and let stand until the sugar is moistened. Add the cream of tartar, cover, and cook over medium heat for 5 minutes. Uncover and cook to 234°F without stirring. Remove from the heat and stir in the butter. Cool. Stir in the rum and cloves. Beat occasionally while cooling to keep a crust from forming. Put over ice water, if necessary, to cool to about 65°F, beating constantly while it is over the water bath. Beat until creamy and just thick enough to spread. Stir in the nuts. Turn out one of the cake layers, top side down, on a serving plate or tray. Spread with the filling, then put the other layer over it, bottom side down.

Icing: *1½ cups whipping cream · 2 tablespoons sugar · ½ teaspoon finely ground coffee · ½ teaspoon vanilla extract*

Whip the cream with the sugar, coffee, and vanilla, only until stiff enough to spread on the cake. Ice the cake with this, decorating it with a pastry tube, if you like. Sprinkle the top with a bit more ground coffee, or some grated chocolate.

   This is a rich, spicy cake, medieval in its feeling, I think, and a slight variation on the Iced Filled Rum Nut Cake from *Italy on a Platter* by Osborne Putnam Stearns.

FRUIT COMPOTE
IN DARJEELING TEA AND SAUTERNES

For 4 servings: *¾ teaspoon Darjeeling tea leaves · 3 cups water · ½ cup Sauternes · ½ cup sugar · 3 ounces dried pears · ⅓ cup (1½ ounces) golden raisins · ⅓ cup (1½ ounces) Muscat raisins, preferably still on their stems: they look very nice in the compote · 2 tablespoons dried currants · 3 ounces dried apricots · 3 ounces unpitted prunes · Sauternes to pour over*

Put the tea leaves in a tea ball or tie in cheesecloth. Bring the water to a boil, remove from the heat, and steep the tea in it for 3 minutes. This should be done in enamel or china, not in metal. Remove the tea and strain the water into a non-corroding saucepan—again, preferably enamel or glass—using a fine strainer to remove any bits of the tea. Add the Sauternes and the sugar and heat to a simmer. Meanwhile blanch any of the fruits that may have been sulfured for 2 to 3 minutes in another pot of boiling water. Usually the pears and the apricots will have been sulfured. The label will tell you, and you can tell by smelling and tasting them.

Poach the pears, covered, in the Sauternes syrup for 10 to 15 minutes, but only until they are tender. Remove the pears with a slotted spoon. Poach the golden raisins for about 4 minutes, or until they puff up. Remove the golden raisins and poach the Muscat raisins for a few minutes until they too have swelled. Remove them and poach the currants until they have puffed. Remove the currants and poach the apricots for about 4 minutes, or until they are tender. Be careful with the apricots—they will get too soft very quickly, and they should still hold their shape after poaching. Remove them and poach the prunes last. Cook them about 10 minutes, or until they puff and the skins are tender when pierced with the tip of a knife. Remove the prunes and cook the syrup down to 1¼ to 1½ cups. Strain over the fruit and chill thoroughly.

Serve a pear and some of each of the other fruits with some of the syrup to each person. Add a spoonful of Sauternes to each serving, if you like. I had a dessert like this the first time I went to Paris and I liked it so much I had to make it when I came back home—but then I grew up on a prune ranch.

PRUNE AND ARMAGNAC ICE CREAM

Makes a generous quart: *½ cup pitted prunes* · *Armagnac to cover* · *1½ cups milk* · *¾ cup sugar* · *4 egg yolks* · *1½ cups whipping cream*

Put the prunes in a container, cover them with Armagnac, cover the container, and let stand several days until the prunes have absorbed a lot of the Armagnac and they are plump and moist.

Make the custard: Warm the milk with the sugar in a non-corroding

222

saucepan until the sugar has dissolved, stirring occasionally. Whisk the egg yolks just enough to break them up and stir in some of the hot milk mixture. Return to the pan and cook, stirring constantly, until the mixture coats the spoon. Strain into a container, add the cream, and chill. Freeze according to the instructions with your ice cream maker. While the custard freezes, chop the prunes fine and measure out ½ cup plus 2 tablespoons. When the custard has finished freezing, stir in the chopped prunes with 1½ tablespoons of the soaking liquid (or more Armagnac if the prunes have drunk it all). Pack into a container and freeze.

Serve this with Lace Cookies. Prunes and Armagnac have a natural affinity, like lamb and rosemary. This is a wonderful dessert after a roast pork dinner, or after cassoulet.

PRUNES POACHED IN BURGUNDY

For 4 to 6 servings: *⅜ cup sugar · 1 cup Burgundy or other fruity red wine · 1 cup water · 1-inch wide strip of orange zest · 12 ounces large unpitted prunes*

Bring the sugar, wine, water, and orange zest to a boil in a non-corroding saucepan large enough to hold the prunes. Add the prunes and bring them to a simmer. Cook, covered, about 25 minutes, or until the prunes are puffed up and the skin is tender when pricked with a fork. Remove the prunes from the poaching liquid with a slotted spoon to a storage container. Cook down the remaining liquid by one-third and strain it over the prunes. Chill thoroughly.

Serve with crème fraîche or cream to pour over, and accompany with Walnut Drops. These are delicious, too, with a few tablespoons of raspberry purée added to the poaching liquid before the prunes are added. This is one of the most popular fruit desserts we serve in the café. Many people ask for the recipe; I think they are surprised that prunes can taste so good.

POACHED SPICED FIGS

For 6 to 8 servings: *1½ cups fruity red wine* · *½ cup water* · *6 tablespoons sugar* · *A 1-inch by 3-inch strip of orange zest* · *6 peppercorns* · *1 whole clove* · *2 allspice berries* · *½ pound dried Calimyrna figs*

Bring all the ingredients but the figs to a simmer in a non-corroding saucepan. Add the figs and cook them at a very slight simmer until they are tender when pierced with the tip of a knife. This will take anywhere from 30 minutes to 1½ hours, depending entirely on the figs. Remove the figs to a container with a slotted spoon, raise the heat, bring the syrup to a boil, and reduce by one-third. Pour it over the figs and chill. They will keep for one to two weeks and will benefit from sitting in their syrup for a few days.

Serve with a little of their syrup and some cream to pour over, or with crème fraîche.

A PROVENÇAL SUNDAE

For 8 to 10 servings: *1 pound dried Calimyrna figs* · *1 cup red wine* · *½ cup water* · *3 tablespoons honey* · *1-inch sprig of fresh or dried lavender* · *Coffee Ice Cream (page 114)*

Cut the tough tips off the stem ends of the figs. Bring the wine, water, honey, and lavender to a simmer and add the figs. Cover and cook slowly until the figs are tender—anywhere from 30 minutes to 1½ hours. Remove the figs to a container and cook the poaching liquid until it makes a thin syrup. Test it by chilling a few drops on a plate that has been chilled in the freezer. Pour over the figs and chill. To serve, slice the figs ¼-inch thick and serve over coffee ice cream. Drizzle with a little of the poaching syrup.

Dried figs, lavender, honey, and good red wine seem to spell Provence. In time they will also spell California; a full-bodied Zinfandel is just as appropriate to this dish as a Cassis or Bandol. This recipe was inspired by Richard Olney's *Simple French Food*; Richard is a great friend of Chez

Panisse, and the Provence-California connection has always been important to our restaurant's development.

PRUNE AND WALNUT DARTOIS

For 8 to 10 servings: *⅓ recipe puff pastry (page 25)* · *½ cup (2 ounces) walnuts* · *1½ cups poached, pitted prunes* · *2 tablespoons sugar, to taste* · *2 teaspoons Cognac, to taste* · *1 egg yolk* · *2 teaspoons whipping cream*

The *dartois* is a filled puff pastry associated with provincial French cooking, where it probably represents a step between an origin in northern Italy and the Danish pastry familiar in so many hotel breakfasts.

Cut the chilled pastry in half and roll one piece into a rectangle 5½ inches by 14 inches and no more than ⅛-inch thick. The bottom sheet of pastry should be thin—if it is thick, its moisture will form a soggy layer under the filling before the pastry bakes. Lay the rolled pastry on a baking sheet and chill while you roll the other piece of pastry into a slightly larger rectangle. This will be the top of the pastry and it can be slightly thicker. Lay it on the baking sheet beside the other strip and chill both strips while you make the filling.

Toast the walnuts in a preheated 350°F oven for 5 to 6 minutes, or until they smell nutty. Cool them and chop coarse. Put the prunes through a food mill to purée them and stir in the sugar and Cognac. I prefer the texture that results from the food mill; the blender or food processor makes too smooth a purée. Stir in the walnuts and adjust the amount of sugar and Cognac to your taste. Spread the prune purée on the chilled bottom layer of the pastry, leaving 1 inch uncovered all the way around. Brush these uncovered edges with water and lay the top layer over the filled bottom layer. Press down gently all around the edges to seal them and trim with a sharp knife, cutting straight down to make the edges even. Cut short parallel slits at regular intervals—½ inch to 1 inch—all around the edge of the tart with the back of a table knife. The slits should cut about ⅛ inch into the edge of the pastry, which will form scalloped notches while it bakes. Beat the egg yolk and cream together with a fork and brush the top with it. Be careful not to let any drip over the edges of the dartois or the pastry will not rise properly. Cut 8 or 10 half-inch slits down the center in a decorative pattern to let the steam escape during the baking, and make a design by incising lines ¹⁄₁₆-inch deep into the pastry.

Bake in the top third of a preheated 400°F oven for 15 minutes, reduce the heat to 375°F and bake 35 to 40 minutes more, or until the bottom is well browned and the pastry is well baked. It will probably look done before it is; it takes a long time to bake and dry out all the layers of pastry on top of the filling. If the top is dark enough before the pastry has baked at least 50 minutes, lay a sheet of foil loosely over it while it finishes baking.

Serve warm with crème fraîche. It should come out of the oven within an hour of serving time, but it can be assembled and kept tightly covered in the refrigerator for several hours before glazing and baking.

To make a Prune and Quince Dartois: Make the prune filling as in the above recipe, substituting ¼ to ½ cup poached quince slices for the walnuts (page 187), diced in ¼-inch pieces.

Another variation of the Prune and Walnut Dartois is called Gateau Niçoise. It is made by substituting the following filling for the prune filling in the above recipe:

¾ cup (3 ounces) whole unblanched almonds · 6 tablespoons soft unsalted butter · 4½ tablespoons sugar · 1½ tablespoons candied orange or tangerine peel (page 64) · ¼ teaspoon finely grated orange peel · 1 or 2 eggs · ½ to 1 teaspoon kirsch, to taste

Toast the almonds in a preheated 350°F oven for 5 to 7 minutes, or until they smell nutty. Cool. Grind with a nut grater or in a food processor or blender, taking care if you use the latter not to grind them to butter. Beat the butter until it is creamy and beat in the nuts. Beat in the sugar and the remaining ingredients, including enough eggs to make it spreadable. Use this to fill the dartois and proceed as in the above recipe.

PRUNE AND ARMAGNAC SOUFFLÉS

For 6 servings: *9 or 10 large pitted prunes* · *Enough Armagnac to cover the prunes* · *½ cup milk* · *1 tablespoon plus 2 teaspoons flour* · *7½ tablespoons sugar* · *5 egg yolks* · *1 tablespoon unsalted butter* · *6 egg whites* · *¼ teaspoon cream of tartar*

Put the prunes in a small container, pour in enough Armagnac to cover them, and let them stand for several days to soften and absorb the Armagnac.

Heat the milk in a small non-corroding saucepan. Mix the flour and 1½ tablespoons of the sugar and gradually whisk in the hot milk. Return to the pan and cook over medium heat, stirring constantly, until the mixture has boiled for a minute or two. Beat the egg yolks until they are light colored and slightly thickened. Carefully beat in a little of the hot milk mixture. Beat the eggs into the mixture in the pan and cook over low heat, stirring constantly, until the eggs are cooked. The temperature should reach 170°F. Stir in the butter and chill in a covered container. This basic mixture can be made several days ahead.

When you are ready to make the soufflés, bring the basic mixture to room temperature while you butter and sugar 6 individual soufflé dishes. Chop the soaked prunes fine and measure ¾ cup. Beat them into the soufflé base mixture with 1 tablespoon of the soaking liquid—if the prunes drank it all, use 1 tablespoon of Armagnac. Warm the egg whites slightly over hot water or swirl above a gas flame until barely warm. Add the cream of tartar and beat them until they stand in soft peaks. Gradually beat in the remaining 6 tablespoons sugar and continue beating until the egg whites hold stiff peaks. Quickly fold about a quarter of the egg whites into the prune mixture to lighten it, then fold into the remaining whites. Pour into the prepared dishes. Bake in a preheated 400°F oven for 7 to 9 minutes, or until they are puffed and light brown and still a little shaky.

Serve immediately with very cold crème anglaise to pour over.

10

CHOCOLATE

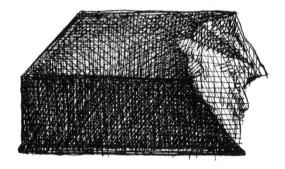

MANY PEOPLE find chocolate irresistible. *Theobroma*, "food of the gods," its botanical name, describes it well. I remember a day spent in Bruges, Belgium, when my husband and I bought samples of every different brand of chocolate we could find and took them to our hotel room to try to taste them in one evening—we couldn't do it. For me, chocolate is just another of the many rich and fascinating flavors available to the pastry chef. In some of Chez Panisse's desserts—the Very Rich Chocolate Mousse and the Rich Chocolate Cake, for example—it is the whole point. Often, though, it is only one among several flavorings, whether very important, as in the Dobos Torte, or just a contributing factor, as in the Marble Cake. Still, I turn to chocolate when I want to make a rich dessert that I know everyone will like. At the restaurant we make chocolate cakes regularly and our customers often request them for birthdays and other special occasions. During the holi-

230

days, chocolate is indispensable for candies, truffled ice creams, and the traditional Bûche de Noël. It is also a great decorating medium. It can be rolled into sheets on a pasta machine to wrap a cake, and the sheets can be cut into noodles to surround a dessert with a silly garnish. If you keep your sense of humor, you can melt chocolate and make Jackson Pollock–like scribbles and drips on top of a cake; since they are not meant to look perfect, they will always be right.

Chocolate can be forced into another kind of whimsy: we served chocolate-covered garlic cloves for one of our garlic dinners, and my daughter Giovanna invented chocolates filled with Fernet Branca, the bitter Italian *digestivo*. The former are still talked about, and the latter were very good indeed as after dinner mints. But on the whole chocolate resists such undignified treatment. We often serve chocolate-dipped nuts, candied citrus peel, coffee beans, or violets with after dinner coffee, or we make chocolate sauces to serve with desserts flavored with nuts or Chartreuse.

Chocolate is available already selected, roasted, ground, refined, and blended. Which kind you choose is very important: the manufacturing process is crucial to its quality, and poor quality chocolate will ruin a dessert. The flavor of chocolate is so strong that it easily overwhelms other flavors. It is important, then, to use the best-tasting chocolate you can buy. I most often use a dark bittersweet chocolate, since the taste I want is that of good chocolate with only enough sugar or other flavors to enhance and amplify it. Rich Chocolate Cake needs only the mellowing effect of butter and nuts to round out the flavor of the chocolate itself.

White chocolate made with pure cocoa butter is a perfect contrast for the sharp bright tastes of raspberries, blackberries, boysenberries, and loganberries. I like to make berry mousses and serve them, or the whole berries, with a white chocolate mousse. Cherries cooked in port wine have a perfect affinity with white chocolate ice cream—a latter-day cherries jubilee. White chocolate truffles can be flavored with most liqueurs to enhance the meal they follow with a mellower taste than that of dark chocolate truffles. Violets and gold leaf enrobed with white chocolate make a simple but unusually elegant candy, one of my very favorites. Chocolate, in other words, can play a more subtle role in dessert making than it often does.

RICH CHOCOLATE CAKE

Makes one 8-inch or 9-inch cake: *1 cup plus 2 tablespoons salted butter · 7 ounces semisweet chocolate · 2 ounces bitter chocolate · 6 eggs · ¾ cup granulated sugar · ⅜ cup brown sugar · ⅜ cup cake flour · 3 tablespoons finely grated almonds · ½ teaspoon cream of tartar*

The flavor of this cake depends almost completely on the chocolate, so be sure to use the best semisweet chocolate you can buy.

Butter the sides and bottom of an 8-inch or 9-inch springform pan. Line the bottom with baking parchment or waxed paper and flour the pan. Melt the butter in a large heavy-bottomed pan. Chop the chocolate in coarse pieces and add to the butter. Stir constantly over low heat until just melted and smooth; be careful not to overheat or the chocolate will turn grainy. It should not get much hotter than 115°F. Set aside.

Separate the eggs and beat the sugars into the egg yolks until just mixed. While the chocolate is still warm, whisk the egg mixture into it, then stir in the flour and the almonds. If the combined mixture has cooled, warm it over low heat, stirring constantly, until it is barely warm. Warm the egg whites slightly by swirling them in a bowl above a gas flame or over hot water—the whites will beat to a greater volume when warmed. Add the cream of tartar to the egg whites and beat until they look creamy and form rounded peaks: if they look at all flaky they are overbeaten. Spread the egg whites over the chocolate mixture and fold them together quickly without deflating the whites. Pour into the prepared pan and bake in a preheated 375°F oven for 30 to 40 minutes, or until the cake is completely set around the sides but still has a soft and creamy circle, about 6 inches across, in the center. The cake will rise and crack around the edge and separate from the softer center. The center should wiggle just slightly when you shake the pan gently; it will continue to cook when you take it out of the oven. Cool thoroughly in the pan.

To serve the cake, turn it out, peel the paper off the bottom, and ice with chocolate icing or powder lightly with vanilla powdered sugar. The cake keeps very well, if not iced, for three or four days. Do not refrigerate or freeze, just cover the pan with foil until ready to use.

This is a synthesis of a number of French recipes for *gâteau au chocolat*.

The cake is very good with Rum, Cognac, or Vanilla Ice Cream, or it can be served with crème Chantilly. Coffee, of course, is welcome afterward.

MARBLE CAKE

For 10 to 12 servings: *1½ ounces unsweetened chocolate · ½ cup unsalted butter · 1 cup sugar · 2¼ cups cake flour · ¼ teaspoon salt · 2½ teaspoons baking powder · 1 cup milk · 1 teaspoon vanilla extract · ⅛ teaspoon baking soda · ¼ teaspoon cinnamon · 1 tablespoon brandy or Cognac · 4 egg whites · ¼ teaspoon cream of tartar · 2 tablespoons sugar*

Butter and flour a 9-inch springform cake pan. Melt the chocolate in a small pan over hot water and set aside. Cream the butter until fluffy. If it is too cold, cut it into slices and melt part of it, let it all stand 5 minutes, and then cream it. Add the 1 cup sugar, then cream again until very light and fluffy. Sift the cake flour, measure it, and sift again with the salt and baking powder. Warm the milk to take the chill off it, add the vanilla, and whisk it into the creamed butter mixture, alternating it with the flour. Beat just until smooth after each addition. Divide the batter into two portions. Stir the baking soda and cinnamon into the melted chocolate and mix it into one portion of the divided batter. Stir in the brandy or Cognac.

Warm the egg whites very slightly by swirling them in their bowl above a gas flame or over hot water. Add the cream of tartar and beat until soft peaks are formed; they should turn over on their tips when you lift the beater from the whites. Beat in the 2 tablespoons sugar and continue beating until the whites hold stiff peaks. Divide the egg whites in half and fold one half into each portion of the cake mixture.

Dot large spoonfuls of the chocolate batter over the bottom of the prepared pan, then a few spoonfuls of the vanilla. Continue in this way until all the batter is used. Swirl a table knife in circles through the batter a few times to marbleize it. Bake in a preheated 325°F oven for about 1 hour, or until a toothpick inserted in the center comes out clean. Cool on a rack in the pan.

Serve iced with Chocolate Icing or with crème Chantilly, and accompany with coffee.

MOCHA CUSTARD

For 6 servings: *2 cups whipping cream · 3 tablespoons sugar · ¼ cup coffee beans (I use mocha-java) · 2-inch piece of vanilla bean · 4 ounces semisweet chocolate · ½ ounce unsweetened chocolate · 6 egg yolks · 2 teaspoons Cognac or brandy*

Choose a pan large enough to hold 6 individual custard cups. Fill the pan about a third full of water and set it into a preheated 350°F oven to warm while you make the custard mixture. Put the cream in a non-corroding saucepan with the sugar and the coffee beans. Split the vanilla bean lengthwise and scrape out the fine black seeds. Add the seeds and pod to the mixture and warm it to about 190°F. Don't overheat or allow to boil or the mixture will curdle. Let it stand about 30 minutes, or until it has a good coffee flavor; reheat if necessary to keep the mixture hot. While the coffee mixture is steeping, put the two kinds of chocolate in a small pan and set over a pan of warm water to melt. Stir and remove from the warm water as soon as it is smoothly melted and glossy.

When the coffee mixture has steeped to your satisfaction, whisk the egg yolks just enough to mix them and pour the coffee mixture into them. Strain, then whisk the coffee-egg mixture gradually into the chocolate. Pour into a pitcher and then into the custard cups. Put the cups into the pan of water in the oven, adding hot water, if necessary, to come halfway up their sides. Lay a piece of foil loosely on top of the cups and bake 20 to 25 minutes, or until they are set ½-inch to ¾-inch in from the edge when you tip the cups slightly. Set the custards on a rack to cool and keep them at room temperature until serving, up to 2 or 3 hours. This custard is best at room temperature because it congeals when chilled; however, it should not be kept at room temperature for more than 3 hours. You can make the mixture a day or two ahead. Keep it refrigerated, and bake it just before you want to serve it.

This is a thick, rich, creamy custard; it can be served as it is or garnished

234

with some coarsely chopped toasted almonds or walnuts. It is also nice with Walnut Drops, or Hazelnut Logs, or Langues de Chat and a brandied cherry.

WHITE CHOCOLATE ICE CREAM

Makes 1 quart: *5 ounces white chocolate · ⅞ cup milk · ½ cup sugar · 1½ cups whipping cream · Vanilla extract to taste*

Melt chocolate with ⅜ cup of the milk in a heavy pan over water that has been heated to 120°F to 130°F—this is usually about the temperature of hot water from the faucet. Heat the other ½ cup milk and dissolve the sugar in it. Cool to 120°F, and carefully add to the melted chocolate. Stir in the cream slowly, add a few drops of vanilla, and chill, stirring every 15 minutes or so until the mixture is cold and a layer of fat (the cocoa butter) no longer forms on the top. Freeze according to the instructions with your ice cream maker.

Serve with blackberries or raspberries, or with warm Cherry Compote, or with cherries cooked in port. Accompany with Lace Cookies or Langues de Chat.

CHOCOLATE TRUFFLE ICE CREAM

Makes a generous quart: *4 ounces semisweet chocolate · 1 ounce unsweetened chocolate · 5 tablespoons unsalted butter · ½ cup plus 2 tablespoons whipping cream · 1 to 2 teaspoons brandy or Cognac or other liqueur, to taste · 1 recipe Vanilla Ice Cream (page 6), ready to freeze*

Melt the chocolate, butter, and cream in a small heavy saucepan over low heat or over hot water, stirring constantly. Add the liqueur to taste. Pour into a small bowl and chill thoroughly. When the chocolate is cold but still malleable, shape small truffles by dipping a half-teaspoon measuring spoon or a melon baller in hot water and scooping a truffle quickly. Lay the truffles on a sheet pan in a single layer. When you have shaped them all, chill them thoroughly. Freeze the ice cream mixture according to the instructions with your ice cream maker and fold the truffles into it. Freeze.

Serve with Lace Cookies or other crisp cookies, or serve with Pistachio Ice Cream in a cookie cup.

CLAY'S CHOCOLATE ICE CREAM WITH WHITE CHOCOLATE TRUFFLES

Makes a generous quart: *1 cup half-and-half · ¾ cup sugar · 6 egg yolks · 5 ounces semisweet chocolate · 1 ounce unsweetened chocolate · 2 tablespoons unsalted butter · 2 cups whipping cream · 1 teaspoon vanilla*
For the truffles: *5 ounces white chocolate · 6 tablespoons plus 2 teaspoons whipping cream · 2½ tablespoons unsalted butter · ¼ teaspoon kirsch*

Warm the half-and-half with the sugar in a non-corroding saucepan until the sugar dissolves, stirring occasionally. Whisk the egg yolks just enough to break them up and stir in some of the warm half-and-half. Return to the pan and cook over low heat, stirring constantly, until the mixture coats the spoon. Strain into a bowl. Break up the dark chocolate and melt it with the butter in a small heavy saucepan over warm water, stirring until it is smooth and glossy. Remove from the hot water and begin to whisk in a little of the warmed custard, a tablespoon or two at a time, until the mixture begins to thin out. Adding the custard gradually to the chocolate will prevent the ice cream from getting little grains of chocolate in it. When all the custard has been incorporated, gradually whisk in the cream. Add the vanilla, taste, and chill.

To make the truffles: Melt the broken white chocolate, cream, and butter over warm water, stirring, until smooth. Add the kirsch and pour into a flat pan in about a ½-inch-deep layer. Freeze in order to shape them more easily. Take quarter-teaspoonfuls and roll into rough truffle-shaped balls with your fingers. Put them in a pan in the freezer until you are ready for them. Freeze the ice cream according to the instructions with your ice cream maker and fold in the truffles when you remove it from the machine. Freeze.

Serve this ice cream with Lace Cookies or with puff pastry cookies.

Clay Wollard thought of adding butter to chocolate ice cream while he was working in our pastry department. It makes this the richest, smoothest chocolate ice cream imaginable.

CHOCOLATE ICING

Makes enough for one 9-inch cake: *4 ounces semisweet chocolate · 1 ounce unsweetened chocolate · 4 tablespoons water or coffee · 3 tablespoons unsalted butter · 2 tablespoons salted butter · Optional: rum, Cognac, Chartreuse, Grand Marnier, or other liqueur to taste*

Chop the chocolate and melt it in the water or coffee over very low heat, stirring constantly. When it is very smooth and glossy, remove from the heat and stir in the butter, bit by bit. Flavor to taste with the liqueur of your choice and cool until the icing holds a shape. Keep at room temperature until you are ready to use it. This icing can be rewarmed slightly if it stiffens too much.

CHOCOLATE LEAVES

Makes 6 to 8 leaves, 2 inches by 2½ inches: *Smooth leaves such as rose, camellia, citrus, or pear · 2 ounces semisweet chocolate*

Clean and dry the leaves. Melt the chocolate over warm water, stirring until smooth. You may temper the chocolate (page 305) if you wish, but I find it is not necessary for decorations that will be used within a few hours. When the chocolate has reached about 88°F it will be ready to use. Brush the backs of the leaves with a thin layer of chocolate. Be sure not to brush over the edges or you will not be able to pull the leaves off. Make a thick enough layer that the chocolate will not break too easily when you remove the leaves—about ¹⁄₁₆ inch.

   Lay the leaves chocolate side up on a baking sheet lined with waxed paper as you paint them. Put them in a cool place to set; when firm, gently pull off the leaves. Try not to handle them too much: the warmth

237

of your hands will melt the chocolate. Keep the leaves in a cool place. Use them to garnish cakes, or make large leaves to set beside servings of ice cream.

CHOCOLATE LACE

Prepare the chocolate as instructed in the Chocolate Leaves recipe. Draw designs on a sheet of white paper and set that under the waxed paper onto which you will pipe the chocolate. When the chocolate has cooled to about 88°F, put it in a pastry bag with a very small round opening. Quickly squeeze the chocolate onto the waxed paper, making scrolls or whatever designs you have chosen. Set in a cool place to firm. Carefully peel off the paper and use to garnish mousses, cakes, or ice creams. If you are clever you can dispense with the guidelines under the waxed paper and pipe freehand designs.

CHOCOLATE BARK

Melt 3 ounces semisweet chocolate. Butter a baking sheet lightly and line it with parchment or waxed paper. Pour the melted chocolate onto the paper and spread to an 8-inch by 13-inch rectangle. Chill briefly. When firm, carefully pull the chocolate off the paper and tear it into strips approximately 1½ inches wide. Tear each strip into 2-inch lengths. Use these to cover cakes, overlapping them in rings in appropriate designs. This recipe makes enough for the top of an 8-inch cake.

DIPPED CHOCOLATES

At the restaurant we sometimes dip coffee beans, nuts, candied peel, various kinds of truffles, or even violets. Chop an appropriate amount of semisweet chocolate and temper it according to the instructions in the appendix (page 305), unless you plan to serve the candies within a few hours. When it is smooth and glossy and has cooled to 88°F, use your fingers or a fork to dip the candies. As you finish, set them on a baking sheet lined with parchment or waxed paper. When they are all dipped, set the chocolates in a cool place to keep until serving time. If you like you can also melt some white chocolate, put it into a pastry bag with a tiny opening, and pipe crisscrossing lines, dots, or other designs over the tops of the dipped candies.

BÛCHE DE NOËL

For 15 servings: For the cake: *2 tablespoons unsalted butter* · *½ cup sifted flour* · *½ cup sifted cake flour* · *A pinch of salt* · *6 eggs* · *¾ cup sugar* · *Powdered sugar* · *1 teaspoon vanilla extract*

This is a very festive cake that looks much more difficult to make than it is, and it can be made well ahead of serving time.

Melt the butter and set it aside to cool. Butter an 11-inch by 17-inch jelly roll pan and line it with baking parchment or buttered and floured waxed paper. Mix the flours with the salt and have ready in a sifter or strainer. Put the eggs, sugar, and vanilla into a mixing bowl and whisk over hot water until they are lukewarm. Remove from the heat and beat until they form a 3-second ribbon. Sift about a quarter of the flour over the egg mixture and partly fold it in. Repeat until all the flour has been folded in. Drizzle the butter on top of the batter and quickly fold it in. Be careful not to overmix the batter or the eggs will deflate. Quickly spread the batter onto the prepared pan and bake in a preheated 325°F oven for 15 to 20 minutes, or until the top springs back when pressed lightly and the cake is golden brown. Sprinkle the top lightly with powdered sugar and cover with a layer of parchment or waxed paper. Lay another baking sheet on top of the cake, hold the two together and invert them. Cool, covered by the pan, for 15 minutes. Remove the top pan, roll the cake lengthwise loosely, and wrap in plastic until you are ready to assemble the cake.

For the butter cream: *¾ cup sugar · ⅜ cup water · 9 egg yolks · 3 ounces unsweetened chocolate · 3 tablespoons triple-strength coffee, or to taste · 1½ cups unsalted butter (or 1 cup unsalted butter and ½ cup salted butter) · A few drops of vanilla extract to taste · 2 teaspoons Cognac, and a little to brush the cake*

Put the sugar in a small saucepan and add the water. Cook over low to medium heat until it reaches the thread stage (230°F to 234°F). Meanwhile beat the egg yolks until they are thick and light. When the syrup is ready, carefully pour it in a thin stream into the egg yolks, beating constantly. Set the bowl over ice water and beat until thick and cooled to about 70°F. Set aside. Melt the chocolate and set aside to cool. Make the coffee and let it cool. Beat the butter, which should be the same temperature as the egg mixture, until it is light and fluffy. Gradually beat in the egg mixture in five or six additions and beat until smooth. Divide into two portions. Beat the cooled coffee and a few drops of vanilla extract into one portion, and the melted chocolate and Cognac into the other.

Unroll the cake and remove the paper. Brush lightly with Cognac. Spread a thin layer of the coffee butter cream on the cake. Roll the cake, starting at the long edge, to make a log shape. Set the cake on a serving tray or a board with the seam on the bottom. Ice the cake completely, except for the ends, with the chocolate butter cream. Slice a short piece at an angle from each end and set them aside. Pull a spatula through the icing roughly to make it look like bark. Press the two end pieces into the icing, pointing the thicker sides toward the top of the log so they look like the stubs of sawed-off branches. Ice them up to the cut edge.

Just before serving, arrange a few clusters of Meringue Mushrooms on the cake or peeking from underneath it, if you like, and garnish with sprigs of holly. Keep in a cool place until serving time.

You can also decorate this cake with chocolate butter cream only, if you prefer, omitting the coffee from the butter cream and adding twice as much chocolate and Cognac as the recipe calls for.

MERINGUE MUSHROOMS

Makes about 20 mushrooms: *1 egg white · A pinch of cream of tartar · ¼ cup sugar · Cocoa to decorate the tops*

Butter and flour a baking sheet. Swirl the egg white above a gas flame or over hot water to warm it slightly, then beat with the cream of tartar until it holds stiff peaks. Gradually beat in the sugar until it holds stiff peaks again. Put into a pastry bag with a ⅜-inch tip. Begin piping rounds for the mushroom tops in varying sizes from ½ inch to 1 inch in diameter, making about 20. Pipe the stems, holding the pastry bag vertical and pulling up to pipe a stem wider at the bottom, pointed at the top, and about ½-inch tall. Vary the diameter of the bottoms so they will fit the different-sized tops you have made. Wet your finger and smooth any points on the tops of the mushroom caps. Bake in a preheated 200°F oven for about 1 hour, or until they are crisp and dry. Store in a tightly covered container until you are ready to use.

To assemble the mushrooms, cut a cone-shaped depression with the tip of a sharp knife in the bottom of the cap. Dip the pointed top of a stem in a little butter cream and join the two sections. Rub the tops lightly with cocoa to color them slightly.

CHOCOLATE MOUSSE

Makes about 3¾ cups: *5 ounces semisweet chocolate · 1 ounce unsweetened chocolate · 2 tablespoons brandy or Cognac · 2 tablespoons coffee or water · 4 eggs · 1 cup whipping cream*

Melt the chocolate with the brandy and coffee or water in a small heavy saucepan over warm water, or in a double boiler. Stir until well melted, smooth, and glossy. Remove the chocolate from the heat. Separate the eggs and whisk the yolks into the chocolate. Whip the cream until it holds a very soft shape. Swirl the egg whites above a gas flame or over hot water until they are barely warm. Beat them until they hold very soft peaks and fold about a quarter of them into the chocolate mixture. Fold in the remaining whites, then fold in the whipped cream. Pour into serving glasses or a serving bowl and chill.

Serve with a rosette of crème Chantilly sprinkled with a little grated chocolate or finely ground coffee. Or spoon into serving dishes or a bowl alternately with White Chocolate Mousse and draw a knife through to make a marble design. Or pour into parfait glasses side by side with Espresso-Cognac Mousse or White Chocolate Mousse. Accompany with Lace Cookies.

VERY RICH CHOCOLATE MOUSSE

Makes 3 cups: *4 ounces semisweet chocolate · 2 tablespoons coffee or water · 4 eggs · ½ cup unsalted butter*

Chop the chocolate into small pieces and melt it with the coffee or water in a small heavy saucepan over hot water, stirring constantly, until smooth and glossy. Remove from the heat. Separate the eggs, put the whites in a bowl, and whisk the yolks one by one into the chocolate until well mixed. Cut the butter in pieces and whisk it in. Let the butter stand a few minutes to soften, if necessary, and whisk in until smooth. Set over the hot water again briefly if the butter doesn't melt. Warm the egg whites slightly over the hot water and beat them until they hold soft peaks, then fold them quickly into the barely warm chocolate mixture. Pour into a bowl or serving glasses and chill.

Serve with lots of crème Chantilly, enough to eat some with each bite of mousse, and with Lace Cookies. This is not a light-textured mousse at all—it is a very rich, heavy chocolate mayonnaise for the unregenerate chocolate lover.

242

WHITE CHOCOLATE MOUSSE

Makes about 1¼ quarts: *9 ounces white chocolate · ⅜ cup milk · 1½ cups whipping cream · 3 egg whites · ¼ teaspoon cream of tartar · ¾ teaspoon vanilla extract, to taste*

Use a good imported white chocolate for this—most of the American ones are made with vegetable shortening instead of cocoa butter, which gives the chocolate its flavor.

Chop the chocolate and melt it carefully over warm water, then stir to smooth it out. It will be well melted and smooth at about 104°F, or when it feels slightly warm to the touch. Warm the milk to about the same temperature and whisk it into the chocolate just until it is smoothly mixed.

Whip the cream until it makes a slight rounded shape when dropped from the beater; it should not stand in peaks or the mousse will be grainy. Warm the egg whites slightly by swirling them in a bowl over warm water or above a gas flame. Beat them with the cream of tartar until they hold softly rounded peaks when the beater is withdrawn. Fold the whites into the chocolate mixture, being careful not to overmix. Then pour the mixture over the whipped cream, add the vanilla, and fold them together quickly. Taste and add more vanilla, if you like, then pour into sherbet cups or parfait glasses. You can use this in a half-and-half mousse by combining it with coffee or chocolate mousse, or with Raspberry or Blackberry Mousse, pouring them in side by side from two pitchers.

Serve garnished with a piece of Chocolate Lace or bitter chocolate shavings, or garnish with strawberries, raspberries, or blackberries. Or drizzle with a little blackberry or raspberry purée.

BLACK BOTTOM PIE

For one 9-inch pie: One 9-inch pie shell (page 23), baked · 4 eggs · 1½ cups milk · 2 ounces unsweetened chocolate · 5 tablespoons light brown sugar · 2⅔ tablespoons flour · 3 tablespoons Cognac · ¼ teaspoon vanilla extract · 1½ teaspoons gelatin · 2 tablespoons cold water · ¼ teaspoon cream of tartar · ½ cup sugar · 1 cup whipping cream · Unsweetened chocolate for garnish

Separate the eggs and set 3 whites aside to warm. Scald the milk. Melt the chocolate over warm water. Beat the 4 egg yolks, 3 tablespoons of the brown sugar, and the flour together in a bowl. Beat in the hot milk gradually and cook in a heavy non-corroding saucepan over low heat, stirring constantly, until the mixture coats the spoon thickly. It will have reached 170°F. Remove from the heat and stir a minute or two until the bottom of the pan has cooled.

Measure out 1⅓ cups of this custard into a bowl and stir in the melted chocolate, the remaining 2 tablespoons brown sugar, 1 tablespoon of the Cognac, and the vanilla. Cool.

Sprinkle the gelatin over the cold water and let it stand 5 minutes to soften. Dissolve over low heat until you can't see any grains of gelatin. Stir this into the remaining custard with the other 2 tablespoons of Cognac and cool the custard over ice water, stirring constantly, until thick enough to coat a spoon heavily. Beat the slightly warm egg whites with the cream of tartar until they hold soft peaks. Gradually beat in the ½ cup sugar and continue beating until the whites hold stiff peaks when you lift the beaters out. Fold the Cognac custard into the egg whites. Spread the chocolate custard on the bottom of the pie shell and spread the Cognac custard mixture over it. Chill 2 to 3 hours, or until the top is set.

Whip the cream and spread a layer over the pie, swirling it decoratively. Shave 1 to 2 tablespoons unsweetened chocolate by drawing a vegetable peeler along a long edge of the chocolate, and sprinkle it over the top of the pie.

Serve this with coffee, or before a glass of Cognac.

DOBOS TORTE

For 16 servings: For the cake: *1 cup plus 2 tablespoons flour* · *7 eggs, separated* · *½ cup plus 1 tablespoon sugar* · *1 teaspoon vanilla* · *⅛ teaspoon salt* · *A rounded ¼ teaspoon cream of tartar*

The Dobos Torte is a handsome, rather formal cake made of seven thin layers of vanilla sponge cake iced with chocolate-hazelnut butter cream. The top layer is characteristically finished with a thin layer of caramel marked into the cake's sixteen servings—often the wedges of caramel are lifted and tilted to produce a fan-like effect. It is my husband's very favorite cake.

The cake can be baked on baking sheets or on the bottoms of 8-inch layer cake pans. If you are using the pans, turn them upside down and butter their bottoms well. If you are using baking sheets, line them with parchment on which you have drawn seven circles 7½ inches to 8 inches in diameter.

Sift the flour. Beat the egg yolks with half of the sugar and the vanilla until they are thick and lemon colored and hold a shape for 1 second. Warm the egg whites slightly by swirling them over a gas flame or by setting the bowl into warm water briefly. Beat them with the salt and cream of tartar until they hold a rounded shape but still look creamy. Beat the remaining sugar into the whites until they hold stiff peaks when you remove the beaters and you can't feel any grains of sugar when you rub a little between your fingers.

Spread the yolk mixture over the whites and start folding them together, sifting the flour over in four portions. Shake your spatula as you lift it through the mixture to break up any flour lumps that may form. Fold until just mixed. Spread about 1 cup of the batter evenly on the bottom of each pan or on the baking sheets and bake in a preheated 350°F oven for 10 to 12 minutes, or until lightly browned. Remove immediately from the pans or the baking sheet to a cooling rack and clean off and re-butter the bottoms of the pans, if you are using them. (The batter will keep its shape long enough to bake it in two shifts, but the second part will deflate more easily than the first when it is worked. Be careful not to overwork it.) Bake the rest of the batter. You should have seven layers.

245

For the butter cream: *18 hazelnuts, shelled · 1⅓ cups unsalted butter · 4 ounces bitter chocolate · ⅜ cup water · ⅞ cup sugar · 8 egg yolks · 2 teaspoons vanilla extract*

Roast the nuts in a preheated 400°F oven for 4 to 5 minutes, until lightly toasted. Skin them by rubbing them in a coarse strainer and grate fine, preferably with a small rotary grater. Have the butter at cool room temperature. Heat the chocolate over warm water just until melted. Mix water and sugar and boil gently, covered, for 5 minutes. Uncover and cook to the thread stage, 230°F to 234°F. Meanwhile, beat the egg yolks until they are thick and lemon colored and hold a shape for a second when the beater is lifted from them. When the syrup has reached the thread stage, pour it slowly into the beaten yolks, beating constantly to keep the syrup from hardening when it hits the cool yolks. Beat over ice, cooling the mixture until it holds a shape. Beat the butter with the vanilla until very light and fluffy and then beat in the egg yolk mixture, a few tablespoons at a time, until smooth. Thoroughly beat in the cooled, but still melted, chocolate. Remove about ¾ cup of the butter cream to use for decorating. (The grated nuts you are about to add will clog most pastry tips, so it is wise to set some smooth icing aside for decorating. If you plan to use a plain round tip you need not worry about this.) Beat the grated hazelnuts into the rest of the chocolate mixture.

Peel off the parchment if you baked the cakes on it. Set aside the nicest looking layer for the top of your torte. Ice the bottom layer with about a ⅜-inch layer of the butter cream and continue until you have iced six layers, using about two-thirds of the butter cream (not counting the portion you have set aside for decorating). Stack the layers as evenly as possible. Trim the sides with a serrated knife, if necessary, to make the cake evenly round. Put the layer you set aside for the top on a baking sheet and use your fingertips to spread butter on the baking sheet around it, a good 2 inches beyond its circumference. Butter a metal spatula and a large knife that you can use to cut the cake pieces apart. (It should have at least an 8-inch blade.) Mark the top of the cake into sixteen pieces by pressing the back of the knife into it. You will need these marks as a guide so you are able to quickly cut the cake into serving-size sections when you put the hot caramel on this layer.

246

For the caramel: *1 tablespoon unsalted butter · ¾ cup powdered sugar*

Melt the butter in a small, light-colored frying pan and stir in the sugar. Cook over low to medium heat, stirring constantly. The sugar will form little lumps, but keep stirring, chopping larger lumps if they appear, until the sugar has melted completely. Cook, stirring constantly, until a light golden brown; then immediately pour this over the top cake layer. Spread quickly with the buttered spatula to make an even layer, and cut through the caramel with the buttered knife to cut apart the sixteen pieces. Quickly cut off any caramel that has run over the edges, and as soon as the caramel has cooled set the pieces on top of the sixth layer of the torte. Ice the sides smoothly with the remaining third of the butter cream. Move the cake to a serving plate if it is not already on one. Put the reserved ¾ cup butter cream in a pastry bag with a decorative tip, handling it as little as possible so that it doesn't melt. Pipe a design around the top of the cake to cover the edge of the caramel, and another around the bottom edge. Put a little rosette in the center of the top where the caramel sections meet if you want to cover that point. Cover and chill. Remove from the refrigerator 30 minutes to 1 hour before serving.

A good Dobos Torte is complete in itself, perfect with a cup of good coffee.

CHOCOLATE TRUFFLES

For 3 dozen 1-inch truffles: *6 ounces semisweet chocolate · ½ ounce unsweetened chocolate · 5 tablespoons whipping cream · ½ cup unsalted butter · ¾ teaspoon Cognac, Chartreuse, Grand Marnier, framboise, or other flavoring, to taste*

Coarsely chop the chocolate and put in a heavy saucepan with the cream and butter. Melt the mixture over hot water, stirring constantly until it is smooth and glossy. Remove from the heat and stir in the Cognac. Pour into a container that will hold it in a 1-inch-deep layer and chill thoroughly. Have ready a cup of hot water. Use a small melon baller or a measuring spoon to shape the truffles. Dip the melon baller in hot water between each truffle. If any chocolates break in the shaping process, pinch them into a rough truffle shape. Chill the chocolate if it softens too much while you work with it.

This will make about 3 dozen truffles—it sounds like a lot, but they won't last long. You may serve them as they are, or rolled in cocoa; or rolled in finely chopped toasted walnuts, hazelnuts, almonds, or pistachios; or dipped in chocolate. You will need about 2¼ cups of finely chopped nuts to coat this many truffles.

Serve after dinner with coffee and liqueurs.

WHITE CHOCOLATE TRUFFLES

Makes 3 dozen 1-inch truffles: *6 ounces white chocolate · 2 tablespoons whipping cream · 2½ tablespoons unsalted butter · 2½ tablespoons salted butter · ¼ teaspoon kirsch, framboise, or other liqueur, or Champagne, to taste*

Chop the chocolate into coarse pieces and melt it over hot water in a heavy saucepan with the cream and butter. Stir constantly until it is smooth and glossy, then remove from the heat. Stir in the flavoring, pour it 1 inch deep into a container, and chill thoroughly. When you are ready to shape the truffles, have a cup of hot water ready. Use a small melon baller or a measuring spoon to shape the truffles. Dip the melon baller in hot water after shaping each truffle. If any break in the shaping process, pinch them into a rough truffle shape. Chill the chocolate if it softens too much while you work with it. If the truffles have softened during the shaping process, chill them briefly.

You can serve these truffles plain or rolled in toasted coconut or in toasted nuts. Be sure you use only white chocolate made with cocoa butter for them; other white chocolate is disappointingly bland.

248

11

WINE
AND
SPIRITS

Winemaking is surely one of the oldest ways of preserving fruit. The distillation of spirits came later, apparently invented by the Arabs; the Greeks and Romans of antiquity had to do without. Spirits were known in Europe during the Middle Ages and they immediately moved into the kitchen, taking their place beside wine. Both wine and spirits distilled from fruit are invaluable resources for the dessert cook. They are a kind of fruit essence that can be used to heighten the flavors of fruits or to provide the central flavor of many ice creams, Bavarian creams, and sherbets. Grain, potato, and cane-based spirits have less inherent flavor than fruit ones; they take much of their flavor from the barrels they are aged in or from added herbs or spices. For this reason they are less useful in the kitchen, although bourbon and rum ice creams are very good.

Spirits are the perfect flavoring for White Chocolate Truffles, and in this form they can echo the tastes or the associations of the dinner that precedes them. A kirsch-flavored sherbet is just right following a dinner of choucroute garnie, the rich sauerkraut dish popular wherever kirsch is drunk. For many of the Provençal menus at the restaurant, we flavor desserts with Pernod, a strong anise-flavored spirit of southern France. Ricard and ouzo are very similar. Pernod complements figs perfectly and it is also a good accompaniment to strawberries and raspberries. Its usefulness even extends to the main course: a bouillabaise is unthinkable without a drop or two.

It is important to buy good quality spirits. You need very little and they keep forever (if you can keep from drinking them). Buy real kirsch from Alsace, real Cognac and Armagnac, and you will be repaid with excellent flavor. In time this country will produce fine spirits, but just now the art is still in its infancy.

The art of winemaking, of course, is not. There is a wide choice of good domestic wines as well as imported ones. The wine you choose need not be expensive, but it should be thoughtfully matched to the dessert in which it is used as well as to the dinner that comes before. Some wines have striking affinities with fruits. At the restaurant we poach pears in Sauternes, and in many dry red and white wines. Prunes and figs, too, are poached in wine and spices, following a good custom that goes back to medieval times. Often we serve desserts made or garnished with Champagne for the festive spirit it lends to almost any fruit. Pears combine beautifully with Late Harvest Riesling Ice Cream, and peaches have a great affinity with Marsala and sherry—but they must be well-made Marsala and sherry: these wines can be artfully rich and complex, or ordinary and dull; worse, the mass-produced versions can taste of chemicals. Of course the time-honored combinations are good—this is why they become clichés: kirsch with pineapple, or pears with cassis. But try to create your own, remembering the affinities of season and region. For instance, Provençal red wines flavored with lavender, rosemary, or thyme make just the right poaching liquid for the figs that are so abundant there; in the same way, Beaumes-de-Venise wine, a gently fortified wine made from Muscat grapes, suits apricots perfectly. If you cannot buy Beaumes-de-Venise, try substituting a French Sauternes or an Italian Verduzzo, but these wines will not have the Muscat flavor of the Beaumes-de-Venise.

Your ideas about what is appropriate will evolve. One of the first sophisticated desserts I enjoyed making was a molded gelatin of crème de cacao and coffee. Now I use wine in a less obvious pairing in a cake invented by one of our most loyal customers—a cake whose flavoring is Sauternes and virgin olive oil. Perhaps it sounds strange, but it is delicate and delicious and accompanies a number of fruits very well; we make it often, occasionally replacing the Sauternes with Beaumes-de-Venise wine.

Finally, there is the possibility of simply serving the wine or spirit *as* a dessert. Spirits are very assertive, of course, because of their high alcohol content, and you have to consider carefully how they will relate to the flavors and aromas of the meal that comes before. An Armagnac is a fine digestive dessert after a cassoulet, or a tiny glass of kirsch and a handful of perfect fresh cherries after that choucroute garnie. Once you begin thinking along such lines, you may find yourself serving the Armagnac with grapes that have been preserved in it. Wine is much easier to serve as a dessert, and a glass of Champagne is always appropriate, especially if it has preceded the meal as well. A fine vintage Sauternes needs only a few fresh almonds as an accompaniment. And a glass of good Zinfandel, red Rhone, or Piedmont wine, perhaps the last of the bottle that accompanied dinner, is delicious with a few biscotti to dip into it.

BEAUMES-DE-VENISE ICE CREAM

Makes 1 quart: *1 cup half-and-half · ⅔ cup sugar · 6 egg yolks · 2 cups whipping cream · ½ cup Beaumes-de-Venise wine*

Warm the half-and-half with the sugar in a non-corroding saucepan, stirring occasionally, until the sugar dissolves. Whisk the egg yolks just enough to break them up and stir in some of the warm half-and-half. Return to the pan and cook over low heat, stirring constantly, until the mixture coats the spoon. Strain into a container, add the cream and the wine, and chill. Freeze according to the instructions with your ice cream maker.

Serve with peaches or nectarines, sliced or stuffed and baked, or with raspberries, acompanied in any case by Langues de Chat.

Beaumes-de-Venise is a slightly fortified wine made from Muscat grapes. If you cannot buy Beaumes-de-Venise wine, try substituting a French Sauternes or an Italian Verduzzo, but these wines will not have the characteristic Muscat flavor of the Beaumes-de-Venise. See the sources for mail order suppliers.

BEAUMES-DE-VENISE SABAYON

Makes 2 cups: *4 egg yolks · 3 tablespoons sugar · ⅜ cup Beaumes-de-Venise wine*

Have a pan of simmering water ready. Whisk the egg yolks and sugar in a copper or stainless steel bowl just to mix. Whisk in the Beaumes-de-Venise and set over the pan of barely simmering water. Don't let the water touch the bottom of the bowl. Whisk constantly until the mixture is thick and holds a shape and there is no liquid left at the bottom of the bowl; to check this, remove from the heat.

Serve this warm as it is, or cold. If you want to serve it cold, whip ½ cup whipping cream until it holds a very soft shape and fold it into the cooled sabayon. Serve with Baked Stuffed Peaches or Nectarines, or with poached peaches or nectarines.

PORT WINE CUSTARDS

For 8 servings: *2⅓ cups whipping cream · ½ cup less 2 teaspoons sugar · 6 egg yolks · ⅔ cup good port*

Heat the cream and sugar in a non-corroding saucepan until the sugar has melted. Meanwhile whisk the egg yolks just enough to mix them—don't let them foam. Pour the hot cream mixture into the eggs, stirring constantly. Stir in the port and taste for flavor balance. Strain, then pour into custard cups, pots de crème, or individual soufflé dishes.

Bake in a hot water bath in a preheated 325°F oven for 15 to 20 minutes, or until the custards are set around the edge but still jiggle slightly in the center when shaken. Cover them lightly with a sheet of foil while they bake so the tops won't brown or form a skin. The top of the custard will turn a lovely café au lait color and the inside will be a soft mauve.

Serve warm or chilled, on a doily with Walnut Drops and a dark Chocolate Truffle.

LATE HARVEST RIESLING ICE CREAM

Makes 1 quart: *½ cup half-and-half · ⅝ cup sugar · 3 egg yolks · 1½ cups whipping cream · 1 cup Late Harvest Riesling wine*

Warm the half-and-half and the sugar in a non-corroding saucepan until the sugar has dissolved. Whisk the egg yolks just to break them up and whisk in the half-and-half mixture. Return to the pan and cook over low heat, stirring constantly, until the mixture coats the spoon. Strain and add the cream and wine. Chill thoroughly. Freeze according to the instructions with your ice cream maker.

Serve with Baked Stuffed Pears. We ate this once after an Alsatian dinner—it was the perfect ending to that meal.

LINDA'S OLIVE OIL AND SAUTERNES CAKE

For 10 to 12 servings: *5 eggs · ¾ cup sugar · 1 tablespoon mixed orange and lemon peel, finely grated · ⅓ cup plus 2 tablespoons extra virgin olive oil · ½ cup good Sauternes · 1 cup sifted flour · ¼ teaspoon salt · 2 egg whites · ½ teaspoon cream of tartar*

Butter and flour an 8-inch springform pan or line the bottom with parchment. Preheat the oven to 350°F. Separate the 5 eggs and beat the yolks

254

with half the sugar until light colored and thick. Beat in the mixed grated peel. Beat in the olive oil and then the Sauternes. Mix the flour and salt and beat into the egg mixture just until it is mixed.

Beat the 7 egg whites with the cream of tartar until they hold soft peaks. Beat in the remaining sugar until the egg whites hold stiff peaks. Fold into the egg yolk mixture thoroughly. Pour into the prepared pan and bake, turning the cake if necessary for it to bake evenly, for 20 minutes. Lower the oven temperature to 300°F and bake for another 20 minutes. Then turn off the oven, cover the top of the cake with a round of buttered parchment, and leave it in the oven for another 10 minutes. Remove from the oven and cool in the pan on a rack.

This cake keeps well for a few days if the pan is covered tightly with foil. It is delicious served with apricot cream, made by whipping cream and stirring in homemade apricot jam to taste. Or serve it with sliced sugared peaches or nectarines and sabayon.

This recipe was printed in *The Chez Panisse Menu Cookbook* as it was developed by Linda Guenzel. I have made a few changes in it to give it a lighter texture. It also works beautifully when Beaumes-de-Venise wine is substituted for the Sauternes.

SAUTERNES SABAYON

Makes 2 cups: *4 egg yolks · ¼ cup sugar · ½ cup Sauternes*

Have a pan of simmering water ready. Whisk the egg yolks and sugar in a copper or stainless steel bowl just to mix. Whisk in the Sauternes and set over the pan of barely simmering water. Don't let the water touch the bottom of the bowl. Whisk constantly until the mixture is thick and holds a shape and there is no liquid left at the bottom of the bowl; to check this, remove from the heat.

Serve warm or cold. If you want to serve it cold, whip ½ cup whipping cream until it holds a very soft shape and fold into the cooled sabayon. Serve with pears or peaches, either baked or poached, or with fresh berries.

ANISE ICE CREAM

Makes a generous quart: *1 cup half-and-half* · *⅔ cup sugar* · *6 egg yolks* · *2 cups whipping cream* · *¾ teaspoon Pernod*

Warm the half-and-half with the sugar in a non-corroding saucepan until the sugar has dissolved. Whisk the egg yolks lightly, just enough to mix them, and stir in some of the hot mixture. Return to the pan and cook, stirring constantly, until the custard coats the spoon. Strain into a bowl and add the cream and Pernod; chill. Taste for the anise flavor, adding a little more Pernod if you would like a stronger flavor. Be careful; the Pernod is very strong and it will sneak up on you. Freeze according to the instructions with your ice cream maker.

Serve with berries or figs, or with warm Fig or Apple Tart.

CRÊPES WITH ANISE ICE CREAM
AND STRAWBERRIES

For 10 servings: *10 crêpes (page 14)* · *Anise Ice Cream (above)* · *1 or 2 pint baskets ripe strawberries, or mixed strawberries and fraises des bois* · *4 tablespoons honey* · *Optional: vanilla powdered sugar (page 4)*

Provençal lavender honey, or a local flower honey, would be delicious for this dessert.

Make the crêpes the day before you need them, or earlier the same day. Make the ice cream a day or two before. When ready to serve the dessert, wash, dry, hull, and slice the strawberries. If they aren't perfectly sweet, toss them with a little sugar. If you are using fraises des bois, keep them separate and don't wash them.

Warm the honey slightly. Warm the crêpes on a rack in a preheated 375°F oven for a minute or two until they are crisp around the edges but can still be folded in half. Cool them. When they are crisp, set them on dessert plates and fill with two or three ovals of the ice cream. Sprinkle the berries on them; dust them lightly with powdered sugar, if you like, and drizzle a little of the warmed honey over the crêpes and berries. Serve immediately.

FROZEN ANISE SOUFFLÉ

Makes 3 pints: *5 egg yolks · ⅝ cup sugar · 3 cups whipping cream · 1¼ teaspoons Pernod, to taste · 1 lemon*

Beat the egg yolks and sugar until stiff enough to hold a shape. Whip the cream to soft peaks. Fold the egg and sugar mixture into the cream. Fold in the Pernod and grate fine shreds of lemon zest into the mixture to taste. Butter the sides of a 1-quart soufflé dish lightly, enough to hold a waxed paper liner in place. The paper should form a collar standing at least an inch above the rim of the dish. Clip the top of the collar together with a paper clip. You may line individual soufflé cups in the same way. Fill the dishes ½ inch above their rims, and freeze.

Before serving, remove the paper carefully and let the soufflé stand 10 to 15 minutes to soften slightly. Garnish the top with a violet and a violet leaf, or with a piece of candied violet. The soufflé is good served with lemon butter cookies.

BOURBON ICE CREAM

Makes 1 quart: *1 cup milk · ¾ cup sugar · 5 egg yolks · 2¼ cups whipping cream · 3 tablespoons bourbon*

Heat the milk and sugar in a non-corroding saucepan, stirring occasionally, until the sugar dissolves. Whisk the egg yolks to break them up and whisk in some of the hot mixture to warm them. Return to the pan and cook over low heat, stirring constantly, until the custard coats the spoon. Strain into a container, add the cream, and add the bourbon to taste. Chill thoroughly; then freeze according to the instructions with your ice cream maker.

Serve in cookie cups or in Pecan Crêpes drizzled with a little maple syrup.

CALVADOS ICE CREAM

Makes about 1 quart: *¾ cup sugar · 1 cup half-and-half · 6 egg yolks · 2 cups whipping cream · 2 tablespoons calvados*

Heat the sugar and the half-and-half in a small saucepan until the sugar has melted. Break up the egg yolks with a whisk, just mixing them without beating them, and stir in the warm half-and-half mixture. Return to the pan and cook over low heat, stirring constantly, until the mixture coats the spoon. Strain into a bowl and add the cream and the calvados to taste. You will probably want the flavor delicate if you are serving the ice cream alone, stronger if you plan to serve it with something like an apple tart. Chill. Freeze according to the instructions with your ice cream maker.

Serve with crisp cookies or with Warm Apple Tart, or make a Pear Sherbet and Calvados Ice Cream bombe.

CALVADOS SHERBET

Makes 1 pint: *2 cups water · ¼ cup sugar · 2 tablespoons corn syrup · ¼ cup 80-proof calvados*

Boil the water with the sugar and corn syrup for 5 minutes. Chill. Add the calvados and freeze according to the directions with your ice cream maker. This sherbet is quite hard at 0°F; serve it by scraping a spoon across its surface, or let it soften slightly before serving. It is a nice complement to a very rich duck dinner.

PROFITEROLES WITH CHARTREUSE CREAM AND WARM CHOCOLATE SAUCE

For 6 servings: *18 small cream puffs (page 18) · ¾ cup whipping cream · 1½ teaspoons sugar · 1½ teaspoons Chartreuse*

Whip the cream with the sugar and Chartreuse. Taste and adjust the amount of sugar and Chartreuse to your taste. Put it in a pastry bag with a tip with a small round opening. When you are ready to serve, pipe the cream into the puffs by breaking a small hole in the bottom of the puff with the pastry tube. Or slice off the top third of the puffs, spoon the cream in, and replace the tops. Put three puffs on a serving plate and drizzle them with Warm Chocolate Sauce.

WARM CHOCOLATE SAUCE

Makes 1 cup: *3 ounces semisweet chocolate · 3 tablespoons water · 1 tablespoon butter · 6 tablespoons whipping cream or crème fraîche · 1½ teaspoons Chartreuse*

Break the chocolate into small pieces and melt them with the water and butter in a small heavy pan over hot water or over very low heat, stirring. Stir in the cream until smooth; using crème fraîche will result in a richer tasting sauce. Stir in the Chartreuse, adding it to taste: remember that it will also be flavoring the cream. Rewarm to serve.

You can also flavor the sauce with any other spirit you like—Cognac, brandy, rum, etc.—to serve with other desserts.

CHARTREUSE ICE CREAM

Makes a generous quart: *1 cup milk · ⅔ cup sugar · 6 egg yolks · 2 cups whipping cream · 1 tablespoon green Chartreuse*

Heat the milk and sugar in a non-corroding saucepan to dissolve the sugar, stirring occasionally. Whisk the egg yolks just enough to break them up and stir in some of the hot milk mixture. Return to the pan and cook, stirring constantly, until the custard coats the spoon. Strain into a container, add the cream and Chartreuse, and chill. Freeze according to the instructions with your ice cream maker.

Serve with Langues de Chat and Warm Chocolate Sauce, or in almond cookie cups.

ESPRESSO-COGNAC MOUSSE

Makes 1¼ quarts: ½ cup boiling water · ¼ cup finely ground espresso coffee, or 1 tablespoon more if you want a very strong-flavored mousse · 1½ teaspoons gelatin · 2 tablespoons cold water · 2 eggs · ⅓ cup sugar · 1⅓ cups whipping cream · Vanilla extract to taste · About 2 teaspoons Cognac

Measure the boiling water into a non-corroding saucepan, bring it back to a boil, stir in the coffee, and heat again until it bubbles slightly around the edges. Let steep for 5 minutes. Strain through a towel or a coffee filter, pressing to remove all the liquid, and set aside. Sprinkle the gelatin over the cold water in a small saucepan and let it stand a few minutes. Beat the eggs and the sugar together until the mixture holds a shape for 3 seconds when you drop some from the beater. Set aside. Whip the cream until it mounds softly when you lift the beater from it; it should not form peaks, or the mousse will have a foamy texture.

Pour the strained coffee over the gelatin and set it over low heat to dissolve, stirring constantly. You will be able to see the clear little specks of gelatin in the coffee, so you can easily see when it has dissolved; the mixture won't need to get very hot. Cool the mixture to lukewarm—over a cold water bath if you are in a hurry.

Whisk the coffee mixture into the whipped cream, being sure to keep the whisk moving through the stream of coffee to avoid making strands or lumps of gelatin when the warm coffee mixture hits the colder cream. Whisk until the mixture is the same texture as the whipped cream was, then fold in the egg and sugar mixture. Fold in a few drops of vanilla and Cognac to taste. Chill.

Serve garnished with a rosette of crème Chantilly, sprinkled with some finely ground coffee or finely grated unsweetened chocolate. Or you can serve it as we did once: make an equal-sized batch of chocolate mousse and pour the two mousses into parfait glasses at the same time from two pitchers so you have a half-coffee, half-chocolate mousse divided down the middle. Or garnish with a piece of Chocolate Lace—but not if it is a warm summer day, as it was the last time we served this. We set the pieces of lace on the first mousses to be served, only to watch them droop immediately and lie flat on the tops of the mousses.

260

COGNAC CARAMEL SAUCE

Makes about ½ cup: *2 tablespoons water · ½ cup sugar · 5 tablespoons hot water · About ½ teaspoon lemon juice · About 1 teaspoon Cognac*

Put the 2 tablespoons water in a small heavy saucepan and add the sugar. Let stand until the sugar is moistened. Cook over medium high heat, swirling the pan occasionally until the sugar turns light golden brown. Remove from the heat and pour in the hot water very carefully to keep it from spattering you. Return to the heat and cook, stirring constantly, until all the caramel has dissolved. Cool. Add a few drops of lemon juice to cut the sweetness, and Cognac to taste.

Serve with Black Walnut Crêpes with Pear Ice Cream, or with puff pastries filled with apples or pears.

HARD SAUCE

Makes ⅔ cup: *4 tablespoons unsalted butter · ½ cup powdered sugar · 1½ teaspoons Cognac or brandy, bourbon, or other spirit to your taste*

Beat the softened butter until it is light and fluffy and gradually beat in the powdered sugar. Beat well and add the Cognac or other liquor. Beat until it is very fluffy and pile into a pretty dish. Cover and chill until it is firm.

Serve with warm Pumpkin Pie or Steamed Fig Pudding.

EGGNOG ICE CREAM

Makes 1 quart: *1 cup milk · ¾ cup sugar · 5 egg yolks · 2¼ cups whipping cream · 2½ tablespoons bourbon · 1 tablespoon brandy · Freshly grated nutmeg*

Warm the milk and the sugar in a non-corroding saucepan to dissolve the sugar. Whisk the egg yolks to break them up and beat in the hot milk mixture. Return to the pan and cook over low heat, stirring constantly, until the mixture coats the spoon. Strain into a container, and add the cream and the liquors. Grate in nutmeg to taste, remembering that its flavor will get stronger as it sits. Chill. Taste again for the balance of liquor and nutmeg flavor. Freeze according to the instructions with your ice cream maker.

Serve during the Christmas holidays with Christmas cookies.

GRAND MARNIER SOUFFLÉS

For 5 individual soufflés: *½ cup milk · 1 tablespoon plus 2 teaspoons flour · 1½ tablespoons sugar · 5 egg yolks · 1 tablespoon unsalted butter · 1¼ teaspoons finely chopped candied tangerine or orange peel (page 64) · 3¾ tablespoons plus 1 or 2 teaspoons Grand Marnier · 5 egg whites · ¼ teaspoon cream of tartar · 4 tablespoons sugar*

Heat the milk in a small non-corroding saucepan. Mix the flour and the 1½ tablespoons sugar and gradually whisk in the hot milk. Return to the pan and cook over medium heat, stirring constantly, until the mixture boils for a minute or two. Beat the egg yolks until they are light colored and slightly thickened. Carefully beat in a little of the hot milk mixture. Beat the warmed egg mixture into the remaining milk mixture in the pan. Cook over low heat, stirring constantly, until the eggs are cooked. The temperature should reach 170°F. Stir in the butter and chill, tightly covered. Soak the chopped peel in a teaspoon or two of Grand Marnier. You may do this much ahead of time.

Butter and sugar 5 individual soufflé dishes. When you are ready to bake the soufflés, whisk the peel and the Grand Marnier into the egg mixture. Warm the egg whites slightly over hot water or swirl above a gas flame until barely warm. Beat them with the cream of tartar until they hold stiff peaks. Beat in the 4 tablespoons sugar until they again hold soft peaks. Quickly fold into the yolk mixture and pour into the prepared dishes. Bake in a preheated 400°F oven for 7 to 9 minutes, or until puffed and lightly brown but still a little shaky if you jiggle them from side to side. Serve with very cold vanilla crème anglaise to pour into them.

262

SAINT-HONORÉ CAKE

This is a very pretty cake—a shell ringed with tiny cream puffs filled with liqueur-flavored cream, with angel hair spun over the top. This recipe makes 10 servings.

Shell: *½ recipe pie pastry (page 23) · 1 recipe cream puff dough (page 18)*

Roll the pie pastry ⅛-inch thick and cut a 10-inch circle from it. Chill. Prick and bake in a preheated 400°F oven for 15 minutes, or until golden. Cool the pie crust on a rack.

Make the cream puff dough. Pipe a circle 10 inches in diameter on a buttered baking sheet using a pastry bag with a ½-inch tip. Then pipe 20 or 22 small puffs about 1¼ inches in diameter and 1-inch high in the spaces and on another buttered baking sheet, if necessary. Put them in the 400°F oven, turn down immediately to 375°F, and bake about 15 minutes for the small puffs. Remove from the oven and prick them quickly with the point of a sharp knife; then dry them in the oven for another 5 minutes. The ring will take about 20 minutes in the oven; then it should be pricked and returned to the oven to dry for 5 to 10 minutes. Cool these on racks.

Put the baked pie pastry bottom on a baking sheet and lightly butter a 2-inch circle around its edge. This will prevent the angel hair, which is the final garnish for the cake, from sticking to the sheet.

Filling: *2 cups vanilla pastry cream (page 7) · 2 teaspoons gelatin · 1 tablespoon water · ¾ cup whipping cream · 1 tablespoon kirsch · 1 tablespoon maraschino · 3 egg whites · 3 tablespoons sugar*

Soften the gelatin in the water for 5 minutes, dissolve it over low heat, cool it slightly, and quickly whisk it into the pastry cream. Whip the cream with the kirsch and maraschino until it holds a very soft shape. Beat into the cold pastry cream just until it is smooth. Beat the egg whites until they hold stiff peaks and beat in the sugar until they hold stiff peaks again. Fold into the pastry cream mixture and set into the refrigerator to chill.

Filling for small puffs: *¾ cup whipping cream · 2 teaspoons sugar · 1 tablespoon Grand Marnier*

Whip the cream with the sugar and Grand Marnier and use a pastry bag to pipe it into the small puffs through their bottoms. Set aside.

Caramel: *¼ cup water* · *¾ cup sugar* · *¼ teaspoon lemon juice*

Put the water in a small heavy saucepan and add the sugar and lemon juice. Let stand until the sugar is moistened. Set over medium high heat and cook, covered, for 5 minutes. Uncover and cook until the caramel is pale gold. Remove from the heat and set briefly into a pan of ice water to stop the cooking.

Before the caramel thickens, quickly dip the tops of the filled puffs into it to make a thin coating of caramel on each one, and set them back on the rack to cool. Be very careful not to let any caramel drip on you. Always have a bowl of ice water nearby when working with caramel: if you do burn yourself you will be grateful for your foresight. Now put a few drops of the caramel dripped from a fork around the edge of the pastry bottom and quickly set the cream puff ring onto it, gluing it in place. If the caramel has thickened, rewarm it slightly to thin it. Carefully dip the bottoms of the small puffs into the caramel and set them in a circle on the ring, fitting them as close together as possible.

Topping: *1½ cups whipping cream* · *2½ tablespoons sugar* · *1 teaspoon vanilla extract* · *Optional: 1 or 2 tablespoons finely chopped candied orange or tangerine peel (page 64)*

Whip the cream for the topping with the sugar and vanilla until it holds a soft shape. Quickly spoon the chilled filling into the shell and pipe the cream decoratively over the top. Sprinkle with the finely chopped peel, if you like. At this point you may decorate the cake with angel hair (page 141). Rewarm the caramel if it has cooled and thickened; when it is syrupy, spin angel hair around the puffs and lightly over the top of the cake.

Slide the bottom of a tart pan under the cake, or use a large spatula to move it to a serving platter. Cut wedges of the cake, allowing two little puffs per serving.

KIRSCH CUSTARDS

For 8 servings: *½ cup sugar · 3 cups whipping cream · 6 egg yolks · 2 tablespoons kirsch*

Choose a baking pan large enough to hold 8 custard cups, pots de crème, or individual soufflé dishes. Fill it about a third full with hot water and set it into a preheated 325°F oven. Heat the sugar in the cream until it has dissolved. Whisk the egg yolks in a bowl until they are broken up, but don't allow them to foam. Pour in the hot cream mixture, stirring constantly. Add the kirsch. Strain the custard and pour it into the cups. Set the cups into the hot water and pour in more hot water if necessary; the water should come halfway up the sides of the cups. Cover the cups lightly with foil and bake for 15 to 20 minutes, or until the custard is just set around the outside but still jiggles in the center when shaken slightly. Using tongs, remove cups from the water bath and let them cool.

Brown the tops, if you like, as follows: Empty the hot water from the baking pan, set the cups back in, and pack ice cubes around them. Fill the pan with cold water halfway up the sides of the cups and set the custards under the broiler for a minute or two, or until their tops are flecked with brown. If you increase the heat to 450°F, you can brown them in the oven in their cold water bath, but it will take longer. The broiler is the better method.

These custards should be thick and creamy rather than solid. Serve them on a pretty plate on a doily with brandied cherries and Sarah's Macaroons.

KIRSCH PARFAIT

Makes a little more than 3 cups: *8 egg yolks · 1 cup sugar · ¾ cup water · 2⅔ cups whipping cream · About 1 tablespoon of kirsch*

Beat the egg yolks until they hold a ribbon for 3 seconds when you lift the beater from the mixture. Meanwhile, cook the sugar and water to 224°F, or until it spins a 2-inch thread when you drop some from a spoon.

Immediately remove the syrup from the heat and pour it in a thin stream into the egg yolks, beating constantly. Try to pour in a very thin stream at first to heat the egg yolks gently so they won't scramble; you may pour it more quickly afterward. Beat over ice water until cool and thick enough to hold a slight shape. Whip the cream until it holds a slight shape when some is dropped from the beaters, and fold in the egg yolk mixture and the kirsch. Taste and add more kirsch, if you like. Pour into parfait glasses and freeze.

Serve topped with a brandied or fresh cherry, and accompanied by Langues de Chat, Lace Cookies, or Sarah's Macaroons.

KIRSCH SHERBET

Makes about a pint: *2 cups water · ¼ cup sugar · 2 tablespoons corn syrup · 2 tablespoons 90-proof kirsch · A few fine gratings of lemon peel*

Boil 1 cup of the water with the sugar and corn syrup for a few minutes. Add the other cup of water, the kirsch, and a little lemon peel. Chill thoroughly; then taste to see if more kirsch or lemon is needed and adjust if necessary. Freeze according to the instructions with your ice cream maker.

This is nice served with fresh fruit after a rich choucroute garnie.

RUM ICE CREAM

Makes 1 quart: *1 cup milk · 2 cups whipping cream · ⅔ cup sugar · 6 egg yolks · ¼ cup dark rum*

Heat the milk, cream, and sugar in a non-corroding saucepan. Whisk the egg yolks just enough to mix them and whisk in some of the hot mixture. Return to the pan and cook over low heat, stirring constantly, until the mixture coats the spoon. Strain into a container and chill. Add the rum, taste, and add a little more if necessary. Freeze according to the instructions with your ice cream maker.

266

Serve with Rich Chocolate Cake or crisp cookies, or use in various bombes.

To make Rum Walnut Ice Cream: Add 1 cup walnuts, which have been lightly toasted and coarsely chopped, to the above recipe. Serve with crisp cookies, or combine with Coffee or Chocolate Ice Cream in a bombe.

To make Cognac Ice Cream: Substitute Cognac to taste for the rum in the above recipe.

FROZEN ZABAGLIONE

For 6 to 8 servings: *¼ cup plus 2 teaspoons dry Marsala · 2 tablespoons sugar · 2 egg yolks · ½ cup whipping cream*

Mix ¼ cup Marsala and the sugar in a small heavy saucepan or a zabaglione pan. Whisk in the egg yolks. Have a pan of simmering water ready and set the pan over it, whisking constantly. Whisk about 5 minutes, until the mixture has become very light and fluffy and there is no uncooked liquid at the bottom. It should hold a shape for a moment when you drop some from the whisk. Whisk over a bowl of ice to chill immediately. Whip the cream with the remaining Marsala and fold into the cooled zabaglione. Pour into a container and freeze in the freezer, not in an ice cream maker. Let soften slightly before serving.

Serve with Baked Stuffed Pears, or Peaches, or Nectarines.

APPENDICES
BIBLIOGRAPHY
INDEX

APPENDIX A

APPLES, PEARS, AND QUINCES

APPLES

The apple is the oldest fruit known to man. A fruit of temperate climates, it probably originated near the Black Sea and the Caspian Sea.

Apples are commercially produced in the United States mainly in the Northwest, Midwest, and Northeast—but are actively produced in thirty-four states, wherever there are warm days with cool nights. However, varieties have been developed for specific climates formerly unsuited to apples: the Gravenstein is grown extensively in Sonoma County, an hour north of Chez Panisse and only a few miles from Zinfandel country. The normal seasons for apples are late summer, fall, and early winter, but these have been extended by ripening in cold storage so that apples are now available up to six months after they have been picked. The apples are kept at low temperatures in an atmosphere that is almost entirely nitrogen. The process, called "controlled atmosphere," is almost universal by now.

Apples have been with us at least since the Stone Age, and have had time to develop at least 5,000 varieties by now—some estimate as many as 20,000. A list of the more popular apples makes your mouth water: Red Astrachan, Baldwin, Spitzenberg, Fameuse, Gravenstein, Jonathan, Macoun, Newtown Green or Yellow Pippin, Northern Spy, Rhode Island Greening, Roxbury or Boston Russet, Tompkins King, Rambo, Idared, Wealthy, York Imperial, Grimes Golden, Winesap, Rome Beauty, Johnagold, Criterion, Mutsu, Melrose, Cortland King, Gala.

Some highly regarded foreign varieties are Cox's Orange Pippin, Granny Smith (but not those picked green to be shipped long distances), Cellini, Grey Rennet, Blenheim Orange, Calville Blanc, Devonshire Quarrenden.

The most commonly available apples commercially are the Red Delicious, the Golden Delicious, and the McIntosh. Of the apples easily available to the restaurant, McIntosh and Gravenstein are the ones I use for most cooking purposes—they stay moist and tender when baked in tarts

270

and they have very good flavor. I like the Summer Rose for its good taste and its white, pink-blushed skin. Others will probably be available in other parts of the country, and it is best to taste and cook with the varieties available to you.

The biggest sellers among apples, as among all fruit, are those that produce copiously and dependably, store and ship well, and look "attractive" in the market. They have been sprayed against the codling moth worm and insects, and often waxed to a high gloss. Taste, alas, is likely to be a minor consideration.

The best apples you get you will probably grow yourself or buy from a local farmer who lets them ripen before picking them. If you are interested in planting a tree, perhaps to graft a few different varieties on, consult the list of sources below—they offer hundreds of varieties, some of them very old, even historic. By growing your own apples, or knowing the people who do grow them, you can exercise greater control over the ripening and the pesticides to which the fruit has been exposed. In the dessert kitchen, apples are nearly always peeled before use, but it is nice to know that you could eat the skins if you wanted to. Fortunately, the success of poisons is their own downfall: resistant strains of pests have developed because of the application of pesticides to apples, and more commercial growers are turning to ecological means of pest control.

When you buy apples, choose firm, unbruised fruits—but the odd blemish or crack or two is of no consequence. Avoid fruit that is noticeably large for its variety; it is likely to have been pushed for size and therefore lack intensity of flavor. Store apples in a cool dry place with good air circulation—the kitchen is not likely to be the best place; the old-fashioned pantry and fruit cellar had their points. The fruit bin in your refrigerator works well for a few days, though, and apples taste a bit better when they have ripened a few days at home after leaving the store.

PEARS

Pears are somewhat younger than apples, originating only 3,500 to 4,000 years ago somewhere between central Europe and northeastern Asia. They became a prized fruit of the wealthy elite and a particular favorite of the French nobility—many varieties retain their French names. There are now an estimated 2,000 to 5,000 varieties.

The most common variety of pear is the Bartlett, a summer pear also known as the Williams. There are both yellow and red Bartletts, the red ones apparently being more disease resistant. They are available from mid-July to early winter. Bosc, Comice, Winter Nelis, Forelle, and Seckel are all winter pears, on the market from October through May.

Unlike apples, pears do not ripen well on the tree. They must be picked when mature but still firm, and ripened off the tree. They are fragile; it is said that growers of Comice pears are becoming rarer because the fruit is so difficult to pick and ship. This is too bad, because the Comice is indeed the "queen of pears," certainly in my kitchen. The flavor is winy and complex, making delicious sherbets and ice creams, and the fine, smooth, buttery texture bakes particularly well. The Bartlett's perfume is also good in sherbets and ice creams, and its flesh holds well when cooked. The Bosc has very good flavor and an elegant shape, which it holds in cooking, making it especially suited to poaching and to tarts. Winter Nelis are even firmer, extremely good baked in upside-down tarts because they hold their shape so well, and have very good flavor.

The Beurre Hardy, or butter pear, can be cooked when treated carefully, but its flesh quickly breaks down when cooked. Its delicious flavor seems more suited to eating fresh. All these pears are suited to eating out of hand, for that matter—when properly ripe. The perfect ripe pear and a slice of Gorgonzola or a Gorgonzola cream make a classic dessert combination.

Choose firm pears unless you plan to eat them within a day or two. They are ripe when they give slightly to gentle pressure around the neck or stem. Refrigerate ripe pears and plan to use them within a few days. They should be ripened in a warm place where the temperature is even— a windowsill is not as good as a spot above the refrigerator.

QUINCES

The quince is a native of Persia and the Caspian areas, where it is still found wild. Quinces that are cultivated there are said to be somewhat sweet and edible raw. The quinces familiar to us are full of starch and a highly astringent compound like that in persimmons. They can be eaten only when cooked, after which the starch is changed to sugar and the astringent compound broken down.

The quince was formerly quite popular in this country; isolated trees are still found in small town family orchards. They remain popular in Europe, Mexico, and Latin America, but have lost favor here—though they are still made into beautiful jams and jellies in this country by those who appreciate the quince's wonderful fragrance and color.

Most but not all quinces turn a deep autumnal red when cooked. This

272

"pinking" phenomenon results when the flesh is heated in cooking. Heat apparently causes changes in pigmentation common to all pomes, as occasional cans of pears and applesauce reveal, but the result is more striking in quinces.

Some of the best varieties are the Apple (sometimes called the Orange), the Portugal, Vrania, Pineapple, and Smyrna. Of these, the Pineapple variety is occasionally distinguished from others in the market. All these quinces are yellow and fragrant when ripe and will keep for several weeks in a cool dry place. They combine especially well with both apples and pears in cooked desserts, and are interesting though still somewhat controversial when used alone—the flavor is highly individual, and valuable for that reason.

CITRUS FRUITS

ORANGES

The orange is one of the oldest fruits, originating nearly 3,000 years ago in India. For centuries it was exclusively the bitter orange. The sweet orange, *Citrus sinensis*, did not arrive in Lisbon from China until the 1630s. It quickly displaced *Citrus aurantium*, now produced chiefly in Spain, whose Seville orange is produced primarily for the marmalade and perfume industries. Early recipes, however, usually called for bitter oranges, since those were all that were available—a point to consider when you think of such dishes as duck à l'orange.

Today's market varieties include the Washington Navel, almost seedless, very easy to peel and to segment, and the Valencias, the chief juice orange. There are also early varieties: the Parson Brown, Hamlin, and Pineapple orange.

Blood oranges are grown especially in Sicily, and are becoming more available here as demand for them increases. Their season runs from January to late spring. Some blood oranges have a red-blushed skin and some don't—this depends partly on the side of the tree they grow on—but the color of the skin doesn't necessarily reflect the flesh.

To choose oranges, look for those with a soft shine, heavy for their size (an indication of sweetness), with a little give. Avoid hard fruit. A little re-greening on the stem ends of Valencias means that they are late-season oranges, quite likely sweeter. Oranges tend to be available all year, but the peak supplies are from December to March.

MANDARINS
Mandarins and tangerines—*Citrus reticulata*—are easily confused. Considered cousins of the orange, they have a sweeter, dryer flesh, are easier to peel, and have looser segments. The available varieties include Fairchild, Clementine, Honey, Kinnow, Page, Dancy, Encore, Mediterranean, and Frua.

HYBRIDS
Some authorities believe the Clementine to be a variety of tangerine. Others think it a hybrid, *Citrus nobilis*, a cross between the tangerine and the orange, said to be descended from a tree found near Oran, Algeria, by Père Clément. Whatever it is, it candies very well indeed.

The tangelo is a cross between the mandarin and the grapefruit, tangy flavored, available from November into the spring. Varieties include Minneolas, Orlandos, and Sampsons.

The Tangor is a cross of mandarin and sweet orange, with large, sweet-tasting fruit.

The Lavender Gem is another citrus hybrid, a cross between the mandarin and grapefruit, small, yellow skinned, with pale pink flesh. It is available in very short supply in December, January, and February.

GRAPEFRUIT
Grapefruits were developed in the early nineteenth century from a mutation of the pomelo, and were not classified a separate species, *Citrus paradisi*, until 1830. One kind or another is available all year; I particularly like the Marsh Ruby. Grapefruits have fortunately not quite displaced the huge old-fashioned pomelo (or pummelo)—it is a traditional part of Chinese New Year celebrations, and we find it easily in early spring, when its unusual flavor perfumes our ice creams.

LEMONS
The lemon, *Citrus limon*, originated in the Far East, reached the Mediterranean courtesy of the Crusades, and was brought to the New World by Columbus. Now half the world's crop is grown in California and Arizona. The standard market variety is the Eureka, egg shaped with a flat nipple at the stem end, a pitted skin, and lots of clear, acid juice. Its

274

peak season is the summer, and it is followed in the fall by the quite similar Lisbon. I increasingly prefer the Meyer, smaller, rounder, thinner skinned and much sweeter to taste. It is hard to find in the market, but grows plentifully in Berkeley back yards.

OTHER CITRUS

I like to make an occasional lime mousse or soufflé, but otherwise find the lime less useful in the kitchen than the lemon—it is, admittedly, a very different fruit. I wish the Key or Mexican lime were more often available in the Bay Area; it is more tart and flavorful than the Persian lime. Kumquats are wonderful eaten out of hand for dessert—their sweet rind and tart flesh complement a glass of gin, vodka, or akvavit—but their flavor easily overpowers other foods. The citron is important for its skin, which candies so nicely and combines well with other candied peels, but don't expect it to have that intense bottle green you admire in commercial fruitcakes, as that results from food colorings.

SELECTION AND STORAGE

Always look for fruit that seems heavy for its size—it is the sugar in the juice that gives it this weight. Don't buy citrus with soft spots in the skin. If you are going to blanch the peel, don't use fruit that has been colored—check the boxes the fruit comes in to see if the telltale words "color added" are there. Unfortunately, they won't always be there. You can't always tell a dyed citrus by looking at the skin, but you can sometimes. Very often a red dye is used that doesn't completely cover the greenish skin underneath. As always, it pays to buy from a merchant you trust—and one who knows if the fruit has been artificially colored, and who, if he *does* know, will tell you. Choose fruit that isn't hard and rigid; such fruit may have been frost damaged. Lemons should have fine-textured skins; rough-skinned ones tend to have less juice. Don't worry about slight patchiness in the skins of Valencias; in general, it is the inside of the orange you are interested in.

Citrus should be stored in the proverbial cool dry place—the refrigerator or a cellarlike room. They should not be stored in plastic, which encourages moistness. Make sure no citrus fruit is beginning to mold; it will ruin the rest very quickly.

Perhaps the first problem of the citrus is that it offers an inedible white membrane between the rind and the flesh. We often use the rind in desserts, to add tang and zest—the word "zest" *means* citrus peel, in fact. And of course the flesh is used for both its juice and meat. But the white pith is to be avoided at all costs. When you grate a citrus, grate it carefully. I usually use a small hand-held grater for the purpose, drawing the fruit across it and letting the fine shreds drop directly into the mixture I want it to flavor. When I want a thin strip of the peel, I use an ordinary potato peeler—a stainless steel one, of course. That way I can easily avoid the pith, but still get a fairly wide strip of peel.

I usually juice citrus by hand, too, using a small electric juicer at the restaurant, an ordinary plastic bartender's juicer at home. The big lever-action orange juicers are nice but expensive, handy when you want a quart of juice, but a nuisance to clean up if you are after only half an orange. They say you can get more juice from a fruit by letting it stand five minutes in boiling water before cutting it, but I haven't tried it—it seems to me you would lose flavor from the peel if you did. Lemons and other hard citrus can be softened to give up more juice by rolling them on the countertop, leaning hard on them to turn them squishy.

All citrus are full of acid and their flesh, juice, and even their zest should never come into contact with corrodible metals. Use glass, enamel, stainless steel, or wood when dealing with them; don't even cut them in half with any but a non-corroding knife.

Save the skins and insides of lemons you have juiced. I use them to clean stains off wooden countertops and breadboards, and off my hands, too, after working with walnuts or huckleberries. My husband uses them with salt to polish the copper pots. And their zests are nice in your coffee, of course, or to flavor a pound or so of sugar.

TROPICAL FRUITS

PINEAPPLES

Modern marketing techniques have made tropical fruits more easily available, and we use them occasionally in the restaurant. The most familiar remains the pineapple—surprisingly, related to Spanish moss, the only edible Bromeliad. Available almost all year, peaking between March and June, it is a dependable fruit, but needs care in purchase. I always use airfreight pineapples, picked ripe in Hawaii; your markets may offer more exotic fruits from Florida, Mexico, or the Caribbean. Contrary to popular opinion, pineapples do not ripen after picking; they should be ripe at the market. Their color is not a reliable indication of ripeness; judge them by scent, weight, and softness, and remember that large ones will have proportionately less shell and core.

PASSION FRUITS

Passion fruits originated in South America and were named by missionaries who saw the fruit as a symbol of the Crucifixion. Purple passion fruit, *Passiflora edulis*, is the most popular—a dark, elongated fruit about the size of a hen's egg, dimpled or wrinkled when ripe. Both seeds and pulp are edible. It is a summer-ripening fruit, best when vine ripened and picked mature. It should be very dark and quite fragrant when you buy it, and, like all tropical fruits, should be used soon after purchase.

MANGOES

The mango, *Mangifera indica*, is related to the cashew. Known since antiquity in India, it has developed a large number of varieties, some of which are specifically suited to Florida, Hawaii, and California. Mangoes average 6 inches or so in length and 10 to 14 ounces in weight, and should have a fragrant, juicy pulp. The rind is variously red or yellow, sometimes even green, and the seed size varies according to variety. Some are large, flat, and quite fibrous, very difficult to remove. Again, color is no sure indication of ripeness. A ripe mango should be soft to touch all over (like an avocado), fragrant, and without many brown spots. It can be stored in the refrigerator, but should be eaten soon after purchase. Mangoes are a good source of vitamins A, B, and C, but their juice can stain very badly and seems impossible to get out of clothing.

Although the seed is often difficult to remove, there is a technique: stand the fruit on its base, narrow side toward you, and slice down completely through it on each side of the seed, cutting the flesh away on both sides and leaving a narrow strip of flesh attached to the seed.

PAPAYAS

The Caribs called this fruit the *ababi*, "fruit of the angels." It has been popular since Columbus found it, corrupting the name to papaya, but a consistent strain was not developed until early in this century when Hawaiian experimenters developed the fruit we know today. Its main source is still Hawaii, though Florida and Puerto Rico also supply the East Coast. They are generally a smallish fruit, 6 inches or so long and 10 to 14 ounces; the larger Mexican varieties are less sweet.

Papayas should be quite yellow when you buy them and give to pressure like an avocado. The skin should be smooth, unbruised and unbroken, without dark spots, especially at the stem end where decay is apt to start.

KIWI FRUIT

Once known as the "Chinese gooseberry," the kiwi was first planted in New Zealand in 1906 and became a commercial commodity by the 1950s; its serious commercial cultivation in California dates only from the 1970s. Rich in vitamin C, the kiwi keeps for months when hard, but yields to pressure (again like an avocado) when ready to use. It should have no bruises or cuts, and a fuzzy, brown, leathery skin.

COCONUT

The coconut palm likes temperatures that never fall below 68°F, 70 inches of rainfall, and proximity to the sea. Almost every part of the tree is used—for wood, roofing, cookware, and the liquid from the nuts for drinking. It grows much faster than other palms, bears fruit from its fifth to seventy-fifth years, and produces 75 to 100 coconuts annually.

When the coconuts are young and the husks still green, the meat can be eaten like a sweet melon and the liquid can be drunk, although it is not coconut milk. Coconut milk is made by steeping coconut meat in water and straining the liquid.

To choose a coconut shake it. If the coconut is fresh, you will be able to hear the liquid sloshing inside.

Coconuts are available nearly all year, with the peak supply in the fall and winter.

COOKERY

All these fruits, except coconuts (but including figs),contain protein-destroying enzymes. The bromelain in pineapples and the papain in papayas are used commercially as meat tenderizers. For this reason, tropical fruits, served raw, are useful both as an appetizer and a digestive, but some people have stomachs too sensitive to tolerate them.

This enzyme attacks proteins quickly, inhibiting protein activity necessary to many desserts. Tropical fruits should therefore not be used raw in any gelatin dessert, or in custards or batter cakes whose structure will

278

depend on protein activity—the gelatin will not set, and the cake will not rise.

Apparently all these enzymes are broken down when heated to 170°F, so these fruits can be incorporated in protein-active desserts simply by heating them to that temperature first.

BERRIES

STRAWBERRIES

The modern strawberry was developed from a chance cross between the Chilean and Virginia strawberries in the mid-eighteenth century. There are two categories of modern hybrid strawberry, the spring-bearing and the everbearing. Strawberry production was revolutionized by intense experimentation in California in the late nineteenth and early twentieth centuries, when the formerly short season and intensely flavored berry were greatly modified through the development of the Shasta strawberry. California continues to raise 75 percent of the berries grown commercially in this country, but Oregon produces quite a few strawberries considered by many to be better tasting than their southern counterparts. Even more than with other fruits, commercial strawberry development concentrated on extending the season, improving consistency of size and maturity, overcoming the many viruses and diseases the plant is prey to, and improving the shipping qualities and market appearance of berries—often at the expense of flavor. Interestingly, my research into commercial varieties turned up only one variety cited for flavor: the Pajaro.

Strawberries are now picked every month except December and January. Berries destined for eastern markets are picked slightly unripe, though the berry does not continue to ripen significantly after picking.

Choose plump, red, well-rounded berries with a natural sheen. The caps should look fresh and bright green. You can keep them a short while in the refrigerator. If they aren't perfectly ripe, they can be left out overnight at room temperature to sweeten somewhat—but they must be perfectly dry or they will begin to spoil. Strawberries should not be washed unless absolutely necessary, certainly not until just before use. They should be washed with their caps still on or they will fill with water, which cannot be drained off, diluting their flavor.

Strawberries are marketed in pint baskets, a dozen to the flat. Each basket weighs just under a pound and contains a little over 2 cups of sliced berries, 1⅔ cups when puréed. Fortunately, strawberries can be grown in many home gardens. Among the good varieties for that purpose are the Benton, Fort Laramie, Hood, Northwest, Olympus, Ozark Beauty, Quinalt (which is the one grown for Chez Panisse), Rainier, Sequoia, and Shuskan.

FRAISES DES BOIS

The Alpine or wood strawberry, usually called fraises des bois these days, is the best tasting of all to my way of thinking—but unsuited to production on a commercial scale. The berries vary considerably in size and appearance, are difficult to pick, and are terribly fragile. They are, however, quite forgiving in the garden, often springing up year after year as volunteers when they find the partly shady, well-watered conditions they like. Just a few of them will flavor a whole bowlful of commercial strawberries, so they are valuable in the kitchen beyond their small visual promise.

RASPBERRIES

There are more than two hundred known species of raspberries in eastern Asia, only one in Europe, and three in North America. Commercial production of raspberries in the United States is concentrated in the Northwest, the Great Lakes states, New York, and New Jersey. In much of the country the season is short, starting as early as May in warmer climates, lasting in some varieties as late as November. The peak season coincides with that of blackberries: June and July.

There are two families, red and black, just as in Stendhal. Favorite Western reds include Canby, Meeker, Willamette, and the mildly flavored Heritage; the Latham and June are found on the East Coast, the Sunrise in the South and Midwest, the Ranere in New Jersey and California. I have found the Indian Summer and Brandywine very nice.

Black raspberries are completely different from red raspberries; they are small, seedy, less juicy, and very highly perfumed. I use the Cumberland as often as I can; the Munger is also available in California, and the Bristol, Shuttleworth, Black Pearl, and Plum Farmer are available in other parts of the country.

Both black and red raspberries grow wild, and fresh-picked wild berries have an incomparable flavor. Like sweet corn, berries seem to lose flavor immediately after picking.

280

A late red raspberry turns up in August—the Amity in the West, the Heritage or August Red in the Midwest and East. Yellow and golden raspberries are now being cultivated. They began as sports of red raspberries and have a subtly different flavor and a much different appearance, which combines nicely with commoner raspberries in compotes and tarts.

Raspberries should be chosen much like blackberries, and should never be washed as they lack the protective cap that would keep water out of the fruit. They should be used immediately on purchase; don't keep them longer than overnight, and then only in the refrigerator.

BLACKBERRIES

The blackberry family includes varieties marketed as boysenberies, marionberries, loganberries, olallieberries, and youngberries, many of them named for their developers. Oregon grows about 85 percent of the commercially marketed blackberries in this country, split about equally between the Thornless Evergreen and the Marion varieties. The Chehalem, Cascade, and Santiam varieties, which are more like wild blackberries, are grown in very limited amounts; producers consider them a special order item.

The olallieberry, a relatively fragile berry, is grown almost exlusively in California. The loganberry, an intensely flavored, deep red berry, retains qualities of its raspberry parent. The boysenberry is one of the best tasting of the blackberry hybrids: big, juicy, and well flavored.

Blackberries grow where the summers are fairly cool and humid: Washington, Oregon, and parts of Northern California. They are unsuited to hot summers and extreme winter cold. Their season runs from May through August; the heavy season ranges from early June to mid-July— midsummer heat ends them just when you really want more.

Blackberries are fragile and generally come in half-pint baskets. Choose plump, nicely scented berries, avoiding those incontinent enough to stain their containers and, of course, any that look at all moldy.

BLUEBERRIES AND HUCKLEBERRIES

Elizabeth White, the daughter of a cranberry farmer in Pine Barrens, New Jersey, developed the large blueberry that is commercially cultivated today. She hybridized wild varieties that had been gathered for generations, developing them into the commercial version introduced in the 1930s. The result is still controversial; many feel the true blueberry has to be gathered wild. Others must disagree, for blueberries are the second largest selling berry in this country; their production increased fivefold in the last ten years. Blueberries are produced in the northern tier of states, the same areas that produce blackberries and raspberries—yet we also get a lot of blueberries from North Carolina. Wild blueberries are smaller and less sweet than the cultivated varieties, and vary more from one region to another. Since it is so recent, commercial production has yet to standardize the blueberry as much as it has other fruits; you should become acquainted with those available in your neighborhood.

Huckleberries and blueberries are considered interchangeable by many, but there is a difference between the berries correctly distinguished by the two names. Huckleberries have large seeds, which are quite hard and noticeable, and are not cultivated. Their name may derive from the English whortleberry or hurtleberry. Other blueberry friends and relations include the bilberry, cowberry, and whinberry in England; the German *Heidlebeeren* and the French *myrtilles* are interchangeable, though not necessarily exactly alike.

CURRANTS AND GOOSEBERRIES

These berries are quite popular in European cooking and are recovering popularity in this country after a long decline during which gooseberries had been restricted largely to jams and pies and currants to jellies. They are closely related to one another.

Their recovery has been hampered by difficulties of production: the vine harbors diseases that attack other plant forms, and the gooseberry is therefore banned in many regions of the country. Check with local authorities before planting them in your garden.

The red currant can be eaten raw, and makes a festive garnish on its green stems—in Florence we were served a pale creamy lemon mousse nicely garnished thus. The black currant is too bitter and must be sweetened to be palatable. Its intense flavor is useful in syrups—it is the basis of cassis, in turn the basis of a popular white wine aperitif—and is therefore well suited to both jams and sherbets. Gooseberries, of course, are mouthpuckeringly sour and generally can be eaten only in a prepared form, but their pungent flavor, reminiscent of rhubarb, stands up well to the intense flavors that may have gone before. They are well suited to dinner desserts for that reason, and also to an accompanying role with a main course, as in North European cookery. Mackerel is traditionally served with gooseberry sauce in France.

Currants and gooseberries are in season for two or three weeks during

282

July. Gooseberries, which are larger and often covered with fine hairs, may come in a variety of colors: red, yellow, green, or white. If firm they will keep several days refrigerated, and you can always serve just a few, quickly cooked into a sauce.

SUMMER FRUITS

APRICOTS

The apricot, *Prunus armeniaca*, is thought to have grown wild in China nearly 4,000 years ago. The Chinese were the first to cultivate it, and Alexander the Great is credited with introducing it to the Greco-Roman world.

California is now the second largest producer of apricots in the world, and the fruit is also grown commercially in Idaho, Washington, Colorado, and Utah. Some of the varieties available are the Royal or Blenheim, Moorpark, Golden Amber, Autumn Royal, Royal Rosa, and Flora Gold.

Tantalizingly, the familiar market apricot is only one of a number of types. There is a famous musk apricot that grows in the South of France, Spain, and North Africa, and there are apricots with the flavor of mixed peaches and apricots that grow wild and in orchards from Persia to Kashmir. Our orchardists have much to learn.

Some apricots ripen in May, and the season continues into early August. Tree-ripened apricots are best, but since the fruit is very fragile it is usually picked for the market while still firm. Where they are grown, it is often possible to find farmers who allow you to pick your own apricots.

Choose the plump, darkest orange apricots, with a velvety feel, and avoid shriveled, pale yellow or greenish yellow fruit. The less ripe fruit will color after it is picked, but it will never have as good flavor as tree-ripened fruit. If you must buy underripe fruit, ripen it at room temperature for several days and use as soon as possible, or refrigerate for one or two days.

Apricot seeds, and indeed those of all stone fruit, have a kernel that in some varieties yields a bitter almond flavor produced by the release of hydrogen cyanide. The flavor permeates an oil that is used as a flavor in liqueurs. A great quantity of this chemical in food can be quite dangerous, but it imparts a noticeably bitter taste before it is present in that amount, and small quantities of the bitter almond oil are apparently harmless even when consumed over a period of time.

NECTARINES

The nectarine, *Prunus persica nucipersica*, is a smooth-fruited peach. California grows 95 percent of our supply. Eighty-five varieties have been developed since World War II, with a change in emphasis from white varieties to yellow-fleshed ones, which have a greater hardiness and suitability to shipping.

Good varieties include May Grand, Spring Grand, Early Sun Grand, Ruby Grand—all the Grands seem to be good tasting—Fantasia, Flavortop, Spring Red, Red Gold, Inland Red, and the white-fleshed Rose Nectarine. California nectarines are available from mid-May through September; Washington varieties from late June through August.

Nectarines should be harvested firm-ripe. They overripen quickly; if you have your own tree, pick when they have good aroma and yield to slight finger pressure, and use them immediately. At the market, choose fruit with a creamy yellow background, well formed with no bruises or cuts, and slightly soft along the seam. The color will vary with the variety from reddish to yellow. A green nectarine should be avoided—it will never ripen. Store them in the refrigerator both before and after ripening—you can ripen them at room temperature in a loosely closed paper bag.

PEACHES

The peach, *Prunus persica* (or *Prunus persica vulgaris*), also originated in China, where it still grows wild—it has been known for at least 4,000 years. The peach thrives in temperate zones, but is a delicate, short-lived tree prone to disease.

There are two varieties of peaches, distinguished by the attachment of their stones to their flesh. The first to appear in the season are generally clings, and they are often used for canning. The more fragile freestone peaches have greater aroma and are the ones I use most. First Lady, Elegant Lady, June Lady, Redhaven, Suncrest, Elberta, Fay Elberta, Fayette, Cal Red, O'Henry, Babcock, Red Babcock, Regina, Empress Hale, Raritan Rose, Cresthaven, and Belle of Georgia are good varieties.

The peach season is long, from April to October, with peaks in late May to early June and mid-July to August. Like most fruit, peaches taste best if they are ripened on the tree. For some of the later varieties, though, earlier picking and home ripening is recommended.

284

Peach kernels, like those of apricots, are used to make liqueurs, and are an important contributor to marzipan-flavored "almond" pastes.

Choose peaches with a creamy or yellowish background color. They should be plump, aromatic, and fairly firm, and yield slightly when pressed between your palms. Avoid bruised, brown-spotted fruit. Peaches will keep refrigerated for a week.

PLUMS

The plum also originated in China, perhaps 2,000 years ago. There are three categories. *Prunus americana* are small fruited, usually tart fruits, very good for jams, jellies, and sherbets; *Prunus salicina*, the Japanese plums, are usually the red, early-blooming types, and they include many of the popular commercial varieties; *Prunus domestica*, the European plum, is usually blue, and is generally used for jams and jellies.

Santa Rosa, Red Beaut, Friar, Laroda, Satsuma, President, Shiro, and Redheart are all Japanese and hybrid plums. Damson, Green Gage, and Italian Prune are good European plums. There are also beach plums native to New England and parts of the Atlantic Coast that make wonderful jam.

The prune is simply a plum dried whole, without fermentation at the pit. The Italian Prune plum is most widely planted for this purpose.

Plums are best harvested firm-ripe but aromatic. They are available from May through October with a peak from mid-July to early August. Look for well-colored plums, firm but with some softening at the tip. They will finish ripening at room temperature in a few days and will keep, refrigerated, for three to five days.

CHERRIES

The cherry family is divided into the sweet cherry group, *Prunus avium*, and the sour cherry group, *Prunus cerasus*. The sweet cherry originated in northeastern Asia, and was carried by the Romans to most of Europe and England. *Prunus cerasus* is thought to have originated in Northern Anatolia and then spread west. Sweet cherry varieties include the Bing, Van, Royal Anne, Black Tartarian, Lambert, and Rainier. Sour cherry varieties are Montmorency, English Morello, and Early Richmond. Many sour cherries are used for canning, but when they are available they make the best pies. Most sweet cherries are used fresh. Sour cherries dominate American production by a two-to-one margin because they are preferred for cooking, canning, and distilling—yet they are hard to find fresh in the markets. Buy plump, well-colored cherries with light-colored stems; refrigerate and use them quickly.

FIGS, MELONS, AND OTHER FALL FRUITS

FIGS

The fig is believed to have originated in the Near East and has spread all over the Mediterranean, to India, China, and the Americas. Figs like regions with mild winters and summers that are not too hot, humid, or wet, and they flourish in barren soils. They have been used dried and in a syrup for sweetening since ancient times. With dates and honey they were important sweeteners for thousands of years before the invention of refined sugar.

There are 600 to 750 varieties of figs including white, brown, purple, and red figs, all taking their name from the color of their skins, not their flesh. Some figs produce one crop a year; others, more generous, produce two. They are available in June and then again from midsummer to October. Good varieties include Calimyrna, Black Mission, Adriatic, Kadota, Genoa, Desert King, Conadria, Brown Turkey, Texas Everbearing, and Brunswick.

Choose soft, dry fruit, or even one that is soft and has begun to shrivel—it will be a sweet fig. If it smells sour, avoid it, and never trust a fig with a nose. Use figs the day you buy them; if they are not quite ripe let stand at room temperature until soft and ripe. If a white milky sap oozes from the stem when they are picked they are not ripe enough.

MELONS

Melons probably originated in Persia at least 4,000 years ago, but were apparently not cultivated in Europe north of Spain until the Middle Ages. Muskmelons, *Cucumis melo*, include the honeydew, casaba, cantaloupe, and the muskmelon. The watermelon is of a different family, *Citrullus lanatus*. The cantaloupe is probably the most popular of these melons, with a dense orange flesh and sweet musky flavor. Of these, the French Charentais is an extremely good one, but unpopular among commercial growers in this country because of its small size and extreme fragility. The Persian melon looks like a large cantaloupe with finer netting, pinkish

286

orange flesh, and mild, sweet flavor. Cranshaw melons are a cross between Persian and casaba melons. They are large, soft, golden-colored melons with pale pink-salmon spicy flesh. Crane melons may be specific to our area and are even better than Cranshaws. Casaba melons are golden yellow with creamy white, juicy flesh. Honeydew melons are large, creamy white melons with green flesh. Now there is also a pink honeydew available. Christmas melons are oval with green skin striped with yellow—their flesh is creamy white and like the casaba in flavor. The Sharlyn and Ha'ogen are other good varieties, and new ones seem to turn up every season—melons hybridize easily.

To choose a good melon, first smell it—it must be aromatic. Cantaloupes should be well netted, the stem end should be smooth, and the melon should give slightly when pressed. Smooth-skinned melons should be velvety or slightly oily to the touch. If they feel hard and slick they were picked underripe; if soft or wet at the stem end they have started to decay. Melons don't gain in sugar after picking, but their flavor mellows if they are kept in a warm dry place for several days. They will keep up to a week in the refrigerator.

PERSIMMONS

Persimmons have been found wild in China and Japan, and also have been cultivated there for centuries. There are two varieties, the American *Diospyros virginiana* and the Japanese *Diospyros kaki*. The Japanese variety, brought here by Commodore Perry in 1855, is larger and of more predictable quality, but those who have tasted the American persimmon seem to prefer it. The Oriental variety grows in California, with the native variety still in Indiana and the South.

Varieties available are the Hachiya, the Fuyu, which can be eaten while still firm, the Tamopan, and the Chocolate, with dark-fleshed fruit. They are available from October through December.

Unripe persimmons contain tannins that make the fruit very astringent. When ripe, enzyme reactions will have transformed the tannic compounds and the fruit will be soft and almost jellylike inside its skin and very sweet. It has great moisture-retaining abilities; baked products using persimmons will usually be very moist. The persimmon is corrosive; always use stainless steel or enamel-coated cookware in its preparation.

RHUBARB

Rhubarb, *Rheum rhaponticum*, also originated in northern Asia; it reached the West about 2,000 years ago, probably with the Tartars. It is botanically a vegetable, but it is most often used as a fruit—so often that in many parts of the country it is known as "pie plant." Rhubarb contains oxalic acid in its roots and leaves, which can be fatal if eaten in large amounts, but there is none present in the stalks. Rhubarb is either field grown or hothouse grown. Field-grown rhubarb usually has dark red stems and green leaves; the hothouse variety has pink stalks, yellowish leaves, and few strings.

Choose firm, crisp stalks and refrigerate and use as soon as possible. The hothouse rhubarb is usually available in late fall and early winter; the height of the season for field-grown rhubarb is April and May, although it is becoming more available year round.

CRANBERRIES

Cranberries, *Vaccinium macrocarpon*, grow wild throughout Europe. The cranberries we buy today are actually selections of the best wild cranberries. They grow mainly in Massachusetts in bogs and marshy areas. They need a very cold climate but fields are flooded after harvesting to keep the roots from freezing. Early Black, Howe, Searles Jumbo, and McFarlin are varieties that are selected wild berries.

The fruit is sorted during the packing process; as long as the berries are firm and unbroken they are good. Store them in their bag in the refrigerator for four to eight weeks or freeze them for longer storage. They are harvested from September to December, with the peak in November.

POMEGRANATES

The pomegranate, *Punica granatum*, is another native of Persia. It was cultivated in Greece, and spread also to India and China and the Mediterranean. Spanish missionaries brought it to California in the late eighteenth century. Pomegranates grow where winters are mild, in the Southeast as well as California, Iran, and Jamaica. A pomegranate tree can live more than 200 years. The fruit color can vary from off-white to purplish or bright crimson. Some varieties grown in this country are Wonderful, Granada, Ruby Red, Foothill Early, Spanish Sweet, and Papershell.

Choose fruits with good color and no cracks or splits. They keep several weeks refrigerated in a plastic bag. To eat, either pull the fruit open and

288

pick out the seeds, or roll the whole fruit on a table until soft, leaning hard on it, and drink the juice through a straw.

GRAPES

The two important varieties of grape are the American variety, *Vitis labrusca*, of which the Concord is the best known, and the European variety, *Vitis vinifera*. Table grapes can be of either variety, and many that are not commonly thought of as wine varieties—the Thompson Seedless, for example—actually make important contributions to less expensive domestic wines.

Thanks to new shipping and storage techniques, grapes are becoming available the year round in this country, but out of season they always seem bland and watery to me. Even in season I find little use in the kitchen for such varieties as Emperor, Cardinal, Ladyfinger, Tokay, and Ribier, all popular for eating out of hand—perhaps because our wine country is so near with its marvelous Chardonnays, Zinfandels, Rieslings, Cabernets, Sauvignon Blancs, and Muscats. Except for the last, these are almost exclusively grown for wine, and they have been developed for a more complex flavor than that of the familiar table grapes. They are perfectly suited to sherbets.

But such grapes are extremely hard to find in the market. Home winemaking is becoming much more popular, so in the short season you may be able to pry a few away from hobbyists—if not, by all means investigate American grapes native to your region: the "fox" grapes (including Concord) of the Great Lakes states, the Scuppernong of the deep South, the muscadines of the Southeast.

Grapes should be chosen for firmness; the stem end offers the first indication of overripeness. The aroma should be distinct, particularly in wine grapes, but that is hard to detect when they are kept chilled in the market. Brown stems indicate old grapes, and clean skins with no trace of bloom—the dusty look of the vineyard—suggest grapes that have been washed or treated. They will keep in the refrigerator for up to two weeks.

NUTS AND DRIED FRUIT

The many kinds of nuts are alike in certain physical characteristics. They are the seed kernels of various plants, surrounded at various stages of growth by a thin membrane, a shell or husk, and a fleshy fruit, often with a leathery outer skin. Like all seeds, nuts have a high oil content, and this volatile oil lends itself beautifully to flavoring desserts. The oils are also wonderful in salads, of course, and subtle connections can be made between the salad and dessert of a single meal. We normally think only of the very inside, impatient to get to the meat of the matter, but getting there can be quite a problem.

Walnuts, black walnuts, pecans, hazelnuts (filberts), almonds, macadamia nuts, and pistachios are the mainstay of nut desserts at Chez Panisse, though we do like to use hickory nuts when we can get them.

WALNUTS

The "English" walnut (really Persian in origin), black walnut, and butternut are closely related. Each is available in a number of varieties. California is the largest producer of walnuts in the world, but black walnuts and butternuts are very hard to find on the market here; we usually count on friends' trees or wild supplies for them. There are mail order firms specializing in unusual nuts.

PECANS

The pecan, *Carya illinoensis*, is more distantly related to the walnut, and is also a member of the Hickory genus. Its name is Algonquin and it is native to North America; its chief production is in the south central states. Again, many varieties can be found on the market—rarely individuated by name. Pecans are remarkably nonstandardized, the result of large numbers of small growers and the lack of a central marketing board.

Many people are allergic to both walnuts and pecans, developing an asthmatic kind of reaction to the slightest hint of oil from the nut. Such people are generally aware of their allergy, but are sometimes surprised to find walnut or pecan present where they didn't expect it. The considerate cook has to find ways of revealing the ingredients of unusual preparations when an allergic response might be a problem.

FILBERTS AND HAZELNUTS

Filberts and hazelnuts—the words are used interchangeably, and considerable controversy rages as to whether they refer to different varieties—belong to the birch family and once covered northern Europe. Their current commercial production is centered on the Black Sea and the Mediterranean, especially Turkey and Italy. As is usually the case, wild ha-

290

zelnuts tend to be smaller and possibly more delicately or characteristically flavored—but vary more from nut to nut.

ALMONDS

Almonds are closely related to peaches and nectarines—the trees can be intergrafted. There are two kinds of almonds. Sweet almonds, available in many varieties, are used for eating out of hand and in cookery; the smaller, hard-shelled bitter almond is used for flavorings and an oil used in cosmetics and pharmaceuticals. The oil of bitter almond generally used in cookery comes not from bitter almonds but from the inner seeds of peaches, apricots, and prunes.

The almond is useful at three stages of its life. We use the blossoms to flavor delicate ice creams and custards; we like to eat the young green almonds as an accompaniment to desserts; and the dried nut is a staple for tarts at Chez Panisse.

MACADAMIA NUTS

Macadamia nuts are a fairly recent addition to our cookery—the only important food source to have come to us from Australia. In our kitchen they are usually used in combination with pineapple or coconut, which seem to have an affinity for them—and, rarely, in a tart inspired by our almond tart.

PISTACHIO NUTS

Pistachio nuts are still produced chiefly in Iran, Turkey, and Italy, where they have been known for centuries. California, however, is making a major assault on the market with several varieties whose physical appearance is superior (but whose flavor is apt to be less intense and refined). The kernel is likely to be an ivory or pale green, which has little to do with the familiar green of artificially colored pistachio ice creams, and the shell is naturally beige blushed pinkish; California producers often dye them a bright pink (which comes off on your hands) to hide minor blemishes.

SELECTION AND STORAGE

Nuts keep, but are best when freshest. They often stay in the market long beyond their prime, with last year's crop still available a month or two after the new crop appears. You can roughly check the age of nuts simply by shaking them: if they rattle, they are too old. The only exception is

291

the almond, which should be dry enough to rattle; any others should be considered suspect.

Nuts are somewhat fragile and quite vulnerable to heat, light, and moisture. They are the natural foodstuffs of a variety of unpleasant small creatures. They should be kept in cold, dark, dry conditions, preferably airtight, preferably in the refrigerator or freezer. They will not last forever, and their oils, when they become rancid, can be very objectionable, easily spoiling a dessert and thus the meal.

COOKERY

The chief techniques for the cook are shelling and toasting. The former process varies widely: almonds present no problem other than blanching to remove the skin; black walnuts, hickory nuts, and butternuts need special devices to crack their tough shells; macadamia nuts can be cracked only with machinery, which may be why they made so late an appearance to Western cuisine.

It is said that hard nuts can be cracked more easily if they are immersed in boiling water for 15 to 20 minutes, but I haven't tried it. Shelled almonds and pistachios can be blanched by dipping them quickly into boiling water, then squeezing off their skins—almonds between the fingers, pistachios by rubbing them in a coarse sieve or tea towel. This wets them, of course, so I then dry them in a 200°F oven until they are crisp but not toasted.

All nuts do improve on toasting, which brings out their flavor. This should be done in a 350°F oven for just a few minutes, until you can smell their nutty flavor. When you want to pop one in your mouth, they are ready to use. Pistachio nuts are often soft and should be toasted at 200°F until they are crisp, but not brown. Be very careful not to overbrown nuts—they burn easily.

DRIED FRUITS

Dried fruits originated naturally and suggested an important method of preserving food. They have become recognized for their own merits, though; sometimes we use dried fruits when the same variety is still available fresh.

At Chez Panisse we use prunes, figs, pears, apricots, and raisins, of course, occasionally using dried cherries for special purposes, and dates for eating out of hand, as accompaniments to desserts. We are in the center of the commercial fruit-drying industry, and we are lucky to be near a

292

number of small producers who dry their fruit with great care. There is a big difference between big and small fruit-drying operations. Most fruits are still sun dried; only prunes are widely dried by artificial heat. Figs and grapes are dried on the tree or vine, and pears and apricots are spread on trays in the sun.

Much of that fruit is treated variously before being dried. Prunes are dipped in sulfur baths, and cut fruit is exposed to sulfur dioxide to preserve color. Vitamin A and C are also preserved by this process, though vitamin E is destroyed. Potassium sorbate is used to prevent mold on prunes and figs. Raisins and dates have no preservatives beyond their natural sugars, but "golden" raisins—really the familiar Thompson Seedless—are bleached with sulfur dioxide.

Dates are the fruit of the date palm, *Phoenix dactylifera*, which may be the oldest cultivated plant. They grew wild in the Stone Age, were in cultivation 4,000 years ago, and are now found in almost all tropical regions of the world.

Dates are classified as either sweet or semisweet moist dates or as dry dates. More than 100 varieties are grown in the Coachella Valley alone, but the Deglet Noor, a semisweet variety, is the main variety grown in California. The Medjhool, a large, moist date considered the premier date, is grown only in small quantities. The Halawy and Khadrawy are also grown in larger quantities.

Choose plump, shiny dates. Most varieties will be smooth skinned, amber colored, with a glossy sheen. The Medjhool dates will be darker colored with a wrinkled skin, and with a fair amount of invert sugar. They may develop a thin white film, which will be reabsorbed with heat.

Dates are available from September through May, with most fresh dates available in November. Dry varieties store well, but softer dates must be refrigerated.

SELECTION AND STORAGE

If you can buy fruits from the people who dry them, so much the better. More and more small farmers are selling them in farmer's markets and roadside stands in the small valleys near the Bay Area and you can also find them often in health food stores. Such fruit may look "unappetizing," because their makers are rightly more concerned with health and taste than with cosmetics and chemicals. Commercial suppliers are often very reliable, however, and the uniformity of their product does have its advantages.

Dried fruit should be kept cold and dry. It need not be as airtight as nuts, but it doesn't hurt to enclose it in airtight containers. Sometimes freezing tenderizes it, and it does keep well frozen. Even in the refrigerator it should last well for a year or two.

Stored in the open, dried fruits, like nuts, can provide food for vermin. A particularly nasty moth came to our house in a supply of prunes, and wasn't happy until it had taken up residence in most of the corks in our wine cellar—an unpleasant experience that we are now careful to avoid.

SOURCES

PLANT SOURCES

A World Seed Service
P.O. Box 1058
Redwood City, California 94064

Angelica seeds available.

C & O Nursery
Box 116
1700 North Wenatchee Avenue
Wenatchee, Washington 98801

Forty-page catalog includes ornamentals and shade trees, as well as fruit trees.

California Rare Fruit Nursery
  Exotica Seed Company
989 Poinsettia
Vista, California 92083

Specialists in subtropicals and mailorder seeds. Catalog, $2.

Fox Hill Farm
444 West Michigan Avenue
Box 7
Parma, Michigan 49269

Angelica plants available.

J. E. Miller Nurseries, Inc.
Canandaigua, New York 14424

Fifty-six-page fruit catalog.

New York State Fruit Testing
  Cooperative Association
Geneva, New York 14456

Thirty-two-page fruit catalog. $5 membership fee.

Nichols Garden Nursery
1190 North Pacific Highway
Albany, Oregon 97321

Angelica plants and seeds available.

Pacific Tree Farms
4301 Lynwood Drive
Chula Vista, California 92010

Twelve-page catalog of subtropicals and low-chilling apple varieties.

Raintree Nursery
265 Butts Road
Morton, Washington 98356

Twenty-four-page catalog of food plants for the Pacific Northwest, including Asian pears.

Sonoma Antique Apple Nursery
4395 Westside Road
Healdsburg, California 95448

Mail order for many varieties of apple and pear trees. Catalog available.

Southmeadow Fruit Gardens
Lakeside, Michigan 49116

Considered the largest source for mail-order fruit trees in the country. They specialize in old varieties. Catalog, $8.

Stark Brothers Nurseries
Box B4225A
Louisiana, Missouri 63353

Sixty-four-page catalog. Nearly 400 varieties of fruit trees, nuts, berries, etc.

ORGANIZATIONS

American Pomological Society
103 Tyson Building
University Park, Pennsylvania 16802

Fruit Varieties Journal, *published quarterly. Write for information.*

California Rare Fruit Growers
Fullerton Arboretum
California State University
Fullerton, California 92634

$10 membership. Write for information.

North American Fruit Explorers
Box 711
St. Louis, Missouri 63188

$5 membership. Write for information.

Northern Nut Growers
  Association
Rural Route 3
Bloomington, Illinois 61701

$10 membership. Write for information.

INFORMATION

State University Extension
  Services

Write to your state university and request a list of publications.

County Agricultural Extension
  Services

Contact local county extension services for local farm buying guides.

296

FOOD SOURCES

American Spoon Foods
411 East Lake Street
Petoskey, Michigan 49770

Wild Missouri pecans, maple sugar, selections of honey and fruit preserves. Write for catalog.

Gowan's Oak Tree
2600 Star Route
Philo, California 95466

Mail-order source for thirty-seven varieties of apples, as well as pears. Contact them at the beginning of the season for information about availability and varieties.

Great Valley Mills
687 Mill Road
Telford, Pennsylvania 18969

Mail-order source for more than twenty kinds of flour. Write for catalog.

Maid of Scandinavia
3244 Raleigh Avenue
Minneapolis, Minnesota 55416

Baking and candymaking supplies, Callebaut and Lindt chocolates. Catalog $1.

Pacific Coast Products
1050 26th Street
San Francisco, California 94107

Guittard and Ghirardelli chocolates, citric acid granules, cocoa powder, and other baking supplies available. Write for more information.

Torn Ranch
1122 Fourth Street
San Rafael, California 94901

Complete line of dried fruits and nuts available. Write for order form.

Willamette Valley Tree Fruit
  Grower's Association
P.O. Box 70
Hillsboro, Oregon 97123

A new group of small growers in the Willamette Valley, they specialize in unusual varieties of peaches, pears, apples, and other tree fruits. Write for information on which growers operate mail-order businesses.

WINE

Kermit Lynch Wine Merchant
1605 San Pablo Avenue
Berkeley, California 94702

Beaumes-de-Venise wine will soon be distributed nationally as a Kermit Lynch Selection imported by Chalone. It may also be ordered direct from Kermit Lynch.

297

CALENDAR OF FRUIT SEASONS

The fruits listed in capitals are at the height of their seasons.

JANUARY: blood oranges, dates, kiwi fruit, kumquats, LAVENDER GEMS, lemons, limes, oranges, papayas, pears, pineapples, TANGELOS, tangerines

FEBRUARY: blood oranges, dates, kiwi fruit, kumquats, lemons, limes, oranges, papayas, pears, pineapples, strawberries, tangelos, tangerines

MARCH: blood oranges, dates, kiwi fruit, kumquats, lemons, limes, oranges, papayas, pears, PINEAPPLES, strawberries, tangelos, tangerines

APRIL: blood oranges, dates, kiwi fruit, kumquats, lemons, nectarines, olallieberries, oranges, papayas, peaches, PINEAPPLES, RHUBARB, strawberries

MAY: apricots, blackberries, blood oranges, blueberries, cherries, dates, kiwi fruit, lemons, limes, mangoes, nectarines, olallieberries, oranges, PAPAYAS, peaches, PINEAPPLES, PLUMS, raspberries, RHUBARB, STRAWBERRIES

JUNE: APRICOTS, BLACKBERRIES, blueberries, boysenberries, CHERRIES, dates, figs, GRAVENSTEIN APPLES, huckleberries, kiwi fruit, lemons, limes, loganberries, MANGOES, nectarines, olallieberries, oranges, PAPAYAS, passion fruit, peaches, PINEAPPLES, PLUMS, RASPBERRIES, RED CURRANTS, strawberries

JULY: APRICOTS, blackberries, BLUEBERRIES, boysenberries, cherries, dates, figs, gooseberries, huckleberries, kiwi fruit, lemons, limes, loganberries, MELONS, NECTARINES, olallieberries, oranges, papayas, passion fruit, PEACHES, pears, pineapples, PLUMS, RASPBERRIES, STRAWBERRIES

298

AUGUST: APPLES, apricots, BLACKBERRIES, BLUEBERRIES, cherries, dates, figs, huckleberries, kiwi fruit, lemons, limes, mangoes, MELONS, NEC-TARINES, oranges, papayas, passion fruit, PEACHES, PEARS, pineapples, plums, raspberries, STRAWBERRIES

SEPTEMBER: APPLES, blueberries, cranberries, dates, figs, kiwi fruit, lem-ons, limes, mangoes, MELONS, nectarines, oranges, papayas, peaches, PEARS, pineapples, plums, pomegranates, pumpkins, raspberries, strawberries

OCTOBER: APPLES, cranberries, dates, figs, kiwi fruit, lemons, limes, mel-ons, oranges, papayas, peaches, PEARS, PERSIMMONS, pineapples, plums, POMEGRANATES, PUMPKINS, QUINCES, raspberries, strawberries, tangelos

NOVEMBER: APPLES, CRANBERRIES, DATES, KIWI FRUIT, kumquats, lem-ons, limes, melons, oranges, papayas, pears, PERSIMMONS, pineapples, pumpkins, QUINCES, strawberries, tangelos

DECEMBER: apples, cranberries, dates, KIWI FRUIT, Lavender Gems, lem-ons, limes, oranges, papayas, pears, persimmons, pineapples, TANGELOS, TANGERINES

APPENDIX B

BUTTER

Butter is made from cream. The best butter we use at Chez Panisse is that which we make by accident when whipping cream. Unfortunately it is expensive and unpredictable. Most of the butter we use is manufactured butter, made by a continuous churning operation that separates, pasteurizes, and churns the butter in one machine, then adds salt and coloring if wanted and sends it cut to the wrapper.

The minimum standards set by federal law require butter to contain at least 80 percent crude fat, and at most 16 percent water, 2.5 percent salt (optional), and 1.5 percent milk solids. United States Department of Agriculture inspectors or state-licensed butter graders grade the butter. It is graded for its flavor, amount of coloring, and salt content.

Until recently butter was graded numerically and by a letter code. The 100-point scale is no longer required, but many manufacturers still refer to it when delivering among themselves. Grade AA or 93-point butter has a delicate sweet flavor, a fine aroma, is made from fresh sweet cream, with a smooth creamy texture and the right amount of completely dissolved and blended salt.

Grade A or 92-point butter may have some flavor defects. It may have acid, aged, bitter, coarse, flat, smothered, or storage flavors to a "slight" degree, and to a greater degree is allowed to have a "feed" flavor.

Grade B or 90-point butter need have only a fairly pleasing flavor, and may have more pronounced flavor defects. It is allowed to have malty, musty, scorched, utensil, weed, or whey tastes to a slight degree, as well as any of the Grade A off-tastes to a greater degree.

Butter varies, as you can imagine, according to the diet of the cow. I remember vividly the butter we churned when the family Jersey feasted on wild onions every spring. Northern California dairy herds are allowed more spring grass feeding than those in Southern California. In general, winter butter is "harder" than spring butter, since cows must eat more grain than grass in winter.

Good butter breaks clean—there are no holes or air spaces within it. A spoon scraped across the surface will not turn up residual whey or water or any other liquid—moisture content causes the butter to spoil faster by providing a breeding ground for various microorganisms. Butter should not taste of buttermilk and should certainly not smell rancid.

The rancidity of butter is directly related to the degree that its fat oxidizes. An initial oxidation can occur without any detectable odor or taste changes, but the second stage of oxidation is more rapid. The fat oxidizes faster according to warmth, moisture, air contact, light, and ultraviolet light, so store your butter in a cool, dry, dark place. And buy it from merchants who do the same. Sweet butter is sold frozen and should be stored that way at home, tightly sealed in plastic or foil, and it should be defrosted as needed. All butter absorbs odors very easily and should always be tightly wrapped in the refrigerator.

Butter is salted to inhibit the growth of certain microorganisms. This has been done for so long that many people, perhaps most people, actually prefer the flavor of salted butter to sweet. I sometimes use one, sometimes the other, and sometimes a blend. Salted butter gives a stronger taste. I use some in my tart pastry for that reason, but I blend it with sweet butter to cut it a bit. My chocolate cake uses only salted butter—chocolate can support the deeper flavor the salted butter supplies. Delicate desserts like puff pastries want the more delicate flavor of sweet butter.

Salted butter often has coloring added in the winter months. Color streaking sometimes results. A coloring agent called "annatto," a dye made from the pulp around the seeds of a tropical tree, seems to be used by most good butter manufacturers these days, though carotene is also allowed. We used to get a package of it with every pound of margarine during the war, when dairy lobbies didn't allow margarine to be colored at the factory. Your butter package should say what kind of coloring is used.

COOKERY

Clarified butter is butter that has been heated to separate the butter oil from the milk solids and watery whey still present. All you need to do is heat the butter gently until it has completely melted, remove it from the heat, and pour it into a container (glass makes it easier to watch the process). After it has stood for a few minutes, skim the foam off the top and save the clear liquid in a clean container, pouring it off the milk solids that have settled to the bottom. Some say this helps the butter to store longer; some say it makes no difference. It certainly changes the quality of coloration the butter takes on—clarified butter simply doesn't brown well. It is the solids that make the color. On the other hand, neither does it burn as easily, and that is the principal reason for clarifying it. However, the clarification process drives off moisture and removes both the milk solids and water-soluble diacetyl, the major flavoring agent of butter.

Besides giving its incomparable flavor to desserts, butter works as a tenderizer and as a leavener. When it is creamed, the air beaten into it acts as a leavening in cakes and other kinds of pastry by expanding in the heat of the oven. When rolled in thin layers between the layers of dough in puff pastry, the moisture in butter turns to steam in the oven and makes the pastry rise. Butter tenderizes cakes and other pastries when it is combined with flour, because its fat is broken into tiny particles rather than dissolved. Distributed among the particles of flour, butter fat particles separate them and tenderize the texture of the baked dessert.

To accomplish this tenderizing, the butter must be well creamed with the sugar. This is best done with the butter at about 70°F, or average room temperature—cooler, the butter isn't plastic enough to trap the air; warmer, it will turn liquid and fail to hold air bubbles. I cream butter with my electric hand mixer, or with a stand mixer if I have a lot to cream. In the home kitchen you can use a wooden spoon, but it takes longer. I incorporate butter into flour, as for tart pastry, with my fingertips, quickly flicking it with my thumb off the tips of my first and second fingers—much like snapping your fingers. You may also cut butter into flour with a pastry blender, with two knives, with a mixer, using the paddle, or with a food processor. I find my fingers handiest.

The flavor of butter is its most important asset in desserts. Other shortenings will leaven and tenderize, but nothing tastes like butter.

CHOCOLATE

Chocolate is made from the beans of the cacao tree, which grows only within 20 degrees of the equator. There are two basic types of bean, the *criollo* from the Americas and the *forastero* from West Africa and Brazil. The latter makes up the bulk of world production, but is considered less delicately flavored, and is therefore less expensive.

Like the production of fine coffee, the making of fine chocolate is an art that depends on the careful selection and blending of beans, and even more careful roasting to bring out the flavors.

When the roasted cacao beans are crushed and ground, heat from the friction releases fat cells in the bean and the mixture is liquefied into chocolate liquor. When cooled at this point, the mixture is sold as bitter baking chocolate.

Some chocolate goes through a second refining process called "conching" (after the shell-like machines originally used in the process). The chocolate is mixed with appropriate amounts of sugar and flavorings—vanilla, among others—ground under pressure in heated tanks, and aerated to make it especially smooth. Conching can take from two to six days, and the finest chocolates are said to take the longest.

The cocoa butter content is an important factor in determining the quality of the manufactured chocolate—the higher the content, the finer the quality. It is listed on European chocolates, but not on American ones. If you want to find an American chocolate comparable to a European one you have tasted, you will have to do a lot of comparative tasting—fatiguing, but rewarding if you like chocolate.

VARIETIES OF CHOCOLATE

Bittersweet and semisweet chocolate are required by United States regulations to contain at least 35 percent chocolate liquor. They have different amounts of sugar added, and both have flavorings added as well, including either vanillin (artificial vanilla) or pure vanilla. Sometimes lecithin is added for smoothness. Lecithin is an animal- or soy-derived fat, considerably cheaper than cocoa butter. It results in increased fluidity and decreased viscosity, and is responsible for strawlike off-flavors most noticeable in milk chocolate.

Milk chocolate must have at least 10 percent chocolate liquor. It has milk solids added to it and so is less intense than I like—I don't use it at the restaurant.

Couverture has a high percentage of cocoa butter and is therefore excellent for chocolate dipping and glazes, as the name implies. It is usually available only in bulk at wholesale, but you can make your own by melting an ounce and a half of cocoa butter (available from pharmacies) into a pound of dark sweet chocolate.

White chocolate can't legally be labeled "chocolate" at all, because it contains no chocolate liquor. It is marketed as "pastel coating," but we all call it white chocolate anyway. It is made of cocoa butter, sugar, milk solids, flavorings, and sometimes vegetable fat, and sold in pastel colors or white. The white chocolate I use has no vegetable fat added.

Cocoa has about 75 percent of the cocoa fat removed. Breakfast cocoa must contain at least 22 percent cocoa fat; other cocoas have considerably less. Cocoa has no sugar added (unless so specified on the label, as is the case with Ghirardelli cocoa).

Dutched, or processed, cocoa has an alkali added to the cocoa to neutralize its acid and make it more digestible. This makes it darker, less bitter, and more soluble. Using it in place of natural cocoas requires more leavening, since it has less acid to react with baking soda.

Either cocoa or Dutched cocoa can be substituted for chocolate, in which case you should use 3 tablespoons of cocoa plus 1 tablespoon of any fat substance (butter, for example) for every ounce of chocolate required.

Chocolate may be substituted for cocoa, but you will need 8 ounces of chocolate for every 5 ounces of cocoa specified in the recipe, and you will have to reduce the shortening called for by half the difference in weight between the chocolate and cocoa. If the recipe called for 5 ounces of cocoa, use 8 ounces of chocolate and reduce the shortening by 1½ ounces. It is easier not to substitute.

STORAGE

Chocolate should be stored wrapped in foil in a dark, dry place at 65°F to 70°F, where it will keep a year or two. Milk chocolate will keep only six months or so, and white chocolates don't keep even that well—and they go rancid very quickly when exposed to light.

Chocolate ages very well, actually improving in its first three months of ageing. Chocolate bought in the fall is likely to be new and should be aged for a few months before using.

TEMPERING

Like iron pots and busy cooks, chocolate has temper. In good temper it handles well and is tractable; in bad temper it will be less cooperative. Tempering modifies the consistency and especially the brittleness of the chocolate, and is important whenever the chocolate is to be used in its pure form without any additional fat—butter, for example, or other shortenings. This will be the case when you are dipping chocolates or making a chocolate glaze for a cake. Bitter chocolate is not tempered in its manufacturing process, as its telltale gray streaks often indicate, but all sweetened chocolates are tempered during manufacturing. Even if the chocolate

304

has been tempered in manufacturing, its temper will be lost when you heat it to melt it—so you have to temper it yourself while melting it.

The cocoa butter is the critical element in the tempering of chocolate. All fat crystals have the capacity to align themselves in either a stable or an unstable fashion. If unstable, the chocolate is out of temper—grayish, dull colored, with what is called a "fat bloom" on the surface and streaks within. If stable, the chocolate will break with a good snap when cracked between the fingers, and will have deep color and high gloss.

The tempering process depends on heat. It must be applied slowly, patiently, and accurately. In the classic method, you melt at least a pound (and up to 5 pounds) of chopped or grated chocolate in a double boiler over water at 120°F. It is essential that no moisture touch the chocolate. If it does, the chocolate will seize and never take a temper. First stir the chocolate until it is melted and heated to 110°F to 120°F. Then change the water in the double boiler to 95°F water and put the chocolate back over it. Continue to stir until the chocolate has cooled to 95°F. Put about an eighth of the chocolate over a bowl of 70°F water and cool the chocolate to 80°F. Now add some of the 95°F chocolate, a spoonful at a time, until the mixture reaches 88°F—the ideal temperature.

There is a simpler way of tempering chocolate. Heat two-thirds of the chopped chocolate over hot water to 115°F and remove it from the heat. Then add the remaining chocolate, little by little, until the mixture is cooled to 80°F. Finally reheat the entire batch to 88°F.

Unfortunately, the longer classic procedure is the only one that will restore temper to chocolate that has gray streaks through the middle or on top. Such chocolate has completely lost its temper and can be retempered only when all of it is heated to 120°F.

Tempering must be done gradually and mustn't be speeded up by putting the chocolate over ice water or in the refrigerator. If you make a mistake you can start over. The only time you have to discard the chocolate is when it has seized from having come into contact with moisture.

White chocolate made from cocoa butter needs to be tempered; that made from vegetable fat doesn't.

BLOOM

Temperature is also a key to the condition known as "bloom," but there are two kinds of bloom on chocolate. Fat bloom makes the chocolate look gray, streaked, and dull, but when you touch the chocolate with your finger, the gray streak disappears and the chocolate feels greasy. Fat bloom results from improper heating, too high a temperature, incorrect cooling methods, warm storage conditions, or pouring the chocolate over cold candy centers or on top of cold pastries—cold profiteroles, for example. It occurs most easily at temperatures between 70°F and 75°F.

Sugar bloom is a result of the effects of moisture on the sugar crystals in chocolate. It looks similar to fat bloom, but the streaks do not disappear when touched with the fingertip, and the surface feels granular or frosty, not greasy.

Sugar bloom occurs when chocolate has been stored in damp conditions, when low-grade or brown sugar has been used, or when the chocolate was not properly covered when removed from cold storage, allowing moisture to condense on the surface of the chocolate.

For these reasons, the cooling of chocolate must be as carefully watched as its melting. When you are dipping candy centers in chocolate they should be at 75°F to 80°F to avoid bloom, and after dipping should be cooled at 55°F to 60°F with air circulating around them for proper set. If you refrigerate them you run the risk of moisture condensing on the surfaces.

Similarly, pastries to be covered with chocolate should be at 75°F to 80°F, and so should any molds you pour chocolate into. They should also set in the open with air circulating around them, preferably at 55°F to 60°F. Chocolate can't be set in a kitchen full of steam or on a hot, humid day.

EGGS

At the restaurant we like to use fresh country eggs the background of which we know. You can't always do this. Almost anyone can keep a chicken or two in the back yard, but not many people like to do that anymore. In Berkeley, we still hear ducks quacking around the corner from our house.

The alternative is to buy factory-laid eggs—eggs from birds that never see daylight, stand all day and night in confining cages, eat formula feed to produce up to 240 eggs in a year, and are then turned into soup. Their eggs have a remarkably consistent flavor.

Eggs are composed of about 10 percent shell, 60 percent albumen (egg white), and 30 percent yolk. Two thin membranes surround the egg under the shell, protecting white and yolk from bacteria. The albumen should be thick and plump, its three parts readily distinguishable: thin toward the shell, a thick white full of riboflavin and protein underneath it, and a thinner white surrounding the yolk.

The yolk is the major source of vitamins, minerals, and protein, and is also about 33 percent fat. When fresh it will be rich in color and will stand upright with very little spread. Blood spots or meat spots have nothing to do with fertility, are not harmful, and disappear with age.

The yolk is anchored to the middle of the egg by twisted cordlike strands called the chalazae. Many people object to their presence, but prominent chalazae, like blood spots, disappear with age and their presence is an indication of freshness.

Eggs are used in desserts for leavening, color, and especially body, but we also eat them for their nutritive value—desserts can be good for you. The yolks contain vitamin A, an abundance of which may be indicated by a darker orange color (and may be related to the quality of the feed and the amount of daylight the hen is exposed to). There seems to be no difference in nutrition between brown and white eggs. In nutrition as well as flavor, eggs vary more according to what the hen eats than according to the variety of chicken (which is what determines the color of the shell). Many people prefer fertile eggs, but there seems to be no evidence that they are more nutritious than nonfertile eggs beyond the possible presence of trace amounts of a male hormone.

Grading

Eggs are graded by size and quality. Size ranges from "Jumbo" to "Pullets," most commonly from "Extra Large" (27 ounces per dozen) to "Small" (18 ounces per dozen). The recipes in this book are based on large eggs (24 ounces per dozen).

Quality is a more complex matter. The egg is inspected for soundness, strength, cleanliness, and shape of shell. The interior is examined by candling machines, which discover large blood or meat spots. (Smaller ones slip past, but can easily be removed from the egg, if you think it necessary, with the point of a knife.)

A fresh grade AA egg will stand up tall and display a firm yolk and a thick white that does not spread out. A grade A egg has a round, up-standing yolk, its thick white is large in proportion to the thin white, and it stands fairly well around the yolk. A grade B egg spreads out more, its yolk is flattened, and there is much more thin white than thick white.

Freshness is an important factor in the quality of the egg, of course. Sometimes eggs are labeled "fancy fresh": this guarantees the egg to be less than ten days old. More often, eggs are sold packaged under codes whose purpose is to tell the storekeeper how old the eggs are—while hiding that information from the consumer. Numerical codes may date the carton to within a day of laying time. "Sell by" codes generally indicate a date three or four weeks after grading.

As usual, oxygen is the culprit in the spoiling of eggs. As it ages, the egg loses carbon dioxide through its porous shell, which is then replaced by air with its higher oxygen content. The acidity of the egg, which helps to protect it from bacterial contamination, is destroyed by oxygen. In a very fresh egg the air spot in the egg is very small. Peeling a hard-boiled egg indicates the size of the air spot, which is larger in older eggs. You don't have to hard boil an egg to check its freshness: a fresh raw egg (unbroken) will sink to the bottom of a container of water and a spoiled egg will float. The quicker or farther it sinks, the fresher it is.

Eggs should be examined carefully when purchased, whether on the farm or in the supermarket. Don't buy a cracked egg—contamination enters such an egg very quickly. If you crack an egg on the way home, use it immediately. If you are lucky enough to be able to buy eggs on the farm, don't wash them until just before use. If you must wash them for some reason, oil the shell lightly with mineral oil. It sounds silly, but commercial egg producers do this—the natural protective coating that is washed off the shell has to be replaced with something to reduce spoilage of the interior.

If you buy eggs from the farm, however, do wash them before cracking them. The salmonella bacteria can be found in the intestinal tracts of most warm-blooded animals, including chickens and cooks. Washing the egg before cracking reduces the risk of bacterial contamination of the food significantly. We use raw eggs frequently at the restaurant, and not only in steak tartare: to give body to mousses, for example. If the eggs have been properly handled, washed, and oiled, if necessary, and there are no cracks in the shell, the possibility of salmonella poisoning is quite remote.

STORAGE

Eggs should always be refrigerated. They deteriorate more in one day at room temperature than in one week refrigerated. I don't buy eggs from merchants who leave them out at room temperature, or in country open-air markets. Store eggs in their carton in the coldest part of the refrigerator

308

(which is certainly not its door). They will keep four to five weeks, but why keep them so long?

Egg shells are porous and eggs absorb odors easily. Don't store eggs near onions unless you like the result. On the other hand, a black truffle kept in a container with a dozen eggs makes a marvelous Christmas morning omelet!

Raw whites will keep seven to ten days in a tightly covered container, and can be frozen for several months. Raw yolks should be covered with cold water, put in a tightly covered container, and used within two or three days. They can be frozen, but the preparation is not worth the bother to me.

EGG COOKERY

Cooking an egg causes its proteins to coagulate, or set, in a process with definite stages. The white becomes jellylike at 140°F and firm at 149°F. The yolk begins to coagulate at 144°F and completes coagulation at 158°F. A whole egg coagulates at 156°F.

The presence of other ingredients changes these temperatures: an egg in a cup of milk sets at 176°F, and sugar also raises the setting temperature. About the highest temperature an egg can reach without coagulating, regardless of the presence of other ingredients, is 190°F.

Eggs are used as thickening agents in custards and creams, as leavening agents in cakes, to lighten soufflés, to add color to pastry, and to add richness. Of all these uses, it is the proper beating of egg whites for leavening that seems most problematic.

When you beat egg whites, you are straightening out their molecules of protein, allowing them to build a gridlike structure that can trap air. When heated in the oven, the air expands and the cake rises. Whites can be overbeaten, in which case these protein molecules lose their elasticity and the egg whites look dry and flaky and can't hold as much air.

The whites you are beating should be at room temperature—that is, slightly warmed beyond their storage temperature. It is hard to separate eggs that have been warmed in the shell, so I use eggs straight from the refrigerator. I take care not to let *any* of the yolk (or any other fat, like butter) get into the whites. I warm the whites slightly in a stainless steel or copper mixing bowl, either putting it over a pan of water on the stove or holding the bowl over the gas flame and swirling the whites to keep them from cooking.

Egg whites beat better in copper, as recent research has proved at

Stanford University. Cooks knew this all along. The copper combines with the conalbumen of the egg white. This makes the coagulation temperature higher than would otherwise be the case. The air bubbles trapped in the beaten egg whites can expand further before the heat of the oven sets them, making a lighter meringue and a higher soufflé. Whites beaten in copper are also more stable and hold more liquid. Cream of tartar produces a similar but slightly different effect and can be used even if you are using a copper bowl. Never beat egg whites until they look flaky; they will not hold air. If you should overbeat them, add another white and beat again only until the whites are creamy and glossy.

The folding process is simple but very important. It must be done quickly and carefully so that the mixture is not deflated in the process, since air is usually providing the leavening in your dessert. To fold properly put the lighter mixture on top of the heavier mixture. Bring a rubber spatula down through the center to the bottom of the bowl, turn the spatula so it is parallel to the surface of the bowl, and bring it up along the side. Give the bowl a partial turn at the same time. You are trying to lift a layer of the heavy mixture over the lighter one. Continue until the mixtures are almost evenly mixed. Don't be concerned about a few unmixed patches; it is more important that the mixture not deflate. Often if you beat a part of the sugar called for in the recipe into the egg whites, they will not collapse so readily.

Egg yolk cookery has its problems, too. Sometimes a 1-second or a 3-second ribbon is called for. Beat the egg yolks with the sugar until they are thick and light and form a slowly subsiding ribbon on the surface when you drop a little from the beater—the mixture should hold the ribbon that long before it blends back in. Like the proteins of egg whites, those in the yolk look like tiny coiled bed springs. Stirring custard mixtures tends to straighten out those coils, allowing them to overlap into a gridlike network that traps liquid (milk, in most cases). The same proportions of egg yolk and milk will produce different custards depending on stirring: baked, it will set; cooked on top of the stove, stirring constantly, it will have the consistency of a sauce. The stirring breaks down the molecular network and allows the custard to retain a fluid feel, rather than baking into a jelled solid.

Of course, sometimes you want one, sometimes the other. A baked Mexican flan and a stirred vanilla crème anglaise are very similar in recipe, quite different in character. Each has its place. Most of the recipes in this

310

book strive for a smooth, rich consistency achieved by constant stirring on the stove "until the mixture coats the spoon"—which means just that. (Pull the spoon out of the mixture and draw your finger across it: if your finger leaves a trail, but not a trough, the custard is just right.)

A stirred custard must be cooked gently, in a heavy pan over low heat or in a double boiler. Otherwise the custard at the bottom will cook much faster than the rest, causing lumps and perhaps even scorching. A stirred custard is cooked at about 170°F and should always be stirred for a minute after you remove the pan from the heat—the pan holds heat, and custard touching its inside surface will continue to cook, as you will find when it comes time to wash the pan and an unpleasant coating is found on its bottom.

FLOUR

There are two basic kinds of wheat used for milling into flour. Hard wheat, grown on Western prairies, has a high protein content. When these flour proteins combine with water they make gluten. This makes an elastic dough, important for pastas and breads but less desirable in pastries. Soft wheat, grown in milder climates, is lower in protein (and therefore gluten) and makes a softer dough whose quality depends on the careful balance of egg and flour proteins. This is done by using a lower protein flour when you use more eggs.

Flour is milled from the wheat kernel, which is made up of three parts: the outer shell (bran), the inner starchy endosperm, and the smaller germ, which is about 11 percent fat. It is this fat that shortens the shelf life of flours that contain wheat germ. Most of the flour called for in this book is one or another kind of white flour, which is made from only the endosperm. I use whole wheat flour, which contains the germ, when making bread and even croissants, but I don't use it in any of the recipes in this book.

Varieties of flour
All-purpose flour (which is what I use most of the time) may be bleached or unbleached. It is made from different combinations of hard- and soft-wheat flours. You should be sure to know the protein content of the flour you use: it is listed on the package. The flour I use has a protein content

311

of about 11 percent, but this may vary from 8 percent to 13 percent in different parts of the country and from one brand to another. If you must substitute cake flour for all-purpose flour, use 2 tablespoons more per cup than the recipe specifies.

Cake flour is made of soft, low-protein wheat and is milled into finer particles than all-purpose flour. A dough made from cake flour will therefore hold more liquid—eggs or milk. Cake flour is heavily chlorinated to destroy its ability to form gluten when combined with these liquids, and this is why it shrinks less while baking than a more elastic dough would. If you must substitute all-purpose flour for cake flour, use about 2 tablespoons less per cup specified.

Pastry flour has a slightly higher protein content—about 1 percent more than cake flour—and is useful for pies, tarts, cookies, and similar pastries where the slightly greater elasticity is desirable. You can make your own pastry flour by mixing 60 percent cake flour with 40 percent bread or unbleached flour.

Bleached flour is put through an artificial bleaching process with potassium bromate to give it the white appearance that unbleached flour takes on when it is exposed to air while ageing in storage. I prefer to use unbleached flour on the general principle that the fewer chemicals used in food the better—certainly for flavor, and probably for health.

Self-rising flour has baking powder and salt added—I never use it.

Rye and buckwheat flours are used in a few recipes in this book. Buckwheat flour is ground from the seeds of plants of the *Fagopyrum* genus to make a dark flour, used especially in Brittany to make crêpes; it also makes good pancakes and blini. Rye flour is ground from the seeds of *Secale cereale* and is used to make dark breads in Central Europe as well as in France. Occasionally I use it mixed with unbleached flour for a slightly richer flavored, darker pastry.

STORAGE
Flour should be stored in a cool dry place, ideally between 65°F and 70°F. The storage area should be well ventilated and free from odors, which are easily absorbed. If necessary, move the flour from its paper or cloth bag to a tightly covered container.

MEASURING FLOUR
It is important to be consistent in the way you measure flour. The best way is to scoop it out of the container and loosely fill the measuring cup.

Fill the cup to overflowing and sweep off the excess even with the top of the cup, using a straight blade—a spatula or the back of a knife. Don't use a cup meant for measuring liquids—its calibrations are different from those meant for measuring solids. And don't tap the cup—even a gentle tap will pack the flour, putting more in the measure than you want. The French weigh out their flour: like most home cooks, I don't. It is usually no longer necessary to sift flour before measuring it, though in damp climates it may be best to sift the flour after measuring it and before incorporating it into the recipe. Older cookbooks often assume the cook will measure flour after sifting it, and you should follow that procedure when working with them. I have specified sifted flour in the few recipes that require it in this book; in all other cases it is not necessary to sift the flour before measuring it.

GELATIN

Gelatin is a water-soluble protein extracted from animal skins, bones, and connective tissues. Of the three types generally available on the market, only one is really used in this book. The sheet gelatin favored by European cooks is not easily found in this country, and the flavored gelatins used in instant desserts have no place at Chez Panisse.

I use the unflavored powdered gelatin that has been familiar in this country since Charles Knox began manufacturing it in 1890. The only use we have for gelatin at Chez Panisse is in making Bavarian creams and some mousses, but for them it is indispensable. Without gelatin they would be thin and runny, impossible to mold—a beverage, not a dessert.

Gelatin is composed of short fibrous molecules that develop meshlike networks like tiny wire screens. That network is what gives structure and firmness to your dessert, and you should be aware that as a gelatin mixture sets, the network grows tighter and tighter. A gelatin dessert will grow firmer overnight in the refrigerator—and will continue to grow firm for up to 36 hours.

Gelatin is always dissolved in cool water at first, then melted in a warmer liquid. It is soluble at 86°F and is completely dissolved at 105°F to 115°F. It should never be heated beyond 150°F: at that temperature it denatures, losing its meshlike network, and will not resolidify when cooled. It should also never be frozen. Freezing it will allow ice crystals to form, breaking the bonds that set gelatin. The recommended temperature for setting gelatin is 38°F.

In general, gelatin packages advise using 1 tablespoon of gelatin powder (1 envelope, usually) for 2 cups of liquid. I prefer to use 1 tablespoon for every 3 cups of liquid, because the resulting texture is more delicate. Sometimes this proportion will be varied—for example, when a fruit with its own jelling properties is also present in the recipe.

I usually soften the gelatin by sprinkling it over cold water—¼ cup or so for every tablespoon of gelatin. I let it stand for a few minutes until it softens, then I stir it over heat until dissolved. It dissolves quickly. The gelatin never makes lumps when I follow this procedure.

Once the dessert is finished, it sets up firm in about 6 hours. If you are making a layered gelatin dessert you will want each layer just barely set before the next is added. If it isn't set, the layers will combine in the mold. But if it is *too* set, each layer will be a separate dessert—as you will discover when you unmold them and they bounce apart onto the table instead of turning out nicely onto your platter.

Some fruits are incompatible with gelatin because they contain an enzyme that destroys the gelatin protein. The result is a dessert that just doesn't set. Figs are among these fruits, and also guavas, passion fruit, papayas, mangoes, pineapple, and kiwi. Other tropical fruits should be considered suspect until you have proven them innocent. Cooking these fruits above 170°F destroys the enzyme, so they can be added to gelatin desserts in cooked form.

The gelatin protein is also weakened, apparently, by the presence of certain acids. Sugar and fruit juices, when used as a principal part of the liquid in which the gelatin is dissolved, have a way of tenderizing the gelatin. For this reason you may want to add more gelatin to the formula when making desserts with a high fruit purée or juice content.

LEAVENINGS

Three kinds of processes contribute leavening to baked goods: a physical or mechanical action, in which air is trapped in the batter; an organic process, in which a gas is generated by a living microorganism (yeast); and a chemical process, in which gas is generated as the result of a chemical reaction involving baking soda, cream of tartar, or one of a number of baking powders.

The first kind of process is most commonly achieved by using beaten eggs and, to a more limited extent, creamed butter. These are by far the most frequently used leavenings in my dessert cookery. The other leavenings I use occasionally are yeast, baking powder, and baking soda.

YEAST

Yeast—the word comes from the Sanskrit *yas*, meaning "to boil or seethe"— is a living microorganism invisible to the naked eye. It eats carbohydrates—in our cookery, sugars and starches. It multiplies incredibly: in a few weeks a single yeast cell can produce hundreds of tons of progeny. All that activity, and the gas it generates, is what makes your savarin rise.

Two forms of yeast are available: fresh compressed ("cake") yeast and active dry yeast. A third type, "instant yeast," has only recently become available to commercial bakers.

Active dry yeast is the most commonly used. It is what I use at home and at the restaurant. It is available without the addition of preservatives, in packages ranging from ¼ ounce (1 tablespoon) to 1 pound, and is easily found in supermarkets, health food stores, and specialty shops. Active dry yeast can be substituted for compressed yeast: use 1 tablespoon (¼ ounce) for every cake of yeast called for (a cake is ⅗ ounce).

Compressed yeast is not as popular as it once was, so the turnover in markets tends to be a little slower than formerly. It is more fragile than active dry yeast, with a shorter shelf life—a couple of weeks in the refrigerator, perhaps three months in the freezer. It should break cleanly, have a creamy color, and smell fresh. If warm, crumbly to the touch, or pungent, it is suspect. If it is dark brown, soft or sticky, and unpleasant to smell, throw it out.

Instant yeast has been dried to a lower percentage of moisture content than active dry yeast. It is finely powdered for good dispersion and combined with an emulsifier and sugar, and has a shelf life of nine to twelve months. It is recommended to be used sparingly—a third as much instant yeast as active dry yeast. I have not used it.

All yeasts should be stored in a cool dry place, preferably the refrigerator.

Yeast is most active between 78°F and 105°F. It goes dormant below about 50°F, begins to die at 120°F, and is completely killed above 140°F.

When using yeast in a recipe, first activate it by putting it in warm water (ideally between 90°F and 112°F). Active dry yeast should be sprinkled on the surface of the water; compressed yeast should be crumbled carefully into it. Stir the liquid carefully to disperse the yeast. After a few minutes, smell the yeast to be sure it has begun to work and look at it to see that it is bubbling. If it isn't, get a new supply of yeast.

Once "activated" in this manner—actually the yeast has been awakened from its dormant state—the yeast has to be fed. You want it to eat and multiply quickly, breaking down starch and sugar to generate the carbon dioxide that will make your dough rise. The activated yeast is generally added to the other ingredients by adding the liquid in which it is dispersed to the flour, mixing it in well. The yeast eats starches like flour as well as sugars. Salt, sugar, and fats inhibit the growth of yeast. An Italian panettone loaded down with butter and eggs makes life very difficult for the yeast that must leaven it. Try to add the yeast to the flour before salt, eggs, butter, or large amounts of sugar are added. Very sweet doughs are especially difficult: if the sugar represents more than 10 percent of the amount of flour (by weight), the yeast will be severely affected.

BAKING SODA

Baking soda is a form of sodium bicarbonate. It gives off carbon dioxide when combined with an acid, and this characteristic gives it two uses. As a leavener it will produce the carbon dioxide whose expansion, trapped in bubbles, makes your pastry rise. Many acids might never be suspected: honey, maple syrup, and some fruit acids combine with soda as actively as sour milk, yogurt, or buttermilk. It also neutralizes acids, however, taking some of the sting out of lemons, for example—which is why it is sometimes called for in recipes that also use baking powder as the chief leavener.

The acids that can be used with baking soda include citrus juice, acid fruits, molasses, brown sugar, honey, buttermilk, sour cream, and yogurt. If you substitute another liquid for one of these you may be removing a vital acid from the leavening process. You must then either replace it with another acid or substitute baking powder for the soda, using 4 teaspoons of baking powder for each teaspoon of baking soda.

BAKING POWDER AND CREAM OF TARTAR

Baking powder is the combination of baking soda and an acid, usually sodium aluminum sulfate and calcium acid phosphate. It also has cornstarch and other ingredients added to act as drying agents to increase its

316

shelf life. Baking powder was one of the earliest convenience foods to be developed, and convenience and shelf life have continued to be high priority qualities to those who manufacture and sell it.

Most baking powder available today is of the double-action type. Two acid salts have been added to the soda. One begins working when the mixture is combined with liquid—when you mix your recipe. The other begins to work only in the heat of the oven.

Single-action baking powder begins its work as soon as it is exposed to liquid, so the cook has to move quickly after incorporating it. Double-action baking powders were developed to allow the cook to work more slowly.

The chief component of single-action baking powder is cream of tartar, made from crystals derived from tartaric acid. This is the crystal you often see clinging to the underside of a cork just pulled from a bottle of cold white wine. Processing tartaric acid is expensive, and it is no longer commonly used in baking powders produced in the United States.

Many people object to the very noticeable metallic flavor of commercial baking powders, and some feel that aluminum, in particular, should not be ingested any more than necessary. Many good cooks feel that commercial double-action baking powders have recently been "improved" beyond the point of diminishing returns, compromising texture and volume for easier handling. Furthermore, the texture produced by tartrate-based leavenings seems definitely finer than that produced by more recently developed baking powders, and they achieve greater leavening as well.

For these reasons and others you should try making your own baking powder. Combine ½ teaspoon baking soda (sodium bicarbonate), 1 teaspoon cream of tartar, and ½ teaspoon cornstarch. Use these amounts to substitute for every 2 teaspoons of baking powder called for, and don't try to make the mixture ahead of time because it doesn't keep well.

All leavenings—eggs, yeast, and chemicals—should be fresh. When stored, they must be stored carefully. Baking soda and powders are no exceptions. You can test baking powder for freshness by putting a teaspoonful into ⅓ cup of any hot liquid—water will do. If fresh, the baking powder will rapidly fizz and bubble.

SUGAR

Almost all the sweeteners used in these recipes are sugar—chemically, sucrose, a chemical union of glucose (dextrose) and fructose (levulose). Although sugar is thought of first for its sweetening properties, it is important to remember that there are other properties as well; these are discussed at the end of this section.

Commercial sugar is obtained from sugar cane or sugar beets. When it is refined it is extracted from the natural juices and fibers present in the cane or beet. It leaves the refinery as 99.994 percent pure sugar, chemically unaltered. Beet and cane sugars are therefore interchangeable.

While sucrose accounts for almost all the added sweetening in these recipes, both glucose and fructose are also present. Fructose, or fruit sugar, in fact, is the essential sweetening in most of the fruit-based recipes; sugar is needed only to heighten the sweetness of ripe fruits. Where sugar is added to ices and other frozen desserts, its presence is important more for its freezing characteristics than for its sweetness.

Glucose is manufactured from cornstarch; we use it in the form of corn syrup. It has a greater solubility than sucrose, and therefore crystallizes more slowly. For that reason we add it to sugar syrups and candies and to some sherbets to keep them from crystallizing.

VARIETIES OF REFINED SUGAR

Sugar is available in a number of forms. White sugar is available in various sizes of particles: granulated and superfine. Powdered, or "confectioners'," sugar is very finely granulated and has 3 percent cornstarch added to retard lumping or crystallization. Cornstarch may be added to some superfine sugars as well. Since cornstarch interferes with the expansion of egg whites, you may want to make your own superfine sugar by whirling granulated sugar in a blender or food processor.

Brown sugar, available light or dark, is white refined sugar with molasses added to it. When substituted for white sugar it imparts a butterscotch flavor, darkens the color, and makes the texture chewier.

Turbinado sugar (also known as Demerara sugar) is often called "raw sugar," but this is a misnomer. It is sugar refined slightly less than white sugar, with a molasses covering and a small amount of impurities left in.

Maple sugar is a crystallized form of maple syrup made from concentration of this sap and is best collected in the early spring, when color and flavor are most delicate.

Honey is an "invert sugar"—a combination of glucose and fructose formed when an enzyme secreted by bees (honey invertase) acts on the nectar they gather from flowers. It retains moisture and will make baked foods heavier than refined sugar would. It caramelizes at a lower temperature than refined sugar, so recipes that include large amounts of honey are baked at a lower temperature than normal. Use ½ or ⅔ cup of honey to substitute for every cup of granulated sugar, if you like, but be sure to reduce the liquid content of your recipe by 2 to 3 tablespoons per cup of sugar. The type of flower makes an important contribution to the flavor of the honey: I use different kinds, depending on the flavor I want.

Corn sugar (available as corn syrup) does not exist naturally. It is produced by changing cornstarch into sugar either chemically or by using enzymes. Since it doesn't crystallize, a small amount added to the other sugars is useful to keep candies, icings, and syrups smooth.

Molasses is a by-product of sugar refining. Its color comes from the concentration of its sugars through boiling. Light and dark molasses have different qualities as well as intensities of flavoring and are not readily interchangeable.

STORAGE
Sugar will last almost indefinitely when it is stored in a cool dry place. It can be flavored in storage by adding herbs or flowers, vanilla bean, or citrus peels. Powdered sugar may develop small lumps in storage; these should be removed before use by passing the sugar through a fine strainer or by whirling it in a food processor or blender.

Brown sugar should be kept in an airtight container, in a cool place or even in the refrigerator. A slice of apple will help keep it moist. If it hardens, sprinkle it with a few drops of water and place in a covered bowl in a 200°F oven for 20 minutes or so.

STAGES OF SUGAR COOKERY
To withstand the high temperature of cooking sugar, use either a stainless steel or a copper pot (copper apparently has trace elements that mix with the sugar to retard crystallization). Start with about 3 parts sugar to 1 part water. The cooking must start slowly; swirl the pot gently to dissolve the sugar. If any remains undissolved it may cause the whole batch to crystallize. When the syrup boils, cover and simmer for 5 minutes to allow

the steam to wash down any sugar from the sides of the pot. Now you may add a little cream of tartar, a few drops of lemon juice, or some corn syrup. This will help somewhat to keep the sugar from crystallizing. Boil a few minutes for a simple syrup. If you continue to cook the syrup, the sugar will go through the following stages in the cooking process.

230°F–235°F—the thread stage: The syrup will spin a thread from a fork or spoon dipped into it.

240°F–245°F—soft ball stage: a little syrup dropped into cold water will form a slightly gummy ball when rolled between your fingers.

255°F–260°F—hard ball stage: A little syrup dropped into cold water will form a hard ball when rubbed between your fingers.

270°F—soft crack stage: When some syrup is dropped into cold water, the sugar will separate into hard threads.

290°F—hard crack stage: When some syrup is dropped into cold water, it will separate into brittle threads.

310°F—caramel: The sugar begins to turn pale gold, then amber, and will quickly progress to dark red brown and then to burned sugar.

It is apparently not possible for the home cook to make invert sugar. However, the following recipe will make a solution of 75 percent invert sugar. The following five things are needed to make invert sugar: sugar, water, acid, heat, and time.

10 pounds cane sugar (cane sugar inverts faster than beet sugar)
4.54 grams citric acid crystals
2 quarts water

Mix in a saucepan. Heat to 212°F and maintain that temperature for 30 minutes. Remove from the heat. Dissolve 5 grams baking soda in a little water and quickly stir into the sugar solution. This will neutralize the acidity. This recipe will yield 5 quarts of invert sugar. Store in the refrigerator.

OTHER PROPERTIES OF SUGARS

In addition to sweetening your desserts, sugar imparts a color to baked pastries, prolongs freshness by retaining moisture in baked goods, acts as a preservative, and gives body to syrups and solutions. It tenderizes cakes by balancing flour and egg proteins. It aids leavening by serving as a nutrient for yeasts and by allowing greater expansion of the air trapped in cake batters.

At the restaurant we poach a lot of fruit and it has always seemed a waste to throw away the syrup with all its good fruit flavors. Cook it down until thick and syrupy and use to glaze fruit tarts or to make dessert sauces, either alone or added to fruit purées in place of sugar syrup, or added to crème Chantilly.

Perhaps the most important other property of sugar to us, though, is its contribution to the texture of frozen desserts. Sugar lowers the freezing temperature of substances, but it also makes ice cream melt faster. The ideal sugar content of ice creams and sherbets is from 14 percent to 16 percent, including milk and fruit sugars. Since the latter can't easily be measured, a certain amount of trial and error has gone into these recipes. More sugar makes a soggy, sticky ice cream; less makes it less creamy, more crystalline. Of course, there are other considerations, especially alcohol content in ice creams flavored with spirits. I found out about this ideal percentage only after developing most of these recipes, and was pleased to discover on checking their measurements that science seemed to conform to practical guesswork.

EQUIPMENT

I have not used much unusual equipment in this book. However, at the restaurant we bake our pastries in pizza ovens with a layer of bricks on the bottom. They are very shallow and the heat distribution is unusual. But we have learned to work with them as I think you must learn to work with your own oven. There is no perfect oven—try to learn where the hot spots in your oven are, where the heat comes from so that you know where in the oven to bake a particular pastry. If you need more heat on the bottom than the top, as you might when baking a pie, put the pastry in the lower third of the oven. All the recipes in this book were tested in my electric oven at home.

Baking stones are nice to have and are usually available in kitchenware shops, hardware stores, or department stores. Quarry tiles or Satillo pavers are less expensive alternatives. Use a baking stone to bake bread, pizza, puff pastry tarts, or anything else for which you want direct heat to the bottom surface.

An ice cream maker is an important piece of equipment. For testing these recipes I have employed a small inexpensive machine that uses ice cubes and table salt. It has worked beautifully, and its small size (although the ice cream can holds two quarts) is very much in its favor. Of course there are many other machines available, some of them very expensive. Try to find out what kind of product the machine will produce before buying one, and note that excessive air in the freezing mixture can ruin the texture of the ice cream.

There are a few other things that are important to your success with certain recipes. Use heavy saucepans that are either stainless steel or enamel coated. Eggs and fruits all react with aluminum and tin. Use glass or stainless steel molds if there is fruit in the mixture you are molding. In general, fruit mixtures should be stored in glass, plastic, or stainless steel. An instant registering thermometer is one of the most useful tools you can have. If you intend to do any sugar cooking, a good candy thermometer is invaluable. A small rotary nut grater is better than any other kind; nuts do not get greasy when grated by hand. A very fine stainless steel strainer is necessary for straining fine seeds out of various fruits or for making really fine-textured purées. Although you can almost always find a substitute, it is much easier to work with these tools:

1 or 2 pie pans, preferably metal
A 9-inch black iron skillet
8-inch or 9-inch layer cake pans
A stainless-steel-lined sauté pan
Individual soufflé dishes or
    custard cups
Wooden spoons
A nutcracker
A nut grater
Cookie cutters
1 or 2 ladles
An electric mixer, hand held or
    table model
Whisks, a small and a medium
    size, sturdy stainless steel
Spatulas, a large and a small,
    stainless steel
Spatula with a flexible blade for
    icing cakes
Rubber spatulas—2 or 3 sizes

Pastry brush—1 or 2
A pear corer
A cherry pitter
A wooden spatula—flat
    bottomed
A stainless steel vegetable peeler
A stainless steel paring knife
A stainless steel chef's knife
A bread knife
A stainless steel slotted spoon
1 or 2 pastry bags and various
    tips
A food mill
A very fine mesh stainless steel
    strainer and a sieve
3 sizes of stainless steel or glass
    mixing bowls
A large ball-bearing rolling pin
A candy thermometer
An instant reading thermometer

Measuring cups and spoons
Storage containers with tight-fitting lids
Heavy stainless-steel-lined or porcelain-lined saucepans, 1 small and 1 medium size
A stainless steel loaf pan or a bombe mold for Bavarians and frozen desserts

A 9-inch springform cake pan
1 or 2 heavy-gauge baking sheets
A 9-inch tart pan with a removable bottom
A crêpe pan
A baking stone
Truffle or aspic cutters
A blender or food processor
Baking parchment

BIBLIOGRAPHY

No cook starts absolutely fresh: there are thousands of contributors to the continuously evolving art of cookery. This list is the core of the collection I have been delighted, inspired, and instructed by over the years; I owe a great debt to them.

Ackart, Robert. *Soufflés, Mousses, Jellies, and Creams*. New York: Atheneum Publishers, 1980.

Ali-Bab. *Gastronomie pratique*. Paris: Flammarion, 1967.

Amendola, Joseph. *The Baker's Manual*. 3d ed., rev. Rochelle Park, N.J.: Hayden Book Company, 1978.

Amendola, Joseph, and Lundberg, Donald E. *Understanding Baking*. New York: Van Nostrand Reinhold Company, 1970.

Andrieu, Pierre. *Fine Bouche: A History of the Restaurant in France*. London: Cassell and Company, 1956.

Bailey, Adrian. *Cooks' Ingredients*. New York: William Morrow and Company, 1980.

Bailey, Liberty Hyde, and Bailey, Ethel Zoe. *Hortus Third: A Concise Dictionary of Plants Cultivated in the United States and Canada*. Rev. ed. New York: Macmillan Publishing Company, 1976.

Beard, James. *Beard on Food*. New York: Alfred A. Knopf, 1974.

———. *Delights and Prejudices*. New York: Atheneum Publishers, 1964.

———. *James Beard's American Cookery*. Boston: Little, Brown and Company, 1972.

———. *James Beard's Menus for Entertaining*. New York: Delacorte Press, 1965.

Beard, James, and Watt, Alexander. *Paris Cuisine*. Boston: Little, Brown and Company, 1953.

Beck, Simone. *New Menus from Simca's Cuisine*. New York: Harcourt Brace Jovanovich, 1979.

Bianchini, Francesco; Corbetta, Francesco; and Astoia, Marilena. *Complete Book of Fruits and Vegetables*. New York: Crown Publishers, 1975.

Boni, Ada. *Italian Regional Cooking*. New York: E. P. Dutton and Company, 1969.

———. *The Talisman Italian Cook*. New York: Crown Publishers, 1950.

Brillat-Savarin, J. A. *Physiology of Taste*. Translated by M. F. K. Fisher. New York: Harcourt Brace Jovanovich, 1978.

Carcione, Joe, and Lucas, Bob. *The Green Grocer*. San Francisco: Chronicle Books, 1972.

Child, Julia. *From Julia Child's Kitchen*. New York: Alfred A. Knopf, 1975.

Child, Julia, and Beck, Simone. *Mastering the Art of French Cooking*. Vol. 2. New York: Alfred A. Knopf, 1970.

Child, Julia; Bertholle, Louisette; and Beck, Simone. *Mastering the Art of French Cooking*. Vol. 1. New York: Alfred A. Knopf, 1961.

Clayton, Bernard, Jr. *The Breads of France and How to Bake Them in Your Own Kitchen*. New York: Bobbs-Merrill Company, 1978.

———. *The Complete Book of Pastry*. New York: Simon and Schuster, 1981.

Conil, Jean. *Haute Cuisine*. London: Faber and Faber, 1953.

———. *Gastronomic Tour de France*. London: George Allen and Unwin, 1959.

Considine, Douglas, and Considine, Glenn D. *Foods and Food Preparation Encyclopedia*. New York: Van Nostrand Reinhold Company, 1982.

Cooking with Bon Viveur: The First Bon Viveur Cookery Book. London: Museum Press, 1955.

Countess of Toulouse-Lautrec [Mapie]. *Chez Maxim's: Secrets and Recipes from the World's Most Famous Restaurant*. New York: McGraw-Hill Company, 1962.

Courtine, Robert. *Feasts of a Militant Gastronome*. New York: William Morrow and Company, 1974.

———. *The Hundred Glories of French Cooking*. New York: Farrar, Straus and Giroux, 1973.

———. *Mon bouquet de recettes*. Verviers: Marabout, 1977.

———. *Les vacances dans votre assiette*. Paris: Fayard, 1971.

Coyle, Patrick L., Jr. *World Encyclopedia of Food*. New York: Facts on File, 1982.

Croze, Austin de. *Les plats régionaux de France: 1400 succulentes recettes traditionnelles de toutes les provinces françaises*. Luzarches: Daniel Morcrette, 1977.

Cunningham, Marion. *The Fannie Farmer Baking Book*. New York: Alfred A. Knopf, 1984.

———. *The Fannie Farmer Cookbook*. New York: Alfred A. Knopf, 1981.

Darenne, Émile, and Duval, Émile. *Traité de pâtisserie moderne*. Paris: Flammarion, 1974.

David, Elizabeth. *French Provincial Cooking*. New York: Harper and Row, 1962.

———. *Italian Food*. New York: Alfred A. Knopf, 1958.

———. *Mediterranean and French Country Food*. London: The Cookery Book Club, 1968.

de Groot, Roy Andries. *The Auberge of the Flowering Hearth*. New York: Bobbs-Merrill Company, 1973.

Dubois, Urbain. *Grand livre des pâtissiers et des confiseurs*. 4th ed. Paris: Libraire E. Dentu, n.d.

Dumas, Alexandre. *Le grand dictionnaire de cuisine*. Paris: Pierre Grobel, 1958.

Elkon, Juliette. *The Chocolate Cookbook*. New York: Barnes and Noble, 1975.

Escoffier, A. *The Escoffier Cook Book: A Guide to the Fine Art of Cookery*. New York: Crown Publishers, 1967.

Escudier, Jean-Nöel, and Fuller, Peta J. *The Wonderful Food of Provence*. Boston: Houghton Mifflin Company, 1968.

Everett, Thomas H. *The New York Botanical Garden Illustrated Encyclopedia of Horticulture*. New York: Garland Publishing Company, 1984.

Firuski, Elvia and Maurice, eds. *The Best of Boulestin*. New York: Greenberg Publisher, 1951.

Fisher, M. F. K. *The Art of Eating*. New York: World Publishing, 1954.

326

————. *Here Let Us Feast: A Book of Banquets*. New York: The Viking Press, 1946.

France, Winifred J. *The New International Confectioner*. London: Virtue and Company, 1979.

————. *The Students' Technology of Breadmaking and Flour Confectionery*. London: Routledge and Kegan Paul, 1982.

Gonzalez, Elaine. *Chocolate Artistry*. Chicago: Contemporary Books, 1983.

Gosetti della Salda, Anna. *Le ricette regionale Italiane*. Milan: Casa Editrici Solares, 1967.

Grigson, Jane. *Jane Grigson's Fruit Book*. New York: Atheneum Publishers, 1982.

Guérard, Michel. *La cuisine gourmande*. Paris: Éditions Robert Laffont, 1978.

————. *Michel Guérard's Cuisine Minceur*. New York: William Morrow and Company, 1976.

Hanneman, L. J. *Patisserie: Professional Pastry and Dessert Preparation*. London: Van Nostrand Reinhold Company, 1971.

Hardin, James W., and Arena, Jay M. *Human Poisoning from Native and Cultivated Plants*. Durham, N.C.: Duke University Press, 1969.

Hazan, Marcella. *The Classic Italian Cookbook*. New York: Harper's Magazine Press, 1973.

————. *More Classic Italian Cooking*. New York: Alfred A. Knopf, 1978.

Hillman, Howard. *Cook's Book*. New York: Raines and Raines, 1981.

————. *Kitchen Science*. Boston: Houghton Mifflin Company, 1981.

Ice-Cream and Cakes: A New Collection of Standard Fresh and Original Receipts for Household and Commercial Use. New York: Charles Scribner's Sons, 1891.

Jones, Evan. *American Food: The Gastronomic Story*. New York: E. P. Dutton and Company, 1975.

Kamman, Madeleine M. *When French Women Cook: A Gastronomic Memoir*. New York: Atheneum Publishers, 1976.

Kotschevar, Lendal H., and McWilliams, Margaret. *Understanding Food*. New York: John Wiley and Sons, 1969.

Lavin, Edwin, ed. and trans. *Traditional Recipes of the Provinces of France Selected by Curnonsky*. Garden City, N.Y.: Doubleday and Company, 1961.

Lewis, Edna. *The Taste of Country Cooking*. New York: Alfred A. Knopf, 1977.

Lewis, Edna, and Peterson, Evangeline. *The Edna Lewis Cookbook*. New York: Bobbs-Merrill Company, 1972.

Le livre des confitures et des confiseries. Provence: Morel Éditeurs, 1975.

McGee, Harold. *On Food and Cooking: The Science and Lore of the Kitchen*. New York: Charles Scribner's Sons, 1984.

MacNicol, Mary. *Flower Cookery: The Art of Cooking with Flowers*. New York: Fleet Press, 1967.

Mapie [Countess of Toulouse-Lautrec]. *La cuisine de France*. New York: The Orion Press, 1964.

Marie, Tante. *La véritable cuisine de famille*. Paris: Librairie A. Taride, n.d.

Martin, Alice. *All about Apples*. Boston: Houghton Mifflin Company, 1976.

Mazza, Irma Goodrich. *Accent on Seasoning*. Boston: Little, Brown and Company, 1957.

————. *Herbs for the Kitchen*. Boston: Little, Brown and Company, 1947.

Meyer, Lilian Hoagland. *Food Chemistry*. Westport, Conn.: AVI Publishing Company, 1978.

Minifie, Bernard W. *Chocolate, Cocoa, and Confectionery*. Westport, Conn.: AVI Publishing Company, 1980.

Montagné, Prosper. *Larousse Gastronomique: The Encyclopedia of Food, Wine, and Cookery*. New York: Crown Publishers, 1961.

Oliver, Raymond. *La Cuisine: Secrets of Modern French Cooking*. New York: Tudor Publishing Company, 1969.

Olney, Richard. *The French Menu Cookbook*. New York: Simon and Schuster, 1970.

————. *The Good Cook: Fruits*. New York: Time-Life Books, 1983.

————. *Simple French Food*. New York: Atheneum Publishers, 1975.

Peck, Paula. *The Art of Fine Baking*. New York: Simon and Schuster, 1962.

Pellaprat, Henri-Paul. *Les desserts*. Paris: Comptoir Français du livre, 1937.

————. *Modern French Culinary Art*. New York: World Publishing, 1966.

Pépin, Jacques. *La Technique: The Fundamental Techniques of Cooking*. New York: Quadrangle Books, 1976.

Potter, Norman N. *Food Science*. 3d ed. Westport, Conn.: AVI Publishing Company, 1978.

Presbyterian Cook Book. Dayton, Ohio: John H. Thomas, 1875.

Ranhofer, Charles. *The Epicurean: A Complete Treatise of Analytical and Practical Studies on the Culinary Art*. New York: Dover Publications, 1971.

Rawlings, Marjorie Kinnan. *Cross Creek Cookery*. New York: Charles Scribner's Sons, 1942.

Reboul, J-B. *La cuisinière Provençale*. Marseille: Tacussel, n.d.

Reich, Lilly Joss. *The Vienna Pastry Cookbook: From Vienna with Love*. New York: The Macmillan Company, 1971.

Rombauer, Irma S., and Becker, Marion Rombauer. *The Joy of Cooking*. New York: Bobbs-Merrill Company, 1951.

328

Root, Waverley. *The Food of France*. New York: Alfred A. Knopf, 1958.

————. *The Food of Italy*. New York: Atheneum Publishers, 1971.

Rouff, Marcel. *The Passionate Epicure*. Translated by Claude. New York: E. P. Dutton and Company, 1962.

Roulet, Auguste J. *Le livre des friandises*. Apt en Provence: Morel, 1977.

Rubenstein, Helge. *The Ultimate Chocolate Cake*. New York: Congdon and Weed, 1982.

Sheraton, Mimi. *Visions of Sugar Plums*. New York: Harper and Row, 1981.

Simmons, Amelia. *American Cookery, or the Art of Dressing Viands, Fish, Poultry, and Vegetables, and the Best Modes of Making Pastes, Puffs, Pies, Tarts, Puddings, Custards, and Preserves, and All Kinds of Cakes, from the Imperial Plumb to Plain Cake, Adapted to This Country and All Grades of Life*. Reprint of the 1796 edition. West Virginia Pulp and Paper Company, 1962.

Stagg, Camille. *The Cook's Advisor*. Brattleboro, Vt.: Stephen Greene Press, 1981.

Stearns, Osborne Putnam. *Italy on a Platter*. Los Angeles: The Ward Ritchie Press, 1965.

Stebbins, Robert L., and Walheim, Lance. *Western Fruit Berries and Nuts*. Tucson, Az.: HP Books, 1981.

Sultan, William J. *The Pastry Chef*. Westport, Conn.: AVI Publishing Company, 1983.

————. *Practical Baking*. 3d ed., rev. Westport, Conn.: AVI Publishing Company, 1982.

Sunset Western Garden Book. Menlo Park, Ca.: Lane Magazine and Book Company, 1971.

Wickson, Edward J. *The California Fruits and How to Grow Them*. San Francisco: Pacific Rural Press, 1914.

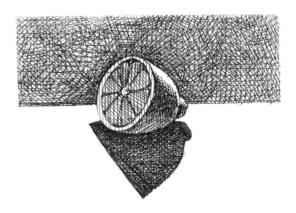

INDEX

C

E

Easter nests, 141
Eggnog ice cream, 261–62
Eggs, 306–11
 coagulation temperatures, 309
Elderberry ice cream, 130
Equipment, 321–23
Espresso-Cognac mousse, 260

F

Figs, dried, 292–94
 poached spiced, 224
 Provençal sundae, 224–25
 pudding, steamed, 183–84
Figs, fresh, 178, 286
 with Beaumes-de-Venise ice
  cream, 180–81
 in caramel, 181–82
 in fall fruit compote, 187–88
 ice cream, 182
 poached in red wine and
  cinnamon basil, 183
 and raspberries with anise
  cream, 180
 tart, 184, 185
  and pear, 55
  upside-down, 57
Filberts. *See* Hazelnuts
Flour, 311–13
Flowers, 100–101
 candied, 105–106
 jasmine ice cream, 103
 mimosa ice cream crêpe with
  buttered honey, 104
 rose petal ice cream, 106–107
  crêpes with, and strawberries,
   106
 violet candies, 107–108
 white plum blossom ice cream,
  104–105
Fool, gooseberry, 132–33
Fraises des bois, 118, 119, 280
 cornucopia of, 130
 ice cream, 131
 sherbet, 131
 spring cake, 140

 timbales Élysées, 144–145
 see also Strawberry(ies)
Frangipane cream, 7
 Butter pear tart with, 54–55
Frozen mousse, 9–10
 caramel, 10–11
Fruit compote
 in Darjeeling tea and Sauternes,
  221–22
 fall, 187–88

G

Gâteau niçoise, 226
Gelatin, 8, 313–14
Gooseberry(ies), 118, 282–83
 curd, 132
 fool, 132–33
Grand Marnier
 mousse, plum sherbet bombe
  with, 172
 soufflés, 262
Grape(s), 179, 289
 muscat, sherbet, 189
 wine, sherbet, 189
Grapefruit, 63, 274
 pink, and Champagne sherbet,
  65
Gratin, blood orange, 74–75

H

Hard sauce, 261
Hazelnut(s), 197, 290–91
 ice cream, 213
 logs, 209–10
 oeufs à la neige, 208–209
 semifreddo, 204
 soufflés, 210–11
 torte, 215
Honey, 319
 -glazed apple tart, warm, 45–46
 lavender, ice cream, 111
 mousse, 102–103
 pears poached in Sauternes and,
  52–53
Huckleberry(ies), 281–82
 ice cream, 133

I

Rum
  babas, 20–21
  ice cream, 266–67
    walnut, 267

S

Sabayon
  Beaumes-de-Venise, 253
  Sauternes, 255
Saint-Honoré cake, 263–64
Sarah's macaroons, 201–202
Sauce
  chocolate, warm, 259
  Cognac caramel, 261
  hard, 261
  peach caramel, 180–81
  plum caramel, 173
  raspberry caramel, 137
  red currant, 129
  wild blackberry, 123
Sauternes
  cake, Linda's olive oil and, 254–
    55
  fruit compote, Darjeeling tea
    and, 221–22
  pears poached in, and honey,
    52–53
  sabayon, 255
Savarin, 19–20
Semifreddo
  almond, 202–205
  hazelnut, 204
  walnut blood orange, 204–205
Sherbet, 6, 321
  apricot, 152
  black currant, 128
  black raspberry, 140
  blood orange, 77
  blueberry, 124
  boysenberry, 126–27
  calvados, 258
  cherry, 161
  cranberry, 188
  Cranshaw melon, 186
  fraises des bois, 131
  grape, 189

grapefruit and Champagne,
    pink, 65
  kirsch, 266
  kiwi, 92–93
  Lavender Gem, 66
  mango, 93
  melon, 186
  Meyer lemon, 69
  muscat grape, 189
  nectarine, 170
  orange and Armagnac, 71
  passion fruit, 95
  peach, 170
  pear, 53–54
    and Armagnac, 54
    and Cognac, 54
  pineapple, 97–98
  plum, 174
  raspberry, 137
  rhubarb, 193
    and strawberry, 193–94
  Santa Rosa plum, 174
  strawberry, 142–43
  tangerine, 84
  tropical, 98
  wild plum, 174
  wine grape, 189
Shortcake, strawberry, 143–44
Short crust pastry, 11–12
Soufflé(s)
  anise, frozen, 257
  apricot, 154, 155
  Grand Marnier, 262
  hazelnut, 210–11
  Meyer lemon, 70–71
  prune and Armagnac, 227
  raspberry, 138
  tangerine, 85–86
Sponge cake, 16–17
Strawberry(ies), 118, 119, 279–80
  Easter nests, 141
  ice cream, 142
  pie, and rhubarb, 192–93
  sherbet, 142–43
    and rhubarb, 193–94
  shortcake, 143–44
  spring cake, 140
  tart, 144
  timbales Élysées, 144–45
  see also Fraises des bois

Sugar, 318–21
  flavored, 4
  see also Caramel
Sunset bombe, 150
Sweet almond oil, 8

T

Tangelo, 62, 274
Tangerine(s), 62, 63, 274
  caramel, 79–80
  ice cream, 81
  mousse, 83
  oeufs à la neige, 81–82
  sherbet, 84
    in tangerine cups, 84–85
  soufflé, 85–86
Tart
  almond, Lindsey's, 205–206
  apple
    country style, 45
    Gravenstein, with cinnamon
      ice cream, 46
    honey-glazed, warm, 45–46
  apricot, 155–56
    and cherry, 156–57
  blood orange, 77–78
  blueberry, with Meyer lemon
    cream, 124–25
  boysenberry, with rose
    geranium cream, 127
  Butter pear, with frangipane
    cream, 54–55
  cherry, 161–62
  fig, 184–85
  lemon, 66–67
  macadamia nut and coconut, 92
  nectarine, 166
  orange, 77–78
  peach, 171, 171–72
  pear, with frangipane cream, 54–
    55
  pear and fig, 55
    upside-down, 57–58
  pear and muscat raisin, upside-
    down, 57
  plum, 175
  raspberry, 138–39
  rhubarb, 194

strawberry, 144
walnut, mixed, 219
wild blackberry curd, 122
Tart pastry. *See* Pie crust; Puff
  pastry; Short crust pastry
Tarte Tatin, 47
  pear, 56
  quince and apple, 58–59
Tea
  black currant, ice cream, 160
  Darjeeling, and Sauternes, fruit
    compote in, 221–22
Timbales Élysées, 144–45
Torte
  almond, 206
  Dobos, 245–47
  hazelnut, 215
  Italian nut, 220–21
  pecan, 214–15
  pistachio, 217–18
  walnut, 215
Tropical fruit, 88–89, 276–79
  sherbet, 98
Truffles
  chocolate, 247
  white chocolate, 248
Twists, 29

V

Vacherins, Valentine, 207
Vanilla, 4
  Bavarian cream, 8
  bean, 4
  ice cream, 6
Violets, 100
  candied, 105
  candies, 107–108

W

Walnut(s), 197, 290
  black
    crêpes, 16
    ice cream, 219
  dartois, and prune, 225–26
  drops, 218

ice cream, 213
    rum, 267
semifreddo, blood orange, 204–
    205
tart, mixed, 219
torte, 215
White chocolate, 231, 303–
    304
    ice cream, 235
    mousse, 243
    and pear bombe with warm
        chocolate sauce, 49
    truffles, 248
        Clay's chocolate ice cream
           with, 236–37

Wines and spirits, 250–52
    see also specific kinds

Y

Yeast, 315–16
    doughs, 19–20, 21–22

Z

Zabaglione
    frozen, 267
    see also Sabayon

ABOUT THE AUTHORS

LINDSEY SHERE grew up on a ranch in Sonoma County, California, and studied French and French culture at the University of California, Berkeley. She has been the pastry chef at Chez Panisse since its opening in 1971, managing a growing staff, continuing to research and create recipes, and tending to her family and her gardens in Berkeley and, recently again, in Sonoma County.

ALICE WATERS founded Chez Panisse fourteen years ago. She wrote the *Chez Panisse Menu Cookbook* in 1982 and co-authored *Chez Panisse Pasta, Pizza, and Calzone* in 1984, the year she opened Café Fanny (named for her daughter, a 1983 arrival). She is working with Chez Panisse's current chef, Paul Bertolli, on a book of Chez Panisse–style Italian menus.

ABOUT THE ILLUSTRATOR

WAYNE THIEBAUD has been teaching and painting for the past forty years. Born in Mesa, Arizona, in 1930, he grew up in Southern California. He worked as a cartoonist, sign painter, and commercial artist for many years before returning to college to complete his bachelor's and master's degrees. Since his first exhibit in 1962 in New York, he has had over a hundred one-man exhibitions, and his work has been shown extensively in this country and throughout the world.